A Time for Consideration

A Scholarly Appraisal
of the Unification Church

Edited by
M. Darrol Bryant
Herbert W. Richardson

The Edwin Mellen Press
New York and Toronto

A TIME FOR CONSIDERATION:

A SCHOLARLY APPRAISAL

OF THE UNIFICATION CHURCH

Edited

M. Darrol Bryant
and
Herbert W. Richardson

Volume Three

SYMPOSIUM SERIES

Second Edition

Copyright © *1978*

by

The Edwin Mellen Press

Library of Congress Cataloging Number 80-81886

ISBN 0-88946-954-7

Printed in the United States of America

TABLE OF CONTENTS

INTRODUCTION

The picture on this volume shows the Rev. Sun
Myung Moon, Founder of the Unification Church, together
with Mr. David Kim, President of the Unification Theological Seminary. The Seminary was established in
1975, enrolls 100 students in a two-year graduate program, and has already graduated two classes of fifty.
That the Unification Church has established such a
seminary is evidence that it considers itself something more than an evangelical or revival movement
preaching church and moral reform.

What, then, is the Unification movement? At
this point, it is not possible to fully answer this
question. It appears to be many things. It seems to
be a reform movement within Christianity since it seeks
to restore unity to the Christian churches. It seems
to be an evangelical movement since it seeks to awaken
us all to the love of God, to rekindle a passion. It
seems to be a social gospel movement since it seeks to
transform the social, economic and political orders.
It seems to be a theological movement since it is developing an insightful and systematic theological stance.
It seems to be a spiritual movement since it is seeking to develop a spirituality which, centered on instruct-
ing and shaping a God-centered heart, will lead to perfection in individuals and families. It seems to be
a cultural movement since it seeks to enlarge our understanding of Christian revelation by interpreting it in
Oriental terms. It seems to be a scriptural movement
since it believes it has discovered the true center

of scriptural teaching. Although all these elements
are present within the Unification Church, it is not
yet clear how to characterize this movement most adequately.

At present we can best proceed by analogy. Consider, for example, what happens if we put just two of
these elements together, namely, the reform and scriptural elements. We know, from the Protestant Reformation
of the sixteenth century, something of the potential significance of a movement which bases itself on new teachings rooted in the discovery of previously unsuspected
meanings of biblical texts. Protestant readings of
Scripture and their consequent theologies led not only
to church reform but also to the creation of new Christian traditions.

The Protestant Reformation is, we believe, a fruitful historical analogue for understanding the Unification
movement. Like Martin Luther, Moon offers a new teaching.
And, like Luther, its newness consists in part in discovering previously unsuspected meanings in certain biblical
texts. Initially Moon's interpretations may appear con-
fusing. Nevertheless, when more closely examined they
reveal a comprehensive theology, sociology and practice
which may perhaps generate a new Christian tradition.
It will also probably have a reformist impact on the
older churches. More than likely, there will be unifi-
cationized Protestants and Catholics, just as by now there
are also protestantized Catholics and catholicized Protestants.

Like Luther, Rev. Moon comes from the periphery of
Christendom. Rev. Moon learned his Christianity from
Presbyterian missionaries. He has sought, however, to
enrich and expand our understanding of the Christian

revelation by reading it in an Oriental idiom. This
new voice disturbs many in the established centers of
Christendom, as did Luther's in his time, because it
does not always speak in the accustomed idiom, nor always
frame its theology and practice in the accustomed con-
ventions.

Unlike Luther, whose scriptural discoveries run
along the axis of God/man-as-individual/church/world,
Rev. Moon's readings of Scripture run along the axis
of God/creation/humankind-as-family/world. For Luther,
then, it is the individual-before-God that is addressed
in his message of justification, whereas it is the human-
family-before-God that is addressed in Moon's message of
restoration. When viewed in relation to earlier movements
within Christianity, the Unification movement comes into
a clearer and more differentiated perspective. It is
for reasons like these that the Unification movement
represents an unusual research opportunity for scholars
and theologians.

The movement itself is disseminating its ideas.
Contrary to the popular impression, this dissemination
is taking place less through active "Moonie" evangelism
than through quiet reading and discussion among business-
men, politicians, professors, and clergy. One might recall that, at the time of the Protestant Reformation, it
was often humanist scholars and political leaders who
carried the seed of the new faith. These men read, deliberated, and then wrote. Some eventually made decisions
that led them to the new faith. Some did not.

In the same way the Unification movement is now
being read about and deliberated about, and eventually

there will be considered decisions. Unfortunately the
thoughtless have already rushed into action. The
National Council of Churches of Christ in the USA has
pronounced an early anathema based on a brief study by
a theologian who did not even meet with one member of
the Unification Church. But Luther too was condemned
by many as a heretic in this same hasty way. Church
bureaucrats are not scholars. Scholars work more slowly.
After Luther's condemnation more reflective people began
asking just why he had been condemned? What were the
arguments, both his and theirs? What were the unspoken
economic and political interests? Where was the world
actually going? Eventually, minds better informed
decided and even changed. The same will happen with
Sun Myung Moon.

These things can be said not out of a religious faith,
but because as historians, sociologists and theologians,
we know that this is the way things have moved and still
do move. There have been many bad reports in the press.
But we should not base our judgments on such reports.
They are typical examples of newspaper sensationalizing:
charges of psychological brainwashing, financial rip-
offs, and power hungry religious leaders. Such stock-
in-trade items are applied by the press to every new
religious group that comes along as well as to many
that have been with us for a long time.

But scholars know that there are deeper reasons
for religious movements that portend large scale institutional developments: reasons that are sociological, philosophical, historical, political, and spiritual.
It takes time to understand all these factors. But

unless we do understand them we do not understand
religious movements.

Inevitably, press sensationalizing leaves people
feeling more confused than ever. The charge that Rev.
Moon is misleading so many bright young people collapses
under its own illogic: how could they be misled if they
were truly so bright? Something, somewhere is wrong.
The back-up tale intending to explain away the illogic-
ality of the original assertion is that "Moonies are
brainwashed." But when this claim is examined by psychologists, sociologists, lawyers, and courts, it collapses too. It also collapses because those who make
this charge cannot agree among themselves who is brainwashed and by whom. The anti-relionists have fingered
Baptists, Catholics, Episcopalians, vegetarians, and
socialists (as well as "Moonies") for deprogramming.

It is precisely because there is so much confusion
today that it is necessary for scholars to begin to
speak. When masses of people have been whipped up to
hysterical fears and hatreds by the media, it is imperative that scholars say "Don't you think we should
analyze the many factors and deeper causes behind this
movement before going off to war?" Only then will the
furor begin to subside and people begin to realize that
they were fearing and hating what, in fact, they themselves knew nothing about. Then it is a time for
consideration.

None of the authors in this volume are members
of the Unification Church. They are all members of other
churches and they are all trained scholars in the field
of religion. For these reasons, parallels to the

practices of other churches and analogies with earlier
developments in history came easily to their minds.
Although there are substantial differences between the
authors of the various essays, they are all concerned
with understanding this movement. Most of the contributors view the Unification Church in relation to the
larger history of Christian traditions. In addition to
studying the writings of the Unification movement, they
have all sought out direct contact with its members.
This field research has involved visiting Unification
institutions: church centers, conferences and the Unification Seminary itself.

Some of the essays in this volume were prepared
specifically for it. Others were first presented on
other occasions. In these cases, we have noted this
fact and allowed references to the original setting to
remain. This means that this volume lacks a certain
stylistic uniformity, yet it also communicates something
of the vitality characterizing the on-going scholarly
debate concerning the Unification Church that is going
on among scholars everywhere.

In this volume we have placed the essays by Professors Shepherd, Sawatsky, Testa and DeMaria under the
heading of cultural analyses. These essays look at
various factors--mythic, historical, institutional and
psycho-social--which condition and shape our responses
to and readings of new religious movements in general,
and the Unification Church in particular. The essays
by Professors Fichter, Flinn, Lewis and Matczak are
placed under the heading of theological analyses.

These essays all seek to appraise the theology and philosophy of the Unification movement within the larger
context of the Christian traditions. The last papers in
this volume by Professors Bryant, Vander Goot and Richardson are placed under the heading of heuristic inquiries.
They provide additional angles of vision and commentary
for the reader in his consideration of the Unification
Church. We believe that, taken together, the essays in
this volume contribute to the construction of a larger
context for on-going scholarly discussion and debate of
this multi-faceted movement.

     Should we fear such debates? We believe not. Many
Unification criticisms of traditional churches have long
been made by traditional Christian theologians themselves.
Others are at the very least new oriental perspectives on
the Bible that a Christian Church still interested in world
mission might find very helpful. Still others are interesting, though minor, points of doctrinal deviation or idiosyncratic church practice of the type which Luther called
"adiaphoria," that is, things in which variety is tolerated
because of personal preference or local custom and about
which ecclesiastical uniformity is totally unnecessary.
To debate the whole range of these questions is both en-
livening and instructive for theology and scholarship.
It clarifies our thoughts and feelings and helps us to
make wiser judgments. Such study will also result, we believe, in a better *Christian* future.

M.D.B.

and

H.W.R.

CULTURAL ANALYSES

THE NEW RELIGIONS AND THE
RELIGION OF THE REPUBLIC

WILLIAM C. SHEPHERD

Sidney Mead is the historian of the religion of the American republic. His perception of the nondenominational religious foundation of American society and polity is of course also captured by Robert Bellah's conception of civil religion in America, and by Will Herberg's treatment of the American Way of Life in *Protestant-Catholic-Jew*. The angle of vision among the three may differ, but the phenomenon is the same: America early on in its short career made religion a social value in a disestablished polity and clothed its political and social experiments with an aura of sacrality drawn from symbols of the Judeo-Christian tradition. This tradition has its own theology, its own saints, its own priests, and all of them are distinct from the theologies of the denominations and sects. Bothered by the fadishness attendant upon Bellah's civil religion argument, Mead has stoutly chosen to go his own way, recognizing Bellah as a kindred spirit but no more than that. History and its methods have their own integrity for Mead and ought not to be dissolved into sociological analysis. On the occasion of having one of his

An earlier version of this essay appeared in the *Journal of the American Academy of Religion,* XLIV/4, Supplement (December 1978) J, pp. 509-525. This version reprinted with the permission of the editor.

articles included in a reader on civil religion, Mead
laconically recalls the case of the man, tarred and
feathered, being treated to an escort out of town. Mead
allows as to how he might prefer simply to walk out alone,
thanks just the same (1975:viii). I think that this
squabble is minor and I shall in what follows treat Mead's
religion of the republic synonymously with Bellah's civil
religion.

The new religions in America, to turn to my other
thematic concern, have received wide journalistic attention, and there is much emphasis in such writing on the
exotic novelty of the new religions—Meher Baba and Teenage Perfect Master Maharaj Ji and the rest do, on the
surface, seem new. Even relatively "scholarly" presenta-
tions of the new religions such as Needleman's *The New
Religions* or Rowley's *New Gods in America* stress the discontinuity between them on the one hand, and both the religion of the denominations and civil religion in America
on the other. I think that there is far more continuity
than discontinuity, and that is the case which I present
in what follows; and I submit that the new evangelicalism
and continuing growth in fundamentalist denominations are
also part of the same picture, complicated though it may
be, of religious life in America today. To understand it,
and even to attempt explanation of it, requires sensitive
exploration of both historical and sociological ways of
seeing, and there is no reason to ignore the insights of
a great literary tradition which, in America, persists
in profoundly ambiguous tension with the religion of the
republic.

Looking first at the American religious situation
on a macroscopic scale, certain facets of historical processes at least since Newton and Kant are evident, although of course there is lots of room for dispute about

microscopic detail. All modern industrialized nations
(including, for example, Japan) are, religiously speaking,
heirs to three interrelated processes of the recent past:
secularization, privatization, and deritualization.
Stated most simply, secularization is a process of in-
creasing institutional complexity or differentiation
among the components of the social system. The factory
replaces the home as the bread-winner's arena of activity.
As an historical fact in the West, medieval Christianity
lost its binding and universal monopoly, and it suffered
weakening from within by internal schism. The effect in
the long run of secularization is not necessarily to dis-
establish one or another form of religion, but to make
all religions one kind of institution among others in a
complex system of institutions (see further, Luckmann).
In Sweden and England, for example, there is still an
established church, but secularization and religious toleration of other denominations have so cut into its authority that extremely small percentages of the popula-
tion participate in either the church or any of the other
available religious organizations on a regular basis. And
atheism is far more in evidence than in America (though I
shall argue that America is no less secularized for all
that.)

      Closely interwoven with the process of seculariza-
tion is that of privatization. If religious toleration
is the policy of the polity, and if religious bodies com-
pete with each other for membership, and if nearly all
social roles are achieved and not ascribed, then religious
allegiance is a matter of private choice regardless of
parental efforts to mold their offspring. Of course children may ultimately adopt the religious role and the system of values suggested to them by parents, but that too
is a matter of choosing, whether more or less self-con-

sciously, on the part of modern adolescents or early
adults. The outcome of private choices must be a precar-
ious religious identity: most religious people in human
history have enjoyed an amount of social support and public encouragement buttressing religious thought and ritual behavior. Not so now.

          Finally, life in modern industrial societies, secu-
larized and privatized, is also, to use another horrific
neologism, deritualized. As Mary Douglas says (passim),
we moderns have relegated ritual to the dinner table and
the bathroom, and Amy Vanderbilt and Emily Post are more
the arbiters of our ritual processes than are powerful
national authorities who have a genuine say with regard
to matters religious and ritualistic. Ritual has become
merely etiquette. In America there are genuinely ritualistic vestiges, but civil religious occasions are less
fueled by commanding historical memories than they used
to be. Memorial Day has given way to Super Bowl Day as
a civil religious occasion for the republic.

          If secularization, privatization, and deritualiza-
tion are the marks of all industrialized nations, how
does one explain the glaringly wide discrepancy between
European nations and America on all indices of religious
membership, belief, and activity? (For statistics, see
Seligman: 290-94, and Argyle/Beit-Hallahmi: 26.) America
is certainly no less industrialized in the main than Europe, but the form of its secularization is strikingly
different, so much so that comparing religious statistics
as between European nations and America is relevant because they bear almost no relation to one another. Since
historical and social developments in American life are
unique, so the course of its secularization has been
unique. America had no feudal past and no peasantry. It
did have such historical experiences as a long move west-

ward, continual territorial expansion, flows of ethnically
distinct immigrations, rapid urbanization and industriali-
zation, the presence of socially marginal groups such as
blacks and indigenous Indians, early disavowal of all attempts to found an established church, revival movements
called "Awakenings," and religious diversity from the beginning coupled with development of sects far exceeding
that in Europe (see further, Luckmann:32).

Sects in America very quickly were transformed from
socially deviant movements to socially characteristic
ones—most sects became denominations in harmony with social life and actually setting the tone for it. No established church against which to protest existed in America,
so the European form of sectarian development centering
around "nonconformity" could not occur in the American
federation. The United States self-consciously chose to
have its political being as a secular nation, offering
religious toleration to all comers. Madison and Jefferson
thought of religion as a man's *opinion,* to which every man
has a natural right, and of ecclesiastical institutions as
nothing more than purely voluntary organizations (Mead,
1976:57-58). As Jefferson puts the case in his *Notes on
the State of Virginia,* America's noble experiment in disestablishment left any and all sects and denominations on
a par.

> Our sister States of Pennsylvania and New York...
> have long subsisted without any establishment at
> all. The experience was new and doubtful when
> they made it. It has answered beyond conception.
> They flourish infinitely. Religion is well sup-
> ported; of various kinds, indeed, but all good
> enough; all sufficient to preserve peace and
> order. (Mead, 1976:59)

But in the same process of guaranteeing religious toleration in a secular state, politically America also sur-
rounded itself with a halo of religious, even specifically

Biblical and Christian, values and meaning.

The new American nation, then, fostered a unique al-
liance of politics and religion, wholly divergent in shape
and tone from the European nations which were the source
of America's populace. Religiously, instead of an established church, America went the denominational or "tamed
sect" way, and that only later became typical of all industrialized, secular societies; politically, however,
America also blessed its venture with religious values
and drew its conception of itself from Judeo-Christian
understandings. America as a political entity not only
still purports to trust in God, but even from the very beginning sought to picture itself as the new promised land,
God's New Israel, and his great experiment with democracy
and toleration. What gathers all Americans together under
a socially shared religious umbrella is not the particular
denomination, but civil religion, the uniquely American
vehicle of religious ideas and values functioning within
the framework of an officially secular state. As Sidney
Mead continually puts it, a deep tension in American life
exists between the denominations and their orthodoxies,
on the one hand, and the religion of the republic, on the
other. Yet because each denomination, no matter how bi-
zarre or apparently sectarian, must make peace with the
republic and, even more, fondle the union's political aspirations, the various American religious bodies had to
become more and more like each other, leveling off the
hard edges of doctrinal conflict. Violent religious conflict *should* be apparent if the denominations took their
orthodoxies really seriously. The fact that it is not apparent is one indication of the priority that the denominations place on consecrating the society and polity in
which they each move and have their beings. The American
Way of Life is civil religion, is the religion of the

the republic, and is, accordingly, not at all the same as
the religious values which are pinned to denominational
orthodoxy. The latter are decidedly backseat passengers
to the former in American Life, but *since America made
religion a social value* ("everybody ought to believe in
something, and I don't care what it is": Eisenhower), religious involvement across a whole spectrum from Catholicism and Orthodox Jewry to Krishna Consciousness and Los
Angeles-style Zen Buddhism continues to flourish in America. Intramural tolerance and support for the civil polity are the marks of the denominations in America. For
all that they have made peace with one another, however,
widespread movement in the direction of ecumenical union
has not occurred. For lingering sectarian reasons, the
denominations persist in avoiding emphasis on the concepts
that a given denomination may actually share with other
American religious bodies, and that in turn gives rise to
distaste for high-level doctrinal generalizing and therefore for theology: "...this built-in aversion to inclusive or cosmopolitan abstractions helps to explain the
oft-noted untheological nature of American religious
groups" (Mead, 1975: 137-38). Against the ideological
backdrop of leveled Americanism, not only the heavy doctrinal exclusivism but also the highly involved theological character of Moon's Unification Church stand out in
clear relief—it is a positively un-American religious
phenomenon, which is why Americans are fearful about
their children getting tainted by it (see Sontag: passim;
and Kim).

        Mead argues that the reality of Herberg's American
Way of Life is hardly new, rather that it is explicitly
inculcated in the theology of the Constitution and the
Declaration of Independence, and in a long series of high
legal opinions (e.g., Justice Clark: "we are a religious

people whose institutions presuppose a Supreme Being"
[Mead, 1975:67]). The Enlightenment deistic convictions
of the Founding Fathers are well known, and Mead in several places documents them extensively. One of his fa-
vorite stories is Franklin's account of leaving the church
with a shrug because he felt that the minister was mis-
takenly trying to make good Presbyterians of his congregation rather than good citizens (Mead, 1977:87). Or
Jefferson's classic formulation of American civil religion, quoted above, to the effect that all the kinds of
religion are "good enough." As Mead has put it recently:

> Assuming that every denominational church taught
> and inculcated in its members the "essentials"
> of every religion, whether they knew it or not
> and whatever might be the particular forms of
> their theology and practice, they might say with
> Jefferson that although there were "various kinds"
> of religion they were "all good enough; all suf-
> ficient to preserve peace and order." (1977:87-88)

An important point, too often overlooked, is that
the Great Awakenings of the late eighteenth and nineteenth
centuries were played out in exactly the same arena and
religiously solidified continuing high religious involvement in America, yet involvement of a very peculiar sort.
While Europeans moved toward outright atheism and the
abandonment of church-oriented religiosity, Americans
moved toward privatism in religious matters. The pivotal
figure in the transformation of Jeffersonian deism into a
depoliticized theology of the inner emotional life was
Jonathan Edwards. Quoting from Herbert Wallace Schneider,
Mead remarks: "While for his New England fathers 'religion had been an objective social institution, preoccupied with public concerns; Edwards...transformed it into
an inner discipline of the emotions.' By him the 'social
and political philosophy' of the early puritans was given
'a private and personal meaning' and wholly 'transferred

to the inner life of the soul.' With Edwards the doctrine of God's absolute sovereignty 'had lost its social
significance.'" (1977:51-52) And Mead's own comment on
that development is characteristically memorable: "This
means that the weight of Edwards' influence was to trans-
fer the wars of the Lord from Cromwell's Nasby fields and
Marston Moors to the inner recesses of individual hearts."
(1977:52). Civil religion, denominational pluralism, and
religious toleration all continue on, but the difference
from an earlier day is simply that the religion of the
republic takes on an individualistic and, at least to
some extent, affect-laden guise; the leveling of doctrinal
discrepancies among denominations occurs no less in the
nineteenth century than in the eighteenth century politically astute Enlightenment form. Both Bellah and Mead bemoan the loss of the public nature of the religion of the
republic, Bellah arguing for its restoration (1975:151),
and Mead analyzing the manifold consequences of that loss,
which of course have continued to the present day. For
Mead the covenant which has been broken is Jefferson's
vision of the polity. Instead the privatization of civil
religion leads to

> the separation of "salvation" from social and
> political responsibility; the appearance of of-
> fering a choice between being an informed and
> loyal citizen of the Republic, with consequent
> bifurcation of the minds of many church members;
> the erosion of the denomination's theology be-
> cause irrelevant to the life of the commonwealth;
> the separation and discrete institutionalization
> of the nations; religious and intellectual lives
> [the churches vs. the universities]; and the
> death of the theologian as significant intel-
> lectual in the society. (1977:133)

Civil religion continues to meet in superficially
different ways psychological needs of the American populace, but social and political needs are not met, except
perhaps in the demonic form of religious nationalism which

sanctioned our buccaneering adventure in Vietnam. Simply
to say, however, that private needs lodged within individual psyches do seem to achieve satisfaction from the mini-
strations of civil religion is not enough. For when its
function, shorn of political and social value, is limited
to psychological impact, civil religion becomes a phenomenon so vague and amorphous that even its restricted
success any more calls for explanation. Sociological
surveys cannot answer the question very well, and neither
can political and social histories of our recent past.
But I believe that the ongoing power of civil religion
may be understood by looking to a resource too often neglected by sociological observers, namely the American
literary tradition.

On the surface of it, that is an odd suggestion,
for no great American writers have accepted civil religion and its God in an uncritical way. Certainly we have
had great patriotic writers, but their understanding of
America have often taken a regional cast. Faulkner's
South is the outstanding instance. Thoreau and Melville
looked at civil religion's banalities with profound ask-
ance, and Walt Whitman among many others directly spoofed
pietistic patriotism. As Leslie Fiedler remarks, even
Whitman in his role as "Booster" exhibits a "duplicity, a
peculiarly American duplicity, that doubleness of our
self-consciousness which our enemies too easily call hypocrisy, but which arises from our belief that what we dream
rather than what we are is our essential truth" (172).
The finest literary tradition in America consistently re-
veals paradox and even negation in its conceptions of
the nation's God. The God of civil religion can survive
in their work, but only when stood on his head, transformed from the saccharine mask covering driving the en-
gines of America's lust for hegemony. Among our contem-

porary novelists, the most thoughtful theologian of civil
religion in Norman Mailer, and to understand that paradox
is to go a long way toward grasping the continuing relevance of the religion of the republic, however privatized
it has become.

Consider, for example, the serenely cerebral and
contemplative vision of God found in John Fowles' British
novel, *Daniel Martin*. Daniel muses, "If there is a God,
he or she (or it) must be supremely and chillingly uncon-
cerned about the number of things to which individual
specks of matter rightly give priority—pain, equality,
justice, and the rest" (271). American individual thinking specks of matter, in the persons of literati such as
Norman Mailer, radiate a wholly different tone, for their
God is the God of civil religion or the religion of the
republic. And as Leo Marx has brilliantly seen, much of
the American literary tradition rests on a fundamental
ambiguity regarding civil religion. Alternating between
adoration and contempt, America's literary response to
civil religion has been *uncivil* in Marx's phrase, and indeed as he shows, positively *obscene* (222-51). Far from
the "no offense" that John Murray Cuddihy sees ensuing
from the religious theologians, the writers heap "offense"
on civil religion, most vividly through obscenity, while
nonetheless shoring it up in a curiously underhanded way
(see further, Cuddihy, 1978).

The obscenity of the writers spins off of the superficially pious sanctimoniousness of civil religion's authority figures. Relying upon obscenity opposes the
"vapid idiom of the official American civil religion"
(Marx:241). Whitman's "a little healthy rudeness" (Marx:
236) turns in the modern period into Mailer's metaphysical death struggle between the God of the republic and
the Devil, but even in Mailer a populist egalitarian

tradition is carried on, unmasking the varied civil lies
upon which civil religion is based. Mailer's crude ob-
scenities are intended to have redemptive value. Mailer
deliberately has spontaneous acts of violence and passion
open new possibilities of salvation (Foster:136). Marx
concludes that the role of obscenity in Mailer "may be
key to another, more authentic, truly democratic, if as
yet inchoate and unrealized form of civil religion" (Marx:
225).

Mailer pits a weak God symbolized by ordinary sexuality and decay against a strong Devil symbolized by anality, buggery, violence, and death; and he argues that
America is the stage upon which the great epic struggle
is being played out in its extreme form. Mailer's interwoven themes are complicated, but he seems to assert that
human liberation in the sense of overcoming repression,
can occur by violence and that is the work of the Devil
and civil religion's God. Waste, feces, disease, and murder are the predominate notes of the whole conflict. In
The American Dream, Mailer's hero, ex-congressman and
philosophy professor Stephen Rojack, achieves a kind of
ecstatic breakthrough in his life only after he brutally
murders his wife and proceeds immediately to bugger the
maid: a work of *der Teufel* he calls it, clearly connect-
ing the symbols of anality, the Devil, and death, all
stronger forces than approved sexuality and the God of
the republic. One theme of *The American Dream* is that
sexual exhilaration in its highest form is achieved
through murder and violence, and only then is what Mailer
calls the cancer inside overcome. But the price is very
high—all the main characters of the novel (Deborah,
Shago, Cherry), with the exception of Rojack himself,
suffer monstrously brutal death (n.d., passim).

Mailer is also quite explicit about the peculiarly

American value of obscenity in *The Armies of the Night*,
his journalistic account of the march on the Pentagon of
October, 1967,

> He [Mailer] was off into obscenity. It gave a
> heartiness like the blood of beef tea to his as-
> sociations. There was no villain in obscenity
> for him, just—paradoxically, characteristically—
> his love for America...so Mailer never felt more
> like an American than when he was naturally ob-
> scene—all the gifts of the American language
> came out in the happy play of obscenity upon
> concept, which enabled one to go back to con-
> cept again. What was magnificent about the
> word shit is that it enabled you to use the
> word noble. (1968:60-61)

Obscenity gives rise to the ability to speak to God. At
the end of *The Armies of the Night,* Mailer soliloquizes
on the anguish of America as he had earlier upon his re-
lease from jail in a public speech: "...we are burning
the body and blood of Christ in Vietnam. Yes, we are
burning him there, and as we do, we destroy the founda-
tions of this republic, which is its love and trust in
Christ" (239). He concludes the volume with the following civil religious exhortation:

> Whole crisis of Christianity in America that
> the military heroes were on the side, and the un-
> named saints on the other! Let the bugle blow.
> The death of America rides in and on the smog.
> America—the land where a new kind of man was
> born from the idea that God was present in every
> man not only as compassion but as power, and so
> the country belonged to the people; for the will
> of the people—if the locks of their life could
> be given the art to turn—was then the will of
> God. Great and dangerous idea! If the locks
> did not turn, then the will of the people was
> the will of the Devil. Who by now could know
> where was what? Liars controlled the locks.
>   Brood on that country who expresses our will.
> She is America, once a beauty of magnificence
> unparalleled, now a beauty with a leprous skin.
> She is heavy with child—no one knows if legiti-
> mate—and languishes in a dungeon whose walls
> are never seen. Now the first contractions of

> her fearsome labor begin——it will go on: no doctor
> exists to tell the hour. It is only known that
> false labor is not likely on her now, she will
> probably give birth, and to what?——the most fear-
> some totalitarianism the world has ever known?
> or can she, poor giant, tormented lovely girl,
> artful and wild? Rush to the locks. God writhes
> in his bounds. Rush to the locks. Deliver us
> from our curse. For we must end on the road to
> that mystery where courage, death, and the dream
> of love give promise of sleep. (1968:320)

Shades of Lincoln's Second Inaugural:

> It may seem strange that any men should dare to
> ask a just God's assistance in wringing their
> bread from the sweat of other men's faces; but
> let us judge not, that we be not judged. The
> prayer of both [sides] could not be answered——
> that of neither has been answered fully.
>   The Almighty has His own purposes. "Woe unto
> the world because of offenses; for it must needs
> be that offenses come, but woe to that man by
> whom the offense cometh"....Fondly do we hope——
> fervently do we pray——that this mighty scourge
> of war may speedily pass away. Yet, if God
> wills that it continue until all the wealth
> piled by the bondsman's two hundred and fifty
> years of unrequited toil shall be sunk, and until
> every drop of blood drawn with the lash shall be
> paid by another drawn with the sword, as was said
> three thousand years ago, so still it must be
> said, "The judgments of the Lord are true and
> righteous altogether." (Stern: 841-42)

Granted, an unlikely pair of bedfellows, Lincoln and Norman Mailer; and yet these two addresses mirror each other,
both subscribing fervently to the God of the republic. In
the same spirit, even the genteel John Updike has his
character Rabbit muse about the American dream: "When he
first heard the phrase as a kid he pictured God lying
sleeping, the quilt-colored map of the United States
coming out of his head like a cloud" (106). This spirit
of American civil religion is utterly distinct from the
far simpler course of secularization by abandonment in
Europe. Americans keep their religiosity in whatever form
because they keep their enthusiastic Americanism, and the

two are intertwined at the core of the American's being.
As de Tocqueville noted in 1835, "It is impossible to
conceive a more troublesome or more garrulous patriotism;
it wearies even those who are disposed to respect it"
(1945, II:236).

What of my claim, then, that America is hardly less
secularized than any European nation? Because the reli-
giousness of Americans, whether in denominational, sectarian, cultic, or self-improvement form, is, in Ernest
Gellner's phrase, "froth rather than substance" (1974:192).
Religious and self-improvement modes of life are what
Gellner calls ironic cultures, fitted as frills on top
of, *but not displacing,* the serious business of what really counts and is acceptable as knowledge:

> The irony is not generally conscious, explicit
> or individual. It resides in the fact that the
> whole of organisation of such cultures, the way
> in which they are implemented and enforced in
> life, the limits within which they are enforced,
> work in a manner which tacitly presupposes and
> admits that they are not to be taken seriously,
> as knowledge. They contain claims, assertions,
> which *sound* cognitive, and which in other, non-
> ironic cultures would indeed have been such; but,
> here, it is somehow understood that they are not
> fully serious, not commensurate or continuous
> with real knowledge. Real knowledge is to be
> found elsewhere; and it does have the cold forms
> which Kant and Weber discerned and anticipated.
> But more colourful, human, cosier worlds and
> thought-styles are at the same time available to
> envelop our daily life, and they have reached
> their quiet accommodation, their tacit division
> of spheres of influence, with the island of
> truth. (193-94)

Exactly the same point has often been made in Bryan Wilson's work:

> The modern world has a supermarket of faiths;
> received, jazzed-up, homespun, restored, import-
> ed and exotic. But all of them co-exist only
> because the wider society is so secular, because
> they are relatively unimportant consumer items....

> In the consciously-planned, and rationally and
> technically constructed social system, which we
> increasingly approximate, religion does not mat-
> ter socially, however much his own religion may
> matter to the individual. (1975:80)

And as even the prophet and advocate of American civil
religion in our day, Robert Bellah, makes clear, the real
values of individualism and utilitarianism are what under-
lie the republic's God (1975: passim).

Both Gellner's and Wilson's point, and Bellah's perspective as well, may be put into recent historical pur-
view. During the sixties we witnessed civil religion at
its best in the civil rights movement; civil religion at
its worst in the Vietnamese War; and a countercultural
rebellion of the young against the tepid values and symbols of civil religion, which was indeed perceived as
trappings decorating real centers of demonic and uncon-
trolled bureaucratic power in America. The decade of the
seventies has assimilated all three movements. Traditional civil religion continues on, still in Mead's tension
with denominational theologies, but in strict continuity
with the patriotic line running from Jefferson through
Eisenhower ("each is good enough"). Evangelical and
Pentecostal movements are not sectarian and can be accommodated, apparently even by Roman Catholics—they are in-
clusivistic and non-dogmatic, instead savoring, perhaps
in Gellner's ironic sense, highs of religious experience.
The new religions are "successor movements" to countercultural ones of the sixties, "adopted by the larger culture because they can be *adapted* in ways which reinforce
existing cultural patterns and do not pose a threat to
dominant institutions. If you spend the weekend in the
ashram, perhaps you can better tolerate working in the
bureaucracy all week" (Robbins: 310). The new religions
are also in tandem with a burgeoning self-improvement

industry, in forms ranging from Erhard Seminars Training
to Rolfing, from Arica to Transcendental Meditation. All
are contemporary manifestations of American civil religion, whether we call it that, or the religion of the
republic, or the American Way of Life, or, more simply,
American religious nationalism. Which phrase we use depends both on our attitudes toward the many-sided phenomenon in general (perhaps, say, on our degree of patriotism), and on whether one is addressing the bright side of
the civil religion (e.g., religious toleration), or the
demonic underside (e.g., military forays undertaken to
save the world from godless atheism).

I have argued elsewhere that the American sacred
canopy is the *form* of their respective religious commitments, recognizing the broad varieties of content. Often-
times our commitments are largely ironic, alterable,
brief, and vague. "Serial adhesion" is a term which
catches the American's willingness to dabble in various
religious movements and to move from one to another without marked psychic dislocation—serial adhesion therefore
catches the diachronic character of the ways contemporary
American civil religion is being played out. As opposed
to conversion, which is deep and perduring, serial adhesion is superficial and transient (Shepherd, 1979).
Polysymbolism catches the synchronic character of the same
phenomenon, the multi-faceted commitment to an array of
differing religious symbols and ideas mixed together by
the individual for his or her own private delectation
(Shepherd, 1974; Hardwick; Kliever). Serial adhesion and
polysymbolism, however, could just as easily apply to Jefferson, Paine, and Franklin as they do today to modern religious styles of life: the forms are similar but the particular contents of faith differ. A counterexample,

touched upon earlier, serves to validate the point. One
of the things which makes the Unification Church of Reverend Moon so threatening to many Americans is precisely
its particularity and exclusivism preached in the cleans-
ing name of unification of all men as brothers. It is
positively *un-American* to be so exclusivistic religiously
and to do everything, including succumbing to an arranged
marriage, for a religious reason. While, to be sure,
there has been an old and continuing tension between denominational particularity and the religion of the republic, what the Unification Church represents is a *threat*
to the complicated balance of tensed allegiances.

     What I have often called polysymbolism is, histori-
cally speaking, simply a way of expressing the old theology, underlying the religion of the republic, which has
always been antagonistic to sectarian and denominational
particularism. It may be nothing all that new. Polysymbolism restates in a generalized way Jefferson's conception of all religions as "good enough." Polysymbolism is
inclusive in the Englightenment spirit of the Founding
Fathers. Polysymbolism articulates pluralism, hetero-
geneity, choice. But it is more independent of patriotism
and the threat of religious nationalism than the old Enlightenment theology of the republic. For that reason it
more accurately reflects the religious privatism which is
in fact the case than the theoretically public deism which
reflects the core values of the Founding Fathers, the
Declaration of Independence, the Constitution and the legal decisions which have affirmed it. So the difference
is polysymbolism's acknowledgement of irony, of self-
consciously and even playfully chosen plural vessels of
individual meaning.

     Our perception of religion in American life can be
deceiving. We can easily see only confusion and prolifer-

ation. But order and meaning may be there if we probe
deeply enough. Mead quotes Bronowski: "For order does
not display itself of itself; if it can be said to be
there at all, it is not there for the mere looking. There
is no way of pointing a finger or a camera at it; order
must be discovered and, in a deep sense, it must be created. What we see, as we see it, is more disorder" (1977:
140). Or Wallace Stevens: "A great disorder is an order."
The problem, religiously speaking, in America is not lack
of meaning so much as it is the wild multiplication of
meaning systems serving what Tom Wolfe calls the "Me Decade." And in that proliferating excess of meanings, the
order to be found is at least partly historical; and it
goes all the way back to the roots of America's being and
the myths of origin which the young country spun to legitimate itself as the New Israel of God. To the extent
that the old rituals of the religion of the republic,
particularly Memorial Day, are no longer powerful solidi-
fying occasions, something public which we once had has
been lost. But perhaps what is taking its place in the
wake of Vietnam is not so much wholly new as it is rather
easily explicable mutant. The "principle of self-deter-
mination," to refer once again to a phrase of Mead, is
still the cardinal and shaping value of the republic.

WORKS CONSULTED

Argyle, Michael and Beit-Hallahmi, Benjamin
   1975   *The Social Psychology of Religion*. London: Routledge
               and Kegan Paul.

Bellah, Robert N.
   1974   "Civil Religion in America." Pp. 21-44 in *American
               Civil Religion*. Ed. Russell E. Richey and Donald G.
               Jones. New York: Harper and Row.

   1975   *The Broken Covenant*. New York: Seabury.

Cuddihy, John Murray
    1978   *No Offense: Civil Religion and Protestant Taste*. New
             York: Seabury.

Douglas, Mary
    1966   *Purity and Danger*. Middlesex: Penguin.

Fiedler, Leslie
    1952   *An End to Innocence*. Boston: Beacon.

Foster, Richard
    1972   "Mailer and Fitzgerald Tradition." Pp. 127-42 in *Nor-
             man Mailer*. Ed. Leo Braudy. Englewood Cliffs:
             Prentice-Hall.

Fowles, John
    1977   *Daniel Martin*. Boston: Little-Brown.

Gellner, Ernest
    1974   *Legitimation of Belief*. Cambridge: Cambridge University.

Hardwick, C.D.
    1977   "Ironic Culture and Polysymbolic Religiosity."
             Theologische Zeitschrift 33: 283-93.

Herberg, Will
    1960   *Protestant-Catholic-Jew*. New York: Doubleday.

Kim, Young Oon
    1975   *Unification Theology and Christian Thought*. New York:
             Golden Gate.

Kliever, Lonnie D.
    1979   "Polysymbolic Religiosity." *Journal of Religion*
             (forthcoming).

Luckmann, Thomas
    1967   *The Invisible Religion*. New York: Macmillan.

Mailer, Norman
    n.d.   *An American Dream*. London: The Book Club.

    1968   *The Armies of the Night*. New York: New American
             Library.

Marx, Leo
    1974   "The Uncivil Response of American Writers to American
             Civil Religion." Pp. 222-251 in *American Civil Reli-
             gion*. Eds. Russell E. Richey and Donald G. Jones.
             New York: Harper and Row.

Mead, Sidney E.
    1975   *The Nation with the Soul of a Church*. New York: Harper
              and Row.

    1976   *The Lively Experiment*. New York: Harper and Row.

    1977   *The Old Religion in the Brave New World*. Berkeley:
              University of California.

Needleman, Jacob
    1970   *The New Religions*. New York: Doubleday.

Robbins, Thomas
    1977   "Old Wine in Exotic New Bottles." *Journal for the
              Scientific Study of Religion* 16 (September): 310-13.

Rowley, Peter
    1971   *The New Gods*. New York: McKay.

Seligman, Lee P.
    1977   "Multi-Nation Surveys of Religious Beliefs." *Journal
              for the Scientific Study of Religion 16* (September):
              289-94.

Shepherd, William C.
    1974   "On the Concept of 'Being Wrong' Religiously." *Journal
              of the American Academy of Religion* 42: 66-81.

    1979   "Conversion and Adhesion." *Sociological Inquiry*
              (forthcoming).

Sontag, Frederick
    1976   *Sun Myung Moon and the Unification Church*. Nashville:
              Abingdon.

Stern, Philip van Doren, ed.
    1940   *The Life and Writings of Abraham Lincoln*. New York:
              Random House.

Tocqueville, Alexis de
    1945   *Democracy in America*. 2 vols. New York: Vintage.

Updike, John
    1971   *Rabbit Redux*. Greenwich: Fawcett.

Wilson, Bryan
    1975   "The Debate over 'Secularization.'" *Encounter 45/4:
              77-83.*

MOONIES, MORMONS AND MENNONITES:
CHRISTIAN HERESY AND RELIGIOUS TOLERATION

RODNEY J. SAWATSKY

Most Americans are aware of the struggle within
the Missouri Synod Lutheran Church in the past decade
over the question of Biblical interpretation, especially at this denomination's seminary in St. Louis.
Fewer, undoubtedly, are informed over the debate
regarding theories of Biblical inspiration in evangelical circles which has recently been focussed by
Harold Linsell in *The Battle for the Bible*. In
these more fundamentalist groups the concern for
Christian orthodoxy is very much alive and the notion
of heresy is still definable with considerable precision.

Cases such as these, however, gain national attention because of their novelty. For much of the
Christian church, heresy is largely passé, and when
the question of correct belief is raised a new headline is born. Contrariwise, our theologians can announce that God is dead, or is a woman, or is living
in Brazil for the Brazilian poor alone, and Christians
smile politely, displaying their lack of understanding
and their unconcern. Correct belief or truth--if you
will--has been relativized to the point where for

An earlier version of this paper was presented in
Berkeley, California, in June, 1977.

much of the church "heresy" has become a meaningless term.

But even for more liberal Americans there seems to be an exception to this general state of affairs. In the reaction to the so-called "new religions", the concept of heresy has suddenly regained a function in society. The term itself may not be used, but the attitude is clear: certain religions are illegitimate within this society.

It seems fair to say that "heresy" or at least "illegitimacy" is involved *not* when theologians spin their fantastic webs in their hallowed halls--these are only idle words; but these terms are called forth the moment common people direct their energies to creating a new order on the basis of new visions-- these are fighting words. Heresy is thus found not in unorthodox ideas *per se* but in perceived challenges to the social status quo.

And it may ever have been so in Christian history. True, to pull apart ideas and actions prior to disestablishment is not entirely legitimate. Furthermore, there is much evidence that correct ideas were important in the history of the church--take the Councils of Nicea and Chalcedon as examples. Yet samplings in the history of Christian heresy suggest that both before and after the establishment of religious freedom, action was taken against a heretical group principally in response to perceived social deviance rather than to error in belief alone. Religious toleration, in turn, is gained only when the threat, real or imagined, of the new religious movement to

the social status quo is minimized. This we will
argue was true for the Mennonites and the Mormons
and may well also be true for the Moonies.

These three religions, each new in their own
time--the sixteenth, nineteenth and twentieth centuries
--differ in many ways but they have in common having
been deemed heretical and illegitimate and have experienced the harsh realities of religious intolerance. Even in America all three have come under severe
censorship. In recent times the cross, the gallows,
the rack, drowning, dismemberment, and so on have
lost their popularity. The methods have been mani-
cured as today the media, the psychiatrists and
the deprogrammers serve as functionaries to maintain
the social status quo. The mechanisms of deconversion
have become much more sophisticated, yet the insis-
tence that steps must be taken against religious
deviance remains--primarily when that deviance is perceived as a threat to normative society.

Our modern heresies vary considerably from each
other. Their relationship to dominant society, and,
by extension, to religious toleration likewise varies.
It is not by chance that the Unification Church, or
the Moonies, have been particularly vilified. As a
primarily Christian and western cult, they pose a particular challenge to the status quo. Eastern religions
like Krishna Consciousness are also feared but are
readily identifiable as "different", and more likely
to be perceived as annoying but not particularly
dangerous, a little like the hippies of old. It is
in their Christian activism, in their Calvinistic

transformationism, that groups like the Moonies are considered dangerous and therefore not to be tolerated.

The Moonies propose to create a new order, a new community of faith, the very kingdom of God on earth. It is this program which, in its deviance from the current American search for the kingdom, places the Moonies in the camp of the dangerous heretics. The Moonies thus stand in a tradition, shared by the Mormons and Mennonites, which seeks a new order on the basis of new vision. They likewise share in the intolerance which follows when the status quo is challenged in favor of a new kingdom, even when that new kingdom is the very epitome of the dominant culture's own ideals.

In the following pages we will document the kingdom quest of the Mennonites, Mormons and Moonies. We will also note the ensuing persecution and the phases of separation and accommodation which followed for the Mennonites and Mormons as they sought to escape persecution. It seems likely that the Moonies too will experience separation and accommodation before their persecution will cease. Our society seems ever able to force aberrant dreamers of dreams to accommodate those dreams to the mythology of the standing order. Today Mennonites and Mormons stand alongside other denominations in the competition for the souls of Americans. What will it take for the Moonies to gain the same legitimation stamp? When will they no longer be deemed heretical in this nation of religious toleration? They will be tolerated only when their dreams and visions are no longer

considered challenges to the present social system.
Their brains will no longer be deemed "washed" when
they stop trying to illegitimately cleanse society.
At least this seems to be the judgment of history.

THE MENNONITES

The Mennonites are instructive regarding new
religions in that they were among the first to imple-
ment the notion of religious toleration; they sought
to create a new community of faith, and therefore
they were among the most persecuted of heretics in
Christian history. Early on the Mennonites were
known as Anabaptists, meaning "rebaptizers," since
they held to adult baptism. The name Mennonite came
from the most able organizer of the movement, Menno
Simons of Holland and North Germany.

The Mennonite story begins in 1525 in Zurich,
Switzerland, amidst the revolutionary upheaval known
by us as the Reformation. Diversity reigned in those
early years as the religious leaders, nurtured in
various contexts in Switzerland, Germany and Holland,
sought to crystallize their new understandings of the
Christian faith. Ever since then division has characterized this people throughout the world, from the
most conservative Old Order Mennonites in their bug-
gies, to the more acculturated arriving at their
speaking engagements in 747's.

But commonalities proved sufficient to weld a
new identity, an identity which sent tremors through
the sixteenth century European establishment and propelled the early Mennonites to the stake. These

radicals sought to re-establish a pure church of
believers only. Believers entered the church upon
adult baptism following confession of faith. The
essence of the believers' life and the characteristic
feature of the pure church was discipleship of Jesus
as taught in the New Testament. The corollaries
quickly followed: if religious choices were made
by adults then religious freedom was implied; following religious freedom came separation of the church
from the state; and recruitment into the church was
by means of missions. Furthermore, Jesus discipleship
included such ethical requirements as pacifism.

In an era of incredible religious turbulence,
why were these particular proposals so heretical?
On the surface these ideas appear harmless enough,
but not so their implications. These early Mennonites
went much beyond the mainline Lutheran, Reformed
and Anglican protestants. These "mainliners" agreed
with the Roman Church that a separation between the
religious and secular functionaries in society ought
to prevail, yet they continued to assume that the
state protected the church while the church provided
the moral fabric which sustained the society as a
unified entity. Infant baptism consequently served
as a rite of passage not only into the church but
also into the state. Heretics or social deviants
were defined as such by either institution and sum-
marily prosecuted and frequently persecuted.

Given these medieval assumptions, separation
of church and state and religious toleration were
alike seditious. To allow all men free choice in
beliefs and to break the church and state asunder,

were perceived as attacks on the unity of society. The
dangerous notions propounded by the Mennonites were
multiplied. A pure church of believers only, gathered
out and separated from the wicked world, to be a sign
of the coming Kingdom, was correctly perceived as
a powerful censure not only of the Roman but also of
the Protestant churches, which continued to embrace
clean and unclean alike in one ark. If the Mennonites
were the path to the Kingdom, Catholics and Protestants
were not. Besides, Mennonite pacifism further undermined the standing order, especially since the Turks
were threatening from the East, and Mennonite refusal
to participate in coercive government implied again
that the magistrates and their supporters were un-
christian.

Here then was not only a religious but also a
social challenge to Europe of the sixteenth century.
Catholics and Protestants agreed that these heretics
needed to be crushed before they spread. They were
imprisoned, deported, beheaded, drowned and burned.
Some recanted under duress, convincing their antagonists
of their rightful use of these deconversion techniques.
Others no doubt were discouraged from joining, and
the movement never became massive. But for many
their suffering reinforced their certainty about the
evil nature of the world and the necessity of separ-
ating into the true church. Indeed, a patent theology
of suffering developed which proposed that the truly
faithful church was marked by the baptism of blood.
A theology of two kingdoms likewise gained credence
as the kingdom of God, suffering nonviolently in its

faithfulness to Christ, was so clearly differentiated
from the sword-brandishing, persecuting, compromising
kingdom of this world.

Protestants also opposed some less overtly sub-
versive elements in Mennonite thought. For one,
regarding religious authority, the Mennonites insisted that *sola scriptura* could permit no compromise
and required a literal compliance to the very details
of New Testament ethical dictates. The Mennonites
insisted furthermore, in opposition to other reformers,
that salvation was not a matter of *sola fide* but
was a more syncretistic process of faith and works in
combination. These were critical issues for the
Reformers but not sufficient reason for persecution.
Luther and Calvin disagreed with each other passion-
ately, but neither called for the extermination of
the other. Faulty ideas alone did not readily warrant persecution, but when these implied a new social
order, action followed swiftly.

A period of separation followed the formative
phase. The push of persecution combined with the
quest for the necessary peace and quiet to create
the pure church of believers, sending the Mennonites
into virtual ghettos in Prussia and Russia, in the Pal-
atinate and Alsace-Lorraine, in Pennsylvania and
Ohio, in Manitoba, Mexico and Paraguay. Withdrawal
eased the tensions somewhat as the threatened societies
saw the problem makers shunted into undeveloped areas.
But resolution was not that easy. Mennonites continued
to pursue their concern to be the true church, the sign
of the kingdom, and accordingly conflicts remained.

The Mennonite quest for the kingdom tended to

insist on separate schools, and always required some
alternative to military service. Besides, the work
ethic and the perfectionism implied in their theology,
combined with mutual aid programs for the needy,
resulted in unusual material success. Almost wherever
they settled, the lands produced abundantly. Taken
together, their refusal to enter all elements of the
dominant culture and their extraordinary prosperity,
made conflict virtually inevitable.

The tactics used to enforce conformity during this
withdrawal phase, from the late sixteenth to late nineteenth centuries, rarely included death, with the
exception of the mass murders of the Russian Revolution. But subtler pressures could be almost as
destructive, with the result that Mennonites constantly
migrated in search of new lands where they might indeed
be the church of God. The more conservative Mennonites
still follow this withdrawal technique as they seek
to be faithful to their understanding of a separate
kingdom.

For most Mennonites conformity followed withdrawal.
Gradually acculturating steps were taken towards the
prevailing ways. Urbanism undermined the more closed
communities, the public educational systems were accepted, and special alternative service programs were
formulated in co-operation with various governments.
Other Christian groups have been affirmed as fellow
sojourners in working for the kingdom, while the
denominational system has become the acceptable means
to pursue the church's tasks.

The Mennonites thus have become just another
American denomination. True, they continue to have

their uniqueness, some of their number are rather
interesting oddities, but they are hardly a threat to
the status quo. But it must be remembered they were
at one time considered heretics, they were hunted
down as animals, they withdrew, and they gradually
accommodated to their present status. The accommodation, however, did not come entirely from the Mennonite side. Before they were accepted, their min-
ority position on religious freedom became normative
at least in most Western societies. Included in this
notion for some Americans, Canadians, and others at
least, is the understanding that counter-cultures may
endeed be legitimate features of a democratic society
and are not necessarily candidates for the wrath
reserved for heretics.

THE MORMONS

Some of the same religious enthusiasm which
characterized the Reformation era was repeated in the
Second Great Awakening, most notably in upstate New
York known as the "burned-over district". In the midst
of this revivalist fervor, a young Palmyra, New York,
man named Joseph Smith was visited by Jesus Christ
and God the Father. Through these heavenly visita-
tions, he learned that existing religious options
were faulty and that he had been chosen as the prophet
of God to bear witness to the full truth for these,
the latter days. The *Book of Mormon,* alongside further
Doctrines and Covenants, was revealed to Joseph and
served together with the *Bible* as the holy scriptures
for this new religion.

The religion the prophet Joseph proclaimed con-
trasted with orthodox Christianity on a number of
key issues. The very role attributed to Joseph's
revelations already distinguished Mormonism as unique
among Christian groups. Other deviations followed.
Man did not fall with original sin, says Mormonism,
but rather man fell in the right direction. Through
the supposed "fall," man received mortal bodies which
are necessary for the attainment of perfection.
Even as God grows in perfection, so too man by a
combination of faith in Jesus Christ and his own
strivings can become like unto God. "As man now is,
God once was; as God now is, man may become", is an
oft quoted Mormon dictum. This perfectionist notion
also had special meaning, for through procreation,
external souls gain bodies through which to strive
towards god-likeness. This concept also provided
one of the reasons for polygamy, for through an abun-
dance of children a family would ever be blessed.
The circle was further enlarged by baptizing for the
dead. Special temple rites were inaugurated to provide the community's blessing on various steps towards
perfection including adult baptism, celestial marriage,
and so on.

These and other Mormon teachings, although considered heretical by the orthodox churches, were
hardly cause for persecution as long as they remained
ideas alone. But these new doctrines were set in a
context that both attracted converts and elicited
intense hostility among the Gentiles--the non-Mormons.
The context was the Mormon proposal to gather from
among the nations of the world a people of God to build
Zion in America, in anticipation of the Second Coming

of Jesus Christ. Joseph did not deny the American
millennial belief fostered above all by Jonathan
Edwards that this nation had a special purpose in
God's providence; he did not deny the quest for a
utopian order on earth urged earlier by Puritans and,
in his day,by Owenites, Shakers, Oneida supporters,
and many others; he did not deny the potential of man's
perfection as maintained by Charles Finney;   rather he
strongly affirmed these common American themes, but
he placed his own unique interpretation on them all.
He held the keys to America's role in building the Kingdom; it was through his church alone that man could
be fully exalted; indeed, no man could fully come to
the Father but through the door of the Mormon Temple.

The Mormon community became virtually a theocratic
state. The church took an active interest in all
affairs of men; nothing was purely secular. Communi-
tarian practices were tried, following Joseph's revelation of the "Law of Consecration and Stewardship".
Economic leveling was never attained, but mutual as-
sistance remained a basic concern. The strong sense
of a separate peoplehood developed especially as
the outgroup placed pressure upon the people seeking
to establish Zion in their midst. The mutuality
and communal solidarity of the Mormons increased
both their material success and the opposition to
them from without.

Almost from the day in 1820 when Smith saw his
first vision, he was derided. The Church, organized in
1830 under the name Church of Jesus Christ of Latter
Day Saints, immediately met mistrust, which encouraged
it to make its first move to Kirkland, Ohio. From

Ohio missionaries moved west establishing new communities, most notably in Missouri. Here in Independence
and Far West the gathering of the Saints faced severe
difficulties including extensive property losses
and even the loss of life. In 1840, Nauvoo, Illinois,
became for some time the city of refuge. Under a
gracious Illinois charter, the city blossomed into
a dynamic centre. However, as internal divisions
combined with the attacks of Gentile detractors, a
crescendo was reached which peaked on June 27, 1844,
with the massacre of Joseph and Hyram Smith in their
prison cells.

     The Mormons were not particularly un-American;
indeed, in many ways they were the most American among
Americans in that they propounded an indigenous American religion in many ways uniquely adapted to new
immigrants taming the western frontier. Neither were
they peculiar in their unorthodoxy. Many heretics of
the day were censured only from the pulpit and in the
written word, for, at least in theory, Americans were
free to believe what they liked. But here was the
rub. They could believe whatever they wanted, but
they could not do whatever they wanted. And Joseph
Smith's new religion challenged the American myth.
Zion was not going to come through orthodox Christianity, through unchecked capitalism, through individuals
killing the Indian in order to take his land. Rather,
Zion was going to come through the gathering of the
Saints according to the Mormon plan. The Mormons
challenged the status quo and successfully established
alternative communities, which stood as glaring
reproaches to all those on the outside. And, with
the Mennonites, the Mormons faced the most severe

persecution, for their heresy challenged the dominant
society.

The loss of their martyred leader caused serious
divisions in the movement but far from shattered
it. The main group came under the strong leadership
of Brigham Young, who led the faithful to a new Zion
in the Great Basin of Utah. Some members of the Smith
family claimed the true heritage and established a
Reorganized Church in Independence, Missouri. Other
schismatics established their kingdoms elsewhere.

By 1844 Mormonism had completed its formative
period and was entering a phase of withdrawal. Utah did
not supply complete separation, however, and indeed
the Mormons sought statehood for Utah for some time.
Possibly the Saints would have been left at peace
had it not been for their peculiar institution--poly-
gamy--practiced openly in Utah, following Young's
example. But again, did all the harassment, the
intolerance, the legislative opposition, even the military action against the Mormon community stem entirely
from polygamy? It is very doubtful. Rather, polygamy
symbolized a community, a highly successful community
at that, which ran counter to normative society.
It challenged the American way of life and therefore
drew upon itself the persecutors' hate.

In 1890, following intense pressure from the
American government, the President of the Saints,
Wilford Woodruff, declared an end to plural marriage.
This also marked the beginning of a phase of accommodation to the dominant society. No longer were all
saints gathered to Zion but rather scattering was
accepted as legitimate. Doctrinal innovations similarly

lessened the critique of Gentile ways.

As the challenge of a new Zion softened, the reaction likewise dissipated. Mormonism became acceptable, a religion to be tolerated. It remains, still proclaiming many doctrines deemed unorthodox and still maintaining that truth is still held ultimately in the church alone, but Mormons are now found throughout society. The critique of Gentile America seems less strident. Once non-Mormon Americans no longer felt their way--their path to the Kingdom--threatened by the Mormon witness, these Saints of the latter days were allowed to exist without persecution.

THE MOONIES

We are living too close to be sure about it, but quite possibly the 1970's represent a time of religious ferment not unlike the Reformation or the Second Great Awakening. True society is not being radically realigned as in the sixteenth century, nor is awakening touching most areas of life as in the early nineteenth century, but the quest for meaning especially through religion is a pervasive concern of the 1970's.

Amidst this ferment, and among the new religious options offered to meet the stirrings of our souls, the Unification Church, or Moonies, have emerged with a high profile. This new religion, most correctly known as the Holy Spirit Association for the Unification of World Christianity, is not entirely new. The first missionaries arrived in America from South Korea in 1959. In the preceding decade the religion was founded

by Rev. Sun Myung Moon, who, like Joseph Smith, received special revelations from God. These visions
resulted in a new theological formulation spelled out
in *The Divine Principle*. This book, primarily a theological construction of the *Bible,* together with the
person of Rev. Moon, serves as the authoritative base
for Unification.

    Like Mormonism, Unification embraces much that
can only be labeled unorthodox, given classical Christian definitions. The central doctrinal tenet is creation. Adam and Eve were created for perfection which
was to be attained through a perfect, loving relationship with each other, with God, and with their offspring.
The attainment of perfection was frustrated by Eve's
adulterous relationship with the serpent. Ever since,
the countervailing forces of "Cain-type" and "Abel-
type" men and nations have struggled to gain pre-eminence
over the world. The Abel side is, however, gradually
proving victorious in God's providential plan of restoration. In this process, Jesus, the Second Adam,
saved man spiritually but not physically, for he did
not fully complete the task in which the first Adam
failed. He did not marry and he had no children.
In these last days God has revealed to man the path
to the kingdom of perfection through the *Divine Principle*. At the Second Coming, the Third Adam who is
among us will become perfect, have perfect children
and, thereby, break the power of the Fall. Unification believes that evidence points to Rev. Moon
as, at least potentially, this Third Adam. If man will
now heed Moon's teaching, develop a heart of God by
loving God and man perfectly, he will be a partaker

of this kingdom.

These teachings have undoubtedly disturbed many
people especially the more orthodox, but in themselves
would hardly justify harassment and persecution. Persecution has been directed at the followers of Moon
because of the social implications of his teaching.
According to Moon, we are living in the most critical
period of history. Extraordinary steps are needed
to herald the new day, to open people's eyes to the
truth. Hence, Moonies, in America at least, devote
all their time, their talents, and their resources
to proclaiming the *Divine Principle*. All is required;
all is given. A communal structure has developed to
embrace this unique situation. The devotees, in turn,
consider this new peoplehood of completely dedicated
servants of God as "The Family". Out of the world
God has called them to be His people, His family.

This family emphasis is at the heart of Unification social organization, and it embraces another
important feature, namely, the formation of perfect
families. Romantic love and western marriage patterns
have not served the attainment of perfect marriages.
Hence, Rev. Moon selects marriage partners for those
converts who have attained a sufficient degree of
perfection to be married. He and Mrs. Moon, as the
first parents, in turn consecrate these marriages,
which in some cases are not consummated for several
years until further perfection is reached. For
the time being, those married as well as the single
Moonies do not follow traditional work patterns for
the most part but remain to witness, to teach, and
to collect financial resources on a full-time basis.

At the same time as the converts are spreading
the word on the street, Rev. Moon is establishing a
financial power base, especially in the eastern United
States. This base is critical, he feels, in order
to gain the necessary hearing to assure that America
will fulfill its role in the coming Kingdom. And
it is all important that America play its role, for
Rev. Moon shares the millennial notion of America
being a chosen nation of God. Although Korea is the
new Israel, America is her defender, and, as the leader
of the Abel forces of this world, it must maintain
its democratic strength--ideologically and militarily--
to shatter the Cain forces of totalitarianism represented above all in communism.

More left-leaning Americans worry about Moon's
militant anti-communism and unfailing belief that
America is called to act on God's behalf. His economic
fervor and his assumed links with the repressive South
Korean regime give them further cause for concern.
But most Americans who call for the repression of
Unification respond less to its politics than to its
blatantly critical commentary on their lives. The
100 per cent dedication of young Moonies, their
self-sacrifice, their communal life-style, their quest
to establish perfect families, their willingness
to enter arranged marriages all underscore weaknesses
in the lives of most Americans and, moreover, challenge
the values central to American life in our time.
The challenge to the status quo is reinforced by
these Moonies' claim that their way is God's way,
when most Americans (including the parents of Moonies)

like very much to think that it is their way that
is God's way.

Why is it that Unification members are being persecuted by deprogrammers, by some psychiatrists, by
the media and even by the law? Are not all religions
free to exist in America? Are these people any more
brainwashed than Billy Graham converts, or Jesuit
priests, or soldiers? It is very doubtful. The
problem with the Moonies is that they are challenging
the status quo. They are giving their whole lives
to their faith. They are seeking perfection, the
kingdom of God on earth. When the majority culture
likes to think that "I'm OK, You're OK," that it is
indeed building God's kingdom, Mennonites, Mormons
and Moonies come along with an alternative proposal--
and persecution begins.

Will the Moonies have to go through separation
and accommodation before they will be fully accepted and
tolerated, and no longer considered heretical or
illegitimate? Speaking sociologically, the Moonies
will probably follow the way of Mennonites and Mormons.
But in the meantime Americans could possibly learn
something from the Mennonite and Mormon experience.
Perhaps these groups do not need to be made into the
image of status quo America before they are tolerated.
Their protests, their alternative kingdoms might,
if allowed to blossom, bring all Americans closer to
the realization of the kingdom--whatever its definition
may be.

SUMMARY

Heresy continues as an influential concept in

this society with the result that certain religious
groups are not granted complete toleration. The problem is not with unorthodox ideas *per se*. If it were,
many of our modern theologians would be lying on psychiatrists' couches or would be entrapped in basements
or motels for deprogramming. Rather, the spectre of
illegitimate religion rises when that religion proposes a notion of the kingdom at variance with the
accepted definitions, and when it proceeds on the
basis of that idea to gather into a new community
disciples of the new way which stands as an obvious
critique of prevailing understandings. Such an alternative community is condemned and the participants
persecuted until it withdraws and/or accommodates.
This has been the experience of the Mennonites and the
Mormons and now appears to be the lot of the Moonies.

PROPOSAL

     At the basis of this state of affairs in America
is the tendency of religion in this country to be
polarized towards the extremes of a privatized religion
of the individuals and of a civil or national religion
of the entire populace. As one element of this civil
religion, America is characteristically seen as playing
a unique role in God's providence with the entire
nation working towards this end. As long as people
maintain their religion in private, or at least
relative privacy, there is no problem. Nor is there
any problem when people hold to a public religion which
is shared by the larger populace. There is little
problem for those religions which have been accommodated

as in the cases of the Mennonites and Mormons.

But a problem looms large for those religions, like the Moonies, who propose a notion of community and who aggressively work towards creation of that community, when the self-definition of that community is deviant from prevailing norms. This is particularly true for a religious movement like Unification which has taken many, if not all, the highest virtues of American society, has repackaged them in such a way as to maximize the critique of the dominant society on issues like the family, with the result that the wish to crush the prophets becomes obsessive.

It seems that societies like America need to learn to tolerate deviance of both orders, intellectual *and* communal. Such toleration is most taxing for a society as Canada knows all too well. Yet true religious toleration must allow for new movements to rise up which claim that it is the will of God to remake our societies, and then aggressively proceed towards that new *telos*. Such true toleration would enrich our world in many ways: at least, it is a better option than destroying the prophets either in cold blood or cooled brains.

MAKING CRIME SEEM NATURAL:

THE PRESS AND DEPROGRAMMING

BART TESTA

> Myth prefers to work with poor,
> incomplete images, where the
> meaning is already relieved of
> its fat...such as caricatures,
> pastiches, symbols, etc.
>
> --- Roland Barthes, *Mythologies*

> "A good kidnapping is like
> fixing a flat tire."
>
> --- Mick Mazzoni ("Not his real
> name") to Josh Freed.

The representation of public controversy is an
important activity of the mass media and particularly
of newspapers. It lies one step beyond factual re-
portage (like news stories on hotel fires) towards
the discussion of abstract ideas (like a science page
feature on new theories in astrophysics). Most
often in newspapers the representation of public
controversy consists of arranging interview materials

An earlier version of this paper was presented to the
Seminar on Media Ethics sponsored by the Toronto School
of Theology and the Institute of Christian Thought
in Toronto in March, 1978. The particular series
analyzed in this article is, in the judgment of the
author and editors, representative of general newspaper coverage of this issue.

and facts from opposing sides of a question in order
to reconstruct the arguments and data relevant to
that controversy. This is most commonly done at
"feature" length and in a more leisurely fashion than
the writing of news stories. The telling of the
"story" itself is subordinated to the *differing
interpretations* of what the facts mean to those who
are interviewed. Such features usually come after
several, and sometimes many, news stories have already
familiarized readers with the relevant facts and
ideas. Such features are intended to sort out information into arguments, and these can concern educational planning, racial conflict, proposed legislation or any number of other questions. Such features
have a model which is very flexible because it alter-
nates viewpoints, the opinions of the people interviewed, which reconstruct the controversy for the
readers.

     But other models for the representation of public
controversy are available and some of these have been
given names that have become familiar such as "in-
vestigative journalism" (the reporter brings to light
new facts which create or change controversies), "advocacy journalism" (the writer chooses a side), or
"New Journalism" (the writer's subjective responses
are made an explicit component of his writing). The
Montreal Star series on deprogramming uses such
alternative models for the representation of public
controversy over the "cults" and deprogramming extensively and effectively. My concern here is to
examine how these alternative models are used in this
series in order to open the question of their ethical

appropriateness in dealing with these issues.

First, some particulars. A newspaper "series" consists of a number of features on one or a few very closely related topics. The *Montreal Star* series on deprogramming appeared for six successive days at the very end of December, 1977, through the first week of January, 1978. The six stories were written by Josh Freed, a *Star* staff reporter. Each of his articles was long, covering almost a whole page, counting the "sidebars." Sidebars are shorter features written either by the same or another writer which supply supplemental information of either an expository or interview kind. In this series, the sidebars consist of two accounts of the Unification Church (the Moonies) and one interview with the Church's San Francisco lawyer, Ralph Baker. The body of each main article differs greatly in style from these sidebars. Whereas the sidebars are "conventional," aside from the occasional "flashback," the articles sustain a single narrative of events to which writer Josh Freed was an intimate witness, and in which he was often a participant. Freed writes almost all of the stories in the first person with close attention to his own reactions to what is going on. In generic form, then, this series is New Journalism: Freed's presence to events is very closely identified with the reader's "presence" to these same events.

After its initial publication in the *Montreal Star*, the series was subsequently run by *The Hamilton Spectator* and *The Calgary Herald* (and perhaps by other Canadian newspapers as well). Sometimes the series

ran with additional sidebars originating with the
paper carrying the series.[1] In each case, the series
was titled *The Moon Stalkers, but only after the first
installment*. With the exception of a far more conventional, interview-model series done in the Toronto
Globe and Mail in early 1978, *The Moon Stalkers* was
the first major series published on deprogramming
in some time and it emerged out of a relative vacuum
of news on the topic.[2]

I was invited to a seminar on Media Ethics to
do a paper on *The Moon Stalkers* because I am a theologian and a journalist, but I am not sure I accepted
for the same reasons I was invited. As a theologian,
I am expected to have competence in the new religions,
but most of the material I have read is inadequate.
This is a real problem. Despite the recent and fascinating example of Harvey Cox[3], theologians conven-
tionally work with texts and rarely work without them.
While some groups, such as Hare Krishna and the Lovers
of Meher Baba, and to a lesser extent the Church of
Scientology, have been studied and we have a few
pieces of work we can depend on, in the case of the Unification Church we are still in a pre-textual situation. *The Moon Stalkers* deals exclusively with this
group, as well as with deprogramming. Moreover,
the controversy surrounding the Moonies concerns
aspects of their religious practice about which conventional theology has little to say. These are
questions concerning recruitment, biographies of the
group's leadership, financial resources, institutional
"fronts" and "life styles." That is why, I think,

the Unification Church has seemed more the province
of journalists than of theologians and I suppose
this is because journalism is the profession that deals
with things for which there are "not yet" specific
"professional" treatments. Journalists are "general-
ists" who write about things before the specialists
have begun their formal enquiries.

As a journalist, I am a specialist. I am not
a news reporter but an entertainment writer. I
review films, books and popular music. More rarely,
I write cultural "think pieces." I am not at all
sure the Seminar on Media Ethics invited me in this
capacity exactly, but it is in this role that I feel
competent to address Josh Freed's series. Like myself, Freed has no apparent theological tools to deal
with the new religions and he evinces no interest in
"hard" news whatsoever. We both tend to see these
new religious groups as pop culture phenomena and I,
at least, see him writing out of a pop perspective.
These are, if I may jargonize a bit, our shared
"conceptual grids."

While this is not the place to theorize about
pop culture, I would like to assert a corner of my
own operative attitude.[4] I think pop culture's
means are trite and do not bear close scrutiny;
but its *effects* on the way we think are serious.
My reading of Freed's series reflects this attitude.
Freed has, in my view, used trite means to achieve
a serious effect. Freed uses trite means to tell
the readers things he takes, and believes his readers
should take, very seriously. In my judgment, what
Freed is doing is not presenting news, but transforming

news into advertising.

Like most journalists,including myself, Freed
is intellectually facile. Journalistic writing is
consumed quickly and does not allow the long reflective
pauses other kinds of writing allow. Put them in
and editors will tell you, "It doesn't *go* anywhere!"
But it seems to me that unlike most good journalists,
Freed is not emotionally cautious. *The Moon Stalkers*
is very passionate writing. Now, the notoriously
"cool," "hardboiled" detachment of journalists is not
a function of cynicism but the result   of "newspaper-
type" writing. The emotional caution embodied by this
writing does not reflect the author's feelings; rather,
it reflects the ethical attitude of ·a style of writing
which precludes a writer's feelings, at least in part,
because it seeks to limit the writer's "emotional authority." As style, newspaper writing rarely says,
"I was there." It says, "Here's what happened."

So too is passionate writing a function of a
certain style that has its own ethics. It forcefully
inserts the writer's commitments because it seeks to
announce the writer as a knowing and feeling presence.

Both kinds of writing have ethical dimensions
because each, as writing, offers a formula for reality.
Newspapers are, of course, one of our crucial media
for grasping the world; their representations of the
world carry immense weight. Most newspaper-type writing
has a highly developed format and is rigorously monitored by editors to give readers the facts, just the
facts. This is because facts elicit an interpretive

response. They do not impose it. In this way newspaper-type writing seeks to limit its authority as
writing, to keep that authority with the reader and his
freedom to interpret. Other types of writing that
appear in newspapers, like "editorial," "opinion,"
"analysis" and "criticism", are clearly labelled as
such. It follows that professional ethics within the
newspaper industry are concerned chiefly with two kinds
of responsibility: truth of the facts and truth of
labelling.

However, problems arise with features. They
are a "second-order" type of writing intended most
often to inform the reader about interpretations of
fact. This aspect, together with the length of features, often requires "invention" in style, and
complexity in form in order to convey a greater rich-
ness of information than is elsewhere usual for newspaper journalism. Sometimes new forms result from
these requirements, and, with them, new ways of structuring reality. This is one way to interpret the
important development of New Journalism, as practiced
by Truman Capote, Norman Mailer or Tom Wolfe in the
1960's.

The controversial new religions have come along at
a time when religious journalism in the commercial
press is at a particularly low ebb. (Did it ever
have a high tide?) The most obvious difficulty for
journalists who have to write about religion is that
it is hard to discern a "fact." Religion is always
interpretation and fact together; its "hard" news
is always intermingled with the "good news." When a

reporter interviews a Hare Krishna "devotee" or an
Anglican bishop, he is immediately aware that he is
not interviewing a fire marshall or even a treasury
official.

The new religious groups have not been handled
at all well by newspapers who have also had to report
on the counter-development of deprogramming at the
same time. Already controversial as separate topics,
the "cults" and deprogramming also are controversial
in relation to each other. The press has found a
typical solution to the complexity that has arisen
from all these controversies: the issues which have
arisen discreetly in new religions and deprogramming
have been re-organized as a grand, simplified antinomy. Journalists now stand back and report, as they
would a war, the fight between the "cults" and the
deprogrammers. As a publicist for one of the new
religions put it to me, "It's a battle of the (P.R.)
flacks." The conventional interview-model feature
has become the field for this "battle of the flacks"
with the result that everyone who is interviewed
sounds like a flack. The reader naturally is led
to the conclusion that both sides are a little mad.

It is in this sense that the new religions and
deprogramming are pop phenomena: they have experienced
a thinning-out of the serious questions into trite
polarities that require one to choose one or the other,
or to throw up one's hands. But, as with all pop
phenomena, when one chooses a polarized side, the
simplified position has complex historical effects.
When chosen, a side regains its density. Where Freed
and I disagree as journalists is that he believes the

serious controversies over the "cults" and deprogramming can be resolved by his choosing to pour his feelings into an act of writing that chooses deprogramming. Freed's series is a problematic example of
"advocacy journalism" because it seeks to choose a
side while also uncovering new facts and revealing
Freed's own feelings. The unusual combination of
these three alternative models--investigative report-
ing, advocacy journalism and New Journalism--results
in Freed writing not news, but an advertisement, or
what Roland Barthes calls a "myth."[5]

In this partial analysis of *The Moon Stalkers*
I will quote generously. Since the series is long
and carefully structured, a preliminary outline will
help place the events and the quotations.

OUTLINE OF THE MOON STALKERS

1. Josh Freed, in Montreal, hears that a friend,
Benji Carroll, has become involved in some strange
project while on vacation in San Francisco. Mike,
another friend, goes off to find Benji and disappears.
Josh and other friends of the two, now worried, do some
investigating and connect the twin disappearances to
The Creative Community Center which they find out
is an alias of Rev. Moon's Unification Church. A
meeting is called. Interwoven into the account of
the meeting are the biographies of Mike and Benji,
both 28-year-old college graduates with solid ties
in the Montreal community where they had lived.

It is decided that money be raised to send a "mission"
out west. But before the mission leaves, Mike returns to Montreal in preparation for moving back to
California permanently. After a few days, however,
he "loosens up" and is persuaded to talk with an ex-
Moonie who persuades him to quit the Unification Church
and stay home. The mission, which includes Josh Freed,
does go to San Francisco and meets with Benji at a
restaurant. Benji is accompanied by two Moonies who
appear to control him; he otherwise appears to be
"a zombie." Freed visits the Moonies' Community Center himself. The sidebar gives the standard account
of Moon and his church, with a few notes on deprogramming woven into the account.

     2. Josh Freed visits the Moonies' San Fran-
cisco Center and goes from there to Boonville, the
Church's "ranch" located about 100 miles north of
the city, where he experiences Moonie indoctrination
first hand. He finds it mentally exhausting and he
leaves after two days, convinced that Benji, who
had been in the group for five months, had undergone a powerful "programming." The series is now
entitled *The Moon Stalkers* and is accompanied by a
curious logo that looks like a hybrid of the Iron
Cross, the Japanese Imperial "setting sun" flag and
a target.

     3. A kidnapping is planned carefully and exe-
cuted in a manner more than a little suggestive of
a farce. This installment ends with a cliffhanger:
the police right on the kidnappers' tails.

     4. Escape from the police to a new hideout is
reported--it seems to have occurred in the ellipsis

between installments 3 and 4. Most of this article
describes the anxious wait for the deprogrammer they
have decided they need. Benji is described as nearly
comatose. Included is a biography of the deprogrammer,
Ford Green, who is said to have "deprogrammed himself"
while in the Moonies. This installment ends with the
apotheotic arrival of Green. The sidebar is about
the Moonies in San Francisco, emphasizing their pre-
sumed questionable fundraising activities.

     5. This article gives a very detailed account
of the deprogramming. For the first time in the series,
Benji speaks at some length.

     6. This article gives an account of Benji's
"recovery period" in the Laurentians in a Quebec
resort area and includes an interview with Benji
"today." The sidebar contains an interview with Unification Church lawyer Ralph Baker who protests the
"improper" kidnapping and deprogramming.

     The first article in the series begins, "The
last time I'd seen Benji Carroll, he was heading
west...". The series begins, then, with the establishment of "places" and "times" as subjective realities, a tendency that deepens as the story unfolds
and that circumscribes both time and space with a
system of values. In the first article, "here" (Montreal) is a place of community, of intimacy, mutual
knowledge and concern. The "west" (California)
is definitely an "elsewhere." Very soon after we
learn Benji and Mike have disappeared, a meeting is
called and the community is mobilized for some action.
Thus, a "we" (the Montrealers) and a "they" (the

California Moonies) are established.

Implied are two different types of human organization: the known Montrealer community and the
reported-alleged one of the "cult." Here are the
reports, on the Moonies--

> The emotional effects were said to be so severe
> that women ceased menstruating and men became
> impotent and even stopped growing facial hair.

and on the community's meeting--

> But worried friends of the two missing Montre-
> alers called a meeting to discuss it. About
> 25 people came--teachers, neighborhood organ-
> izers, community doctors, unemployed. All were
> bewildered and somewhat shaken.

Who are Benji and Mike?

> Benji and Mike were bright college graduates of
> 28, with close family ties and many friends.
> There was nothing in their backgrounds to lead
> them to a cult.

Two kinds of human organization are described here,
and a person leaving one joins another. One cannot
belong to both; one has to choose. After his return
to Montreal, Mike talks to an ex-Moonie on the phone:

> The conversation lasted only a hour, but friends
> listening could sense the whole idea turning in
> Mike's head and by the time he had hung up, he
> had agreed to stay in Montreal.

Mike's subsequent description of his stay among the
Moonies makes two points: he "knew nothing of Rev.
Moon" and his"mind was swimming... I thought it would

burst." Freed then informs us specifically that "On
the morning of the fourth day, Mike seemed to see things
with a new clarity." The reader had not previously
been aware that Mike was being monitored on a close,
day-to-day basis, or that, after deciding to stay in
Montreal, he had shown any signs of being unclear.
This passage, then, serves both to emphasize the in-
tensity of the Montreal community's concern for its
members and to indicate that something really strange
was going on "out there" in California.

Mike's second description, after the "new clarity,"
of his experience in Boonville is far more assertive
than the first:

"Something came over me...destroyed my critical
thinking," he told us..."I think I was brainwashed."
This is a report. It specifies, through Mike, the
vague allegations mentioned above. It also specifies
in the person of Mike two kinds of human organization
and their methods of eliciting commitment from members:
community/clarity and cult/brainwashing. This is a
good example of Freed's writing method: the writing
stays on the level of experience while inscribing
that experience and the talk he hears with the global
structure of a basic polarity between community and
cult.

If Freed were a film director (and he does allude
later to film techniques), what follows would be called
a "jump cut:"

A week later I was sitting in a tiny coffee
shop in San Francisco looking at the pallid,
expressionless figure that bore no resemblance
to the Benji I had known.

The "jump cut" is an accelerated version of the "mon-
tage of attractions," editing in which one shot attracts itself to the next. "Brainwashing" attracts
itself to Freed's being in California looking at Benji,
without anything intervening. It is an ellipsis.
It is also more generally a "motivated cut." Mike's report was so scary that Freed and the reader are propelled immediately to San Francisco. The text in
this way imitates the charge of concern that has built
up in the Montrealer community.

      Freed and another Montreal friend, Marilyn, are
at a meeting with Benji, but "he did not come alone...[and]
showing none of his usual warmth and wit, remained
silent and detached through most of the meal, gazing
across the room as if through some kind of trance."
Between these two sentences, which I have elided
together, Freed describes Benji's "family" companions
as "lively." Benji, however, is underweight and
uninterested in the community at home; in short,
he is inert. The reader, sharing Freed's confusion
as he accumulates his impressions, wants to know why.
Freed cannot yet tell us, but he does speculate:

      It seemed impossible. I thought I knew Benji
      but this just wasn't him. The body was his but
      someone else was pulling the strings.

For Freed, these are just impressions. His writing
registers dismay and tells us he must find out more.
The community he and Marilyn (who never speaks),
represent has failed to touch Benji. Why? The allegations reported in the earlier part of the article
now seem to have some basis in Freed's empirical
experience of Benji and the "family" members. The

two competing human organizations do seem radically
different. What is this difference really? What has
so affected Benji?

I'd like to note that my analysis reads like an
analysis of a fictional text, with the usual emphasis
on voice, space and time because Freed's text is written
this way--as a series of impressions in time. "And
then, and then..." is the mode. What little discursive
writing appears reports what wonderings Freed feels,
along with the reader who wants to know what is happening. But, for the most part, the writing is literal.

At the end of the first article, Freed begins a
journey into the Moonie world to find out what it is
really like. He does find out, in the second article,
during his two-day visit to "Boonville Ideal City Ranch
-- training headquarters and alleged 'brainwashing'
centre for Rev. Sun Myung Moon's Unification Church."
The article actually begins with a brief "mood piece":

> The seemingly endless gravel road halted abruptly
> at a high barbed-wire fence and a wooden sentry
> post...

If this sounds like an evocation of a concentration
camp, so does this 'report' Freed read from a colleague:

> and the only reporter whose first-hand account
> I had read had collapsed vomiting and hallucinating
> on fleeing the camp after 48 hours.

When Freed tells us he is nervous, we readers are
worried for him. As the narrative itself begins,
Freed meets "the spitting image of a young Jack Nicholson." The only word spoken by the otherwise uniden-
tified 'Jack Nicholson' is "Bi-zarre!" Twice. Whether
it is just impression or not, the presence of a Jack
Nicholson is also an evocation, like that of the

concentration camp. Aside from his role in *One Flew
Over the Cuckoo's Nest,* in which he played a spirited
individualist finally destroyed by a mental hospital,
Nicholson always plays an alienated man who can name
the world around him even as it oppresses and sometimes kills his soul. It is precisely this role that
Freed himself plays (or writes for himself later)
at Boonville. Whether intended or not, this evocation
of the movie actor informs us of the right attitude
one should have while visiting among the Moonies.
Who could disagree?   Jack Nicholson is cool all
the time and anywhere. It is keeping that internal
cool that is Freed's struggle in the hours to come.

     As a reader I myself identified with all this,
and I understand why. Boonville provides a great
opportunity for Josh Freed (and me, too) to stand
alone against a whole organization and outwit it.
(It will not be the last opportunity the series gives
us to do this. The structure of the kidnapping story
works the same way.)

     Here is how Boonville seemed to Freed. I quote
at some length:

> Constant activity, enthusiastic discussions and
> holding hands soon proved to be the most notable
> feature of life with the Moonies.

Here is Freed's response after 90 minutes (by his own
count) after arrival:

> I was as eager for a breather and some personal
> space as I was for food. But even meals were
> another link in a chain of totally structured
> activity that continued unbroken to day's end.

The implication is clear--the Moonies try to break
down individuality by constant group activity. This
is how Freed interprets "sharing":

Sharing required each person to divulge a bit
about his or her life story and inner feelings.

But the invasion of Josh's personal space is not only
verbal:

> ...my food was salted for me, my coffee doused
> with cream and everything done for me but the
> positioning of the fork in my mouth...As well,
> my hands were being held as though they were
> communal property.

Next comes a lecture which he relates to "sharing"
by suggesting that the lecturer begins by explaining
that custom:

> "Nowadays people are used to doing their own thing."
> (...)

> ...the lectures struck me as being meticulously
> prepared...They were absorbing, humorous and
> thought-provoking, but ideas wheeled past far too
> fast to reflect on them critically.

But the lectures are more than lectures. They are
another kind of personal invasion:

> If my attention wandered from the lecturer for
> even an instant, a "helpful" family member would
> prod me politely and say: "Josh...try to listen.
> This part is very important."

The representation of such invasions is full and
systematic, though Freed presents them narratively.
Two events break up what we read as "a dizzying stream
of singing, 'hooching' (cheering) and hand-holding":
a short interview with a Moonie and a sports event.
Josh tries to be alone:

> I hadn't taken three steps when a clammy hand
> came down on my shoulder and a voice asked:
> "So, how do you like it so far, Josh?"

> The voice belonged to a chubby fellow in thick
> glasses and a stunned smile quite common to many
> Moonies--a dull, hallow look in the midst of
> apparent enthusiasm that reminds me of one of

the androids that fetch Boris Karloff's coffee
in late-night films.

Being alone--to reflect--at Boonville is clearly impossible. Or rather, it becomes a mode of rebellion:

I paused to collect my wits, then stared at him
as intently as I could. "NO," I declared, then
turned and walked quickly away.

Two women nearby spotted me within seconds
and came rushing over bubbling, "Josh! Josh!" as
though I were a boyfriend they had not seen in
years.

The women pulled my unwilling hands from
my pockets, fondled them lovingly and minutes
later I was back in the lecture hall again.

The "kickball" game is all chanting, rendered in "caps":

"BOOTWITHLOVE BOOTWITHLOVE BOOTWITHLOVE! CATCH
WITH LOVE! CATCHWITHLOVE! CATCHWITHLOVE!"
shrieked the other team, as the two cheers
drowned each other into meaningless, deafening
sound.

This chanting continued for two hours. It
did not rise and fall with good and bad plays.
It simply continued like a TV set accidently left
on at maximum volume.

Finally, Freed analyzes his responses and tells us
about his resistence to the indoctrination:

...Like so many other *techniques* at Boonville,
the purpose of the mind-numbing chant was to keep
you from "spacing out"--finding seconds to day-
dream and possibly to entertain "negative" or
"unproductive" thoughts about life at the camp.
(...)

Only my original cynicism kept me *consciously
resisting*... Fortunately, by this time, I had
developed a number of small tricks to preserve
my sanity--minute gestures that somehow helped
me *to keep my sense of self*. [emphasis mine]
(...)

> It is astonishing how important these trivial
> tricks seemed when I felt every fibre of my person
> being sucked into this anonymous collectivity.
> The pull of the group was so strong that, at times,
> inexplicably, I felt like giving in myself--
> despite what I knew.

His overall evaluation of the process suddenly leaps
into a medical discourse, hooked to the term "programming." Freed's evaluation proceeds through three steps.

> [one], Several bright and normal people who came
> up with me were clearly swayed by the group's
> *indoctrination techniques, shredding their cri-
> tical faculties* quickly in the intense environ-
> ment. [emphasis mine.]

> [two], Reality somehow shifts a few degrees.
> Isolation, dwindling sleep, little protein and
> no time to re-evaluate what is happening cause
> you increasingly to lose perspective. You never
> really decide to stay--you simply defer indefin-
> itely the decision to leave.

> [three], As effective as this 'programming'
> technique is, it can be interrupted fairly easily
> in its early stages.

Interwoven with this evaluation is an analysis of the
steps in becoming a Moonie. The first, *influence,*
so the life at Boonville seems normal; second, *shift
in reality* so that when Moon's name comes up, "it
doesn t seem to matter as much as it might have;" and
third, *enlightenment* identification with Moon and his
church--"You have become a Moonie." This is the full
"programming" seen as a progressive disease: its early
stages and full tumescence.

Freed's rebellion takes the form of interrupting
the process for his fellow visitors at Boonville, including Jack Nicholson who is present. Freed flusters
his "group leader" by the mere mention of Moon's name,

causing her to deliver "a lecture that usually comes
two weeks later." But the lecture fails; the name alone
was enough to interrupt the "programming." "Within an
hour Jack Nicholson and two other recruits had hitch-
hiked out. Among them was...a huge Colorado mountain
man--sort of a hippie Paul Bunyan I had taken a liking
to..." "Paul Bunyan", whose real name is Keith, as
we learn in the third article in the series, gets a
bit part in the kidnapping, but a flat tire prevents
him from actually participating.

Having detailed Freed's sojourn into the Moonie
world to find out what it is really like, I would like
to make two observations. Freed writes as if he were
naive about the whole issue of the "cults" and deprogramming. For a newspaper reporter, he seems unaware that the rhetoric he uses is commonplace in the
rather copious journalism extant on these subjects.
Moreover, he does not seem conscious that the structure
and language used in his narrative is identical to
that of the early chapters of Ted Patrick's book, *Let
Our Children Go!,* in which the noted deprogrammer tells
how he found his vocation after a visit to a Children
of God center prompted by his son's conversion to the
group.[6] This raises the question: Is Freed really
an open and naive observer? Can we believe this when
he has mentioned "scouring" newspaper files and has
conducted an interview with an "anti-cultist", a middle-
aged San Francisco pharmacist?

Freed's writing would have the reader believe
in the "innocence" of its author, who is merely a representative of his community. The writer argues this
innocence by refusing to disclose his rhetoric

as rhetoric, as a systematic contending, and instead
pretending to use the rhetoric of narration: the rhetoric of events and Freed's response to events.

I do not object to the truth of Freed's account. I
have never been to Boonville myself and I have no reas-
son to doubt Freed's story. It sounds like something
I might have written myself. I, too, tend to identify
with Jack Nicholson and have felt my share of hostility
towards religious persuaders (Catholic mostly) who
presume to intimacy. But one has to question the
"innocence" of a style which falls so neatly into an
argument that converges on the term "programming,"
which seems to have a "merely" symmetrical relation to
"de-programming." Freed's is not just an innocent first-
person story. It is also an argument based on a theory.
If Freed tells the reader all about his inner mental
processes, why doesn't he tell the reader about the
formulation (and sources) of the theory that underlies
his argument?

My second observation concerns the title *The
Moon Stalkers*. The third story in the series goes to
great lengths in recounting the kidnapping of Benji
Carroll to include all the details it can to make the
venture into a farce perpetrated by a band of well-
meaning but rank amateurs. Yet the title of the series
is a sign of a certain kind of professionalism. We
find this kind of title frequently in pulp fiction,
such as Donald Hamilton's "Matt Helm" books, like
The Destroyers. These titles are formed by making a
verb into a proper noun. "To stalk" becomes "stalker."
Such neologisms are ironic. They express the terms
under which an ordinary man becomes something else,

becomes a professional something-else.

The plot of much pulp "action" fiction tells us how a regular guy is propelled into dangerous circumstances and has to come to a moral decision, in the midst of intrigue and danger, to act within the terms of those circumstances to reach a moral end. Much of these novels is taken up with defining these terms and "proving" to us that the hero has no choice but to accept these terms to be effective. He has to become a temporary professional. But the profession is limited to one "unique" action wholly defined by the plot, and hence the hero's new name, the title, becomes a verbal-name.[7] A recent example of such fiction is the now-defunct TV series *The Night Stalker* which stars Darren McGavin as a newspaper reporter who accidently discovers a "classic" monster living in an American city (Dracula in Las Vegas, Werewolf in Phoenix). McGavin does serio-comic battle with these monsters, and with his editors who never believe his story. *The Night Stalker* is an ironical title because Darren McGavin is such a fumbler. He can no more "stalk" than do karate. He is a farcical night stalker (he bangs his head or stubs his toe every episode) who is more like a night stumbler.

The Moon Stalkers is a title in this tradition, and certainly not in the tradition of newspaper headlines. It fits, too. Freed and friends are unwilling "Moon Stalkers" who act out of the imperative of community feeling. They did not seek this job. They just want to get their friend back.

This title, together with the innocence of the writing, permits the reader to deflect attention from

questioning the complex issues the series raises and
encourages him to focus on plot. The title embodies
only one personalized conflict-- that between the
community and the cult. This stylistic deflection
increases enormously in the third article, which treats
the most controversial, indeed illegal, event in the
series, the kidnapping. It is, I should point out,
written as farce.

It begins, "They were hardly the Magnificent Se-
ven." In fact, they are amateurs, to a man. The team
consisted of a Jungian psychologist, two "kidney, not
kidnaps" specialists, an "aging hippie general prac-
titioner," Benji's father, the "hippie Paul Bunyan"
Keith, a consulting private eye and "us", Garry, Lenny
and Josh. The private eye is the one who tells Freed
that a kidnapping is like fixing a spare tire. "There's
no point in doing it if you don't do it right." Wrong,
but that's how it seemed at first:

> Our plan was to lure Benji back to his mother's
> and sister's hotel--and snatch him fast. (We'd
> often seen it on television.)

It is curious that Freed and friends have often seen it
on television when such a plan has never been executed
on TV. Kidnappers do not lure people to mother's and
sister's hotel.   People who hold surprise parties
(maybe on the *Mary Tyler Moore Show*), do. This may
be the befuddled rhetoric of amateurism, but the plan
itself is standard deprogramming procedure, as encoded
by the press and by Patrick's book. By the way, how
was contact made with all these doctors? Freed does
not tell us, but the reader might wonder what inspired
all these amateur kidnappers.

As I said above, the form of the article is farce.

It is written from Freed's limited point of view.
Yet lest the reader forget the deeper seriousness of
the venture, Freed interrupts the rollicking narrative
with passages like this:

> ...Lenny and Simon arrive, grabbing Benji from
> the front, as he flailed his arms to escape--
> his eyes registering a terrifyingly blank ex-
> pression.
>
> Then momentarily, he noticed Simon, and for
> an eerie second he seemed to return to the Benji
> of old. He stopped, as in a freeze frame in a
> movie, and said:
>
> "Hi Simon--what are you doing here?"
>
> But an instant later his eyes were distant
> again and he was fighting to escape as though
> we were total strangers.

The Benji who can recognize reality (i.e. his friends)
has flashed out of the Moonie-Benji for a moment, a
"freeze frame," before the "possessed one" returns
to his previous condition, expressed through his eyes.

The farce ends with a cliff-hanger, with the police about to close in, and line, "'My God,' she [the
hotel clerk] whispered the blood draining from her face.
"'They're standing right behind you now.'"

The fourth and fifth articles deal with the deprogramming itself. Actually the fourth, a very sombre
piece, deals only with the wait for the deprogrammer,
who arrives only at the very end. The fourth article
is sombre for a good reason: amateurs may make a farce
out of their kidnapping and still manage to pull it
off. There is nothing mysterious about that. It requires no special expertise, no real professionalism.
But now that they have Benji Carroll, they do not

know how to reach him. The community of Montrealers
fail again, just as they did in the coffee shop:

> "Benji...why don't you just talk? "

> It was like speaking to a corpse. Hour after
> hour he sat there rigid as a block of concrete,
> gazing into space as though we weren't there.

> It was uncanny and frightening: for the
> first time since the strange odyssey had begun
> five weeks earlier, we knew we had done the right
> thing.

> And we now knew as well that we needed a
> "deprogrammer" if we were ever going to reach
> him [Benji] again.

Here, for the first time, the word "deprogrammer"
is mentioned, and with it comes the first explicit
identification of a professional person. Prior to
this we have met only the bumbling, well-meaning friends
of Benji and the mystified Moonies, of which Benji is
now one. As if cued by the mention of the need for
the deprogrammer, Rev. Moon makes his sole appearance
in the series--on TV, right there in the room with Benji,
Lenny and Josh. Benji is sleeping. The deprogrammer
has been called on the phone. Rev. Moon appears on
TV, having "rented an hour of television time to 'talk
to America.'" As described by Freed, Moon's show was
a thoroughly fascist affair:

> "MAN-SEI!!" shrieked 1,500 Moonies kneeling be-
> fore him, saluting skyward with clenched fists
> that seemed to come from a single body.

The next morning the police have arrested Benji's
father. Following this, the newspapers, the local
police and the FBI are described as mobilized and clo-
sing in, under the guidance of the Moonies themselves.
The headline for article four is "Police Help the Moonies". The community, indeed, seems frail before this

massed power pressing down on them. But,

>   We had come this far...we were going to stick
>   it out to the end.

One can almost hear the wagon wheels creak as the circle
is formed to do hopeless battle with the enemy. There
is no question about the right: Freed has now thinned
down his prose to an extraordinarily tense enumeration
of events. If the third article in the series ends
in a cliff-hanger, the fourth is the dawn before the
final assault. There is only one hope:

>   Several hours later we finally reached a depro-
>   grammer. He was Ford Green, a 27-year-old ex-
>   Moonie who had gotten into the Moonies training
>   camp to retrieve his sister, and succumbed him-
>   self.

Green was in the Moonies for "eight mindless months"
before he "unbrainwashed" himself. The reader can ap-
preciate Green's strength and heroism after Freed's
very brief visit to Boonville: Ford Green has passed
through the most vigorous vocational rite of passage
a deprogrammer possibly could. Even Ted Patrick himself only suffered through one weekend of the Children
of God. Green was (mentally) dead for eight whole
months before he resurrected himself. Freed doesn't
make a big thing out of all this, just:

>   We had talked to Ford briefly over the phone,
>   and he certainly sounded like a tough customer.
>
>   "If you want me, I have to be in complete
>   charge," he stated bluntly, in a voice that
>   singed my ear...
>
>   There wasn't much choice, so we agreed to
>   his terms. Then we sat down to watch the news
>   and to wait to see who came first---Green or
>   the FBI.

Green may be tough, but he is not a man without personal
pain, the source of even higher motives than his own

experience:

> ...he and his parents face a $15.6 million law-
> suit for allegedly trying to deprogram his own
> sister. During the session, his sister slashed
> her wrists--sideways--and was rushed to the hos-
> pital where the Moonies recovered her. Today
> they use her as a virtual saint in church pro-
> paganda.

Freed had explained earlier that Moonies have been taught
that it is better to die than to be deprogrammed and
have been instructed how to commit suicide, "down to
the precise angle at which to slash one's wrists:
across for the hospital, down for death."

Green, then, has both professional credentials
and personal reasons to be after the Moonies who "identify him as the 'special servant of Satan.'" At this
point the reader may well be delighted that Freed finally reached this deprogrammer, and neither asks
"Where did he get the phone number?" nor notices that
Ford Green's biography is an entirely conventional one
for deprogrammers, right down to the demonic status he
enjoys among the Moonies. Such questions hardly matter
when Green speaks--and Freed listens. Green's arrival,
which Freed uses to close the fourth article with
a gasp, is nothing short of an apotheosis:

> As the door cracked open, a gaunt six-foot figure
> leaned around and peered in. A pale face with
> fresh scars and stitches, he wore a dark patch
> oveɪ one eye.
>
> The other eye stared out unblinking, burning
> into Lenny's forehead--while the mouth smiled
> and whispered "Ford Green."
>
> Lenny hardly heard the words. Just waking
> up, as though still dreaming, he squinted into
> the doorway, and felt as if a cold wind were
> blowing, over his whole body:

"My God," he said to himself, "It is the devil."

The fifth article deals with the deprogramming itself and it divides into two parts. After a fast recap of the fourth article, there is a "battle" between Benji and Green and, then, the "essence of any deprogramming" which, in Freed's account, is not Green's work but a community affair.

First, the "battle order." Green and his assistant, Virginia, are described through a succession of aligned "professional" metaphors which are chosen really to say something about Benji's state. This "order" is how the first part of the deprogramming is narrated. Benji "is a dead man," says Green;"They've got you good...But don't worry. I'm here to give you a life transfusion...a soul injection." Freed calls Green "exorist." The metaphor and the dialogue are both theological. *The Exorcist* itself uses this kind of metaphor for the mystical bringer of freedom. But today, advertising uses the same metaphor for the bringer of household cleaners. Freed, I think, is closer to the more recent usage. I don't know what Green's religious self-image is. Ted Patrick means it literally when he uses religious language, but it is likely that Freed and Green use it to parody Benji's own understanding, which at this point is religious, or,as his opponents see it, pseudo-religious. The point is that Benji, metaphysically at any rate, is a zombie.

Then Green momentarily disappears (from Freed's prose) and Virginia appears, "like a summer breeze."

> Like a shy child opening to a stranger, Benji
> began to respond to Virginia--nodding or shaking
> his head at first, then grunting out terse sen-
> tences as if by rote.

This childhood-mother metaphor begins Benji's gradual recapitulation of his power of speech. It is the first time he speaks in the whole series. Then, "like a fire catching, Benji and Green begin a debate." The metaphors of fighting now proliferate--"in a psychological sword fight with no quarter given." Here is Green's finest hour:

> Standing, kneeling, pacing and whirling, Ford swept to the attack, his gestures lurching yet graceful--like the thoughts they were punctuating.

Freed can only follow the physical movements because this was a fight between adepts and "no one could understand what they were talking about." Gradually it becomes a battle between equals, but not before Freed's explanation that:

> It was a painstaking process: winding the doctrine, *unraveling* the knots in Benji's mind, *untwisting* the half-truths that had seemed so logical at Boonville, where little sleep, less protein and no time alone had weakened him to the point where anything could slip in. [emphasis mine]

Then, Ford acknowledges that he has met an equal:

> "He's smart, "Ford gasped, sweating, during his first break four hours later. "The smartest *I've ever gone against*...the dumb ones are easy." [emphasis mine]

> Then back into the ring with Benji again, with encouraging slaps on the back and a glassful of water to carry the next round.

Not only are the metaphors action-packed, but so is Freed's prose. Yet what is really supposed to be happening is a debate, a discussion. This style, I think, conveys the peculiar irony of deprogramming in the descriptions written by its supporters. They tell us

its main quality is reasoned discourse, but whenever
one reads a detailed description, there is little re-
porting on what is said. Rather, we read metaphors of
aggression, of battle. This is true here, and everywhere else where the celebrants of the technique of deprogramming put their descriptions down on paper. Freed
differs, however, in that he locates the "essence" of
deprogramming elsewhere: in a "caesura"--"Lots of food,
lots of rest," says Green.

The battle resumes the next day, this time in
gentler language. In the middle of the second day, "He
[Benji] asked to see our press clippings on Rev. Moon's
wealth and political connections. *Everyone left the
room,* and he knelt to pray." [emphasis mine]

This moment of private reflection, an obvious contrast to Freed's Boonville trip, is the dividing line.
After this, Green gradually recedes from Freed's prose
and members of the Montreal community take his place,
but not before this last, crucial exchange:

> "So Benji, which one is it going to be?" he
> [Green] *concluded* lurching toward him, his
> voice falling to a near whisper. "Only you
> can make the decision!" [emphasis mine]

There follows an exchange between Lenny and Benji on
choosing during which Lenny says, "I'm not evil. None
of us is evil." The exchange is emotional, an appeal
from the community for Benji's return. Finally, "The
next thing we knew..." the entire gathering has leapt
into a loving group-grope that concludes with this:

> ...Virginia appeared in the doorway shouting
> delightedly: "Welcome home, Benji...welcome
> home!"
>
> The metamorphosis in Benji, once he stopped
> crying, was immediate and startling.

What follows is a long description of the "new"
Benji who is also the "old" Benji:

> It was as though a new person had stepped into
> his body. As different as he was, he was nothing
> new to us--just the Benji *we had known before,*
> [emphasis mine]

That is, he is again the Benji of the community. In
Freed's account the key task in Benji's deprogramming
is to get Benji to choose between the cult and the
community. But, as he has shown us in his Boonville
story, no one "chooses" the cult; one becomes a Moonie
by failing (deferring) to choose. Hence, what, according
to Freed, distinguishes the cult and the community is
the former's technical destruction of the power of
choice. Deprogramming simply restores that power so
that one can choose the community, which is the only
choice anyone would make as soon as they can again
choose at all. But, since the Boonville community is
so effectively technical (i.e., professional) in its
destruction of the power to choose, a counter technician
is needed to re-evoke, and so restore, the power to
choose. That is the deprogrammer, the one who "unravels"
and "unwinds" the (obviously) bonded mind. Once this task
is finished, the deprogramee is really "brought back"
into human relationship by his community who comes in
to make its legitimate claims on the person. For Freed,
these claims are infallible; no one would desert a real
community like that formed by Lenny, Mike, Marilyn,
and Josh, who went up against the whole system (the
FBI-Moonie-etc. system) to save Benji. This is why the
community can perform the real deprogramming, by forcing
a true choice, the only one worth making, to be "free."
There is a fascinating passage, just before Benji reaches

his "breaking point" (Freed's term) and the community
group-grope begins. Freed sees into Benji's mind and
writes, "Images of his parents in jail, his friends
kidnapping him, the concern and feeling in it all
flashed through his mind."

Freed could not have known this, could he?
It is a fictional device, but a very astute one given
the notion of what a "person" is in this series: a
member of a tightly knit community which literally
has given him life again. Ford Green promised a
"life transfusion." The blood came from the community
--Benji's true mother. Another passage at the "breaking point" expresses this notion very well:

> Suddenly Benji shuddered, then burst into a
> wretched sob. He grasped Lenny like a life
> preserver and collapsed in his arms.
>
> Outside in the living room we heard a
> high-pitched wail, *like a newborn baby's first
> scream.* The door opened and Ford, *like a
> doctor,* told us, "Get in there fast...he needs
> you all." [emphasis mine]

The community immediately loses itself in the "mess
of tears and affection." Child-fighter-blood-tears-
feelings--this complex of images used by Freed are
the community's claims. They circumscribe personal
life and demonstrate possibilities. What else would
there be to choose? Clearly nothing.

This is fascinating when one recalls the repression in this series of all traces of pre-existing
texts, of any mention of organizations or anything
else that might have been involved in Benji's kidnapping and deprogramming except the "organic" presence
of the community and the specialized technical task

that Green had to perform. But, at the crucial moment, even Green disappears, for in the community vs. cult paradigm that undergirds the structure of Freed's narrative, the deprogrammer as a technician must disappear after his minor technical task is done.

This repression of texts is Josh Freed's writerly "innocence" made into a structuring principle. Not only is he innocent of all knowledge of the cult controversy and the deprogramming controversy, but the whole world is just as innocent, when you get down (with him) to these "organic basics." The sources for the phone numbers, the sudden materialization of "helpers," the "new hide-out" (a private house without apparent owners but with a TV), the desperate decision to call Green--these seem to be functions of writing naively from direct experience. The reader tends not to ask about such "details" when co-witnessing the far more compelling saga of the community regaining and giving a new life. In fact, to ask at a TIME LIKE THIS would be sacrilegious, like asking where the pastor got his gold chalice during the elevation of a Catholic Mass. The community, in Freed's articles, is sacred, just as Rev. Moon is decidedly not sacred. The mere mention of Rev. Moon's name at Boonville can interrupt the "programming" process if it is done before recruits have lost the power to choose.

The cult mirrors the community, almost point-by-point, in Freed's series. I have mentioned only a few of the more salient points where this mirroring is especially sharp and focussed. Needless to say, this formulation of reality, which Freed has performed with consummate skill and elegance, is systematic --

more systematic than reality itself could ever be.

The last article in the series consists largely
of an interview with Benji Carroll, back in Montreal
after his "recovery period" with Green's assistant,
Virginia. Deprogrammers call this the "floating period"
and Freed's description is the standard one-- "junk
books," rest, the company of a friendly deprogrammer
of the opposite sex, a secluded resort area. What is
equally standard among deprogrammers is to enlist former
members of religious groups they have deprogrammed
into the ranks.

Benji's interview provides a first-person account that nicely "footnotes" many of Freed's speculations about what must have happened to Benji when
he was a Moonie. For example, at Boonville:

> I went along with it to be polite, and I kept
> meaning to leave.
>
> But somehow, as the days went by, my ideas
> changed and I became convinced that those parts
> of me that were annoyed were just old concepts
> that I had to get rid of.

Of his deprogramming Benji says:

> When you're a Moonie, you're locked into
> a kind of living death. It's unfortunate,
> but the only way to reach you is against your
> will.
>
> In retrospect, Benji sees deprogramming
> as a kind of Boonville in reverse--but "much
> more gentle and human."

And, finally, on the community nature of the deprogramming he says:

> All these people willing to put out their necks
> in the belief that underneath all that garbage
> somewhere was the real me. It was very moving...

> In the end it was as though a dam had burst
> in my head.
>
> I felt good about the people I knew be-
> fore the whole experience...but now I have
> even more faith about people in general and
> my friends in particular.

Having rejoined his community, in Montreal, Benji is
"now angered at the difficulty other parents are having
in reaching their offspring in the Moonies." In fact,
Benji is now acting on that anger, talking to parents
and Moonies both.

> For the future, the 28-year-old Benji thinks
> he will be tied up in cult-related activity
> for some time because he is "fascinated" by
> the whole field of mind control.

He has been avidly reading books on the subject. One does not find Benji's decision to go into
cult-related activity disturbing, or at least not as
disturbing as Josh Freed's persisting "innocence."
The fact is that deprogramming is a profession and that
there are organizations of anti-cultists. Freed, at
this point at least, has to know about them, but he
presents Benji as an almost casual private "researcher"
who does some counselling out of his own experience,
on the side.

Josh Freed is a professional newpaper reporter
for the *Montreal Star*. Freed has repressed information
germane to his story, information about the at least
loosely organized opponents of the new religious groups.
A case could be made for his doing so in the first
five stories of his series: they tell of his own
experience, and before this experience, he might have
known nothing about all the controversy surrounding
deprogramming. When he sat down to write his stories,

he might have felt that he should stick to his own
experience because it was only through that experience
that he found out about these things. But in the last
article, the pretense of innocence does not serve any
such New Journalism purpose. Rather, it serves to sustain the identification of the anti-cult movement and
deprogramming with what he considers to be community.

Most journalists, as I said above, have chosen
to see the cults and the deprogrammers (and other anti-
cultists) as antagonists in a kind of "war." Reporters
write about this "war," and do so as if it were in a
foreign country. This is problematical because it
reduces the complex issues within the separate phenomena
of new religions and deprogramming (which touches
others besides members of "cults") to a simplistic
antinomy within our society and treats the controversy
as if it were outside "community" concerns. Although
this view is simplistic, and we expect better from our
journalists, it is not exactly unethical to see the
"war" as one fought by two opposing minorities who
appear to have equal legal artillery. The view is
not very sophisticated, but then other institutions
within our society have been unable to choose between
the cults and their enemies, and that includes the
conventional churches. Journalists seldom break out
of such a consensus situation, especially when they
have, to a large extent, generated it, as in the case
of the cult/anti-cult antinomy.

But what Josh Freed has done is to identify
the deprogrammers with the community. In his portrayal
of Ford Green, the deprogrammer is called in as the
technician who restores the power of choice so that

the community can make its claims anew on a person,
and thus restore a person to his "natural" condition.
Deprogramming, as Freed depicts it, is a re-natural-
ization of the mind to a condition of freedom; what one
chooses after that is the deprogrammed person's business. But "everyone" chooses his community, so the
deprogrammer becomes a servant of the community, the
"natural" place for a person to be.

The whole thrust of Freed's highly impressionist
writing is towards the de-politicization of deprogramming and towards its "naturalization." As we saw in
the fourth article, when you are desperate, you need
something or someone extraordinary to restore things
to normal, to freedom of mind in this case, and there
is nothing "political" or strange about that. All
that happened to make Green a deprogrammer is his own
self-restoration; it is a "natural" process at which
he is now adept. And we readers "saw" all this step-
by-step, line-by-line, without any intellectual or
ideological interpolations on Freed's part. Everything is written out of natural, pure, direct, unadult-
erated, etc, etc. experience. They are innocent
articles, a "personal expression." Of course, this
becomes less and less true once we as readers begin to
question these articles. Then they become mythic texts
that utilize discernible forms from TV shows, "rites
of passage," from labels and literal names drawn from
pop culture. We begin to see how inscribed within
this "innocent" writing is an extremely rich range
of subtexts and imagery that culminate in "arguments."
One of the most powerful, but seldom analyzed of
these arguments is a political one. It concerns the

"hero" who arrives at the "last" desperate moment to
restore things to their natural condition, to restore
a community to its pre-political condition.[8] The
hero in this piece is, of course, Ford Green and the
community is Montreal. Within Freed's mythology the
Moonies alone are political, and politically powerful
in that "other place," California. They have all the
legal artillery. Worse, the Moonies have crudely
politicized the community with their pseudo-religious
parody of its natural order: their indoctrination
divides the world up into "MOON" and "SATAN", an unnatural and deceiving division of the natural order
of the world. Why is it unnatural? Because the world
in its real nature is what I choose and what I don't
choose, and is made up of communities which are separate but not exclusivistic and divisive. The Moonies
are a parody of community, a "cult", because they
do not respect this nature of the world. Thus, their
members have first to be deprogrammed back into choosing, the central "natural" power of a person. It is
understandable, then, that Benji Carroll would, back
in Montreal, become fascinated with "mind control"
(this political term was reserved by Freed for his last
article) since he has lost the power to choose and
regained it. The same happened to Ford Green and, if
only slightly, to Josh Freed as well. It is a rite
of passage that makes them heroes, for heroes are those
who have "died" and been reborn into something super-
natural, or "twice-natural", and thus live to serve
nature.

        This is a pop-theology analysis of Freed's
series, I suppose, because Freed's series is a mythic

narrative that serves as an apologetics for deprogramming that makes it seem a heroic, or super-natural
extension of the natural human community. In commercial terms and I mention them because anybody can hire
a deprogrammer and this is a newspaper series--we
call this advertising. We never call it news.

[1] The sidebar run by the *Hamilton Spectator* along with
the fourth article in the series, for example, is
"Moonie Was Almost on Cafic's Staff." The "Cafic
case" involved the deprogramming of John Biermans which
was arranged by Norm Cafic, the federal Multi-Cultural
Minister of the Canadian government. The story broke
in February, 1978, about a month after the series had
run in the *Montreal Star*. This new sidebar hooked
nicely into the fourth article, which ran under the
headline, "Police Help Moonie," and concerns the
cooperation between the Moonies, the police, the FBI
and the media in finding Benji and his abductors,
including Josh Freed.

[2] The whole "deprogramming" story seemed dead in Canada
for most of 1977. The banning of the most famous deprogrammer, Ted Patrick, from Canada seemed to close
the issue. *The Globe and Mail's* series, for example,
was written pretty much as a "back burner" affair mostly
concerned with the controversies about the new religions themselves, although one article was taken up by
an interview with local Toronto deprogrammer Brian Curry.
News stories about "the cults" at the time mostly came
from the U.S. over the wire services, or were intermingled
in a newer controversy over various kinds of unorthodox
psychological therapy groups, like PSI, and the proposed legislation for their control in Ontario.

[3] See Harvey Cox's *Seduction of the Spirit, The Use
and Misuse of People's Religion* (New York, 1973).
In both books Cox develops a method, sometimes mistaken
for autobiography, of theologizing in which his own
experience--he calls it "participation"-- in religious
events and movements is given greater importance than
the texts consulted. Cox, in the second book, treats
several new religions, though his principle concern is
Zen Buddhism in America, which is not ordinarily
considered to be one of the new religions.

[4] See *Mass Culture,* eds. Rosenberg and White, (New
York, 1957), Griel Marcus, *Mystery Train* (New York,
1975), Roland Barthes, *Mythologies* (1957; London,
1972) and Robert Jewett and John Shelton Lawrence,
The American Monomyth (Garden City, N.J., 1977).

5 Barthes, pp. 109ff.

6 Ted Patrick, with Tom Dulec, *Let Our Children Go!*
(New York, 1976).

7 Hamilton's Matt Helm is a classic example. An
American businessman living in the Southwestern
United States, Helm finds his "past" as a World
War II secret agent catching up with him. The "unique
national emergency" of the war that gave him his "profession" is renewed by a ripple in the "cold war."
A new emergency invades his hometown. Helm's entire
personal world is overturned. As Helm explains
endlessly (the novels are first-person narratives),
he has to adopt a new, paranoid morality and become
of The Destroyers. The rest of the series is based
on the similar tension between Helm's human feelings
and the feelings needed to do the jobs he has to do.

8 See Jewett and Lawrence, especially p.x. "A community
in harmonious paradise is threatened by evil; normal
institutions fail to contend with this threat; a
self-less superhero emerges to renounce temptations
and carry on the redemptive task; aided by fate, his
decisive victory restores the community to its para-
disal condition; the superhero recedes into obscurity."

A PSYCHO-SOCIAL ANALYSIS OF RELIGIOUS CONVERSION

RICHARD DeMARIA

My interests in the Unification Church are those
shared by anyone who is concerned about spiritual growth,
and especially that of the young. The day on which a
student of mine withdrew from college in order to dedicate
himself totally to the religion of Rev. Moon was the day I
began to question seriously the dynamics, the attraction,
and the consequences of membership in the Unification
Church. As someone engaged over the years in spiritual
guidance, I was concerned with the effect on personality
and spirituality which membership in the Church might involve. I read the theological writings of the Church and
questioned the members about their lifestyle against the
backdrop of traditional spiritualities. In this paper I
would invite the reader to share the questions and thought
that have occured to me during this time of reflection. I
is not the purpose of this paper to arrive at conclusions,
but rather to apply a frame of reference from the social
sciences and from the history of spirituality which may
be useful to those who,for one reason or another, are concerned about membership in this new movement. Much of
what is discussed applies to any religion and to the commitment it evokes. That is no coincidence; for one purpose of this paper is to show that the dynamics and method
the values and dangers, of the Unification Church are thos
one finds repeatedly in the history of religion and spirituality.

It may be of value to mention at the outset two pre-suppositions with which I approached this study. The first is a theological presupposition which, for me, because of my Roman Catholic affiliation, is articulated in the deliberation of the Second Vatican Council: namely, that God uses many religions, both Christian and non-Christian, to bring people to salvation and to growth. Therefore, without raising questions of ultimate truth or fullness of truth, I could approach the Unification Church with the hypothesis that it *might be for its members* an important path of spiritual growth. Whether this was in fact the case remained to be seen. I knew that the majority of the reports in the media regarded the movement as the work of a dangerous or deranged man; I knew that many observers viewed membership in the Unification Church in terms of an enforced captivity. But a familiarity with the history of American reactions to new religions cautioned me against an uncritical acceptance of these early, popular opinions.

Americans have repeatedly ridiculed, misrepresented, and persecuted new religious groups that have arisen in their midst. Gamaliel's advice to the Sanhedrin has not found many imitators among the American public. To mention but a few examples of this: Our Puritan forefathers, having themselves fled England in order to escape persecution, had barely settled in the New World when they drove out the religious innovators Anne Hutchinson and Roger Williams. Joseph Smith and his followers were, in their early years, driven from city to city by neighbors who resented their success or feared their enthusiasm.

Smith and his brother were eventually shot to death in
Illinois, where the Mormons had settled after a small
scale "Mormon War;" but from there as well they were
eventually driven away. John H. Noyes and his earliest
Perfectionist co-religionists were driven from Putney,
Vermont, in the early nineteenth century by an enraged
populace. They eventually settled in Oneida, New York,
where their lifestyle was continuously misrepresented and
attacked in the press, until they finally dissolved their
communal life under the threat of legal conviction for
their unusual socio-religious practices. More recently,
the Koinonia Community in Americus, Georgia, was sabotaged
and embargoed by the people of the surrounding towns because it allowed blacks and whites to live together com-
munally. And the examples could be multiplied. I mention these only to account for my second presupposition:
that one should not uncritically credit the reports of the
media without reading, thinking and investigating for oneself.

SUDDEN CONVERSION EXPERIENCES

The first question that had to be considered about the
Unification Church concerned the suddenness with which
people become members. The overnight conversions of so
many to this new religion have caused many Americans to
question the validity of the religious experience and to
conclude that some rather malevolent dynamics are being
used by the leaders of the movement to bring this about.
One must consider, in other words, the oft-heard charge

brainwashing.

The phenomenon of sudden conversion is not something
w; in fact sudden conversion experiences have been recog-
zed as valid in almost every religion. To limit my com-
nts to Christianity: Paul of Tarsus is but one figure
ong many in the early Church who embraced this new reli-
on within hours. Indeed, throughout the history of
ristianity, there have been sects which not only en-
rsed the validity of conversion experience but which
ld that a sudden and radical religious metanoia is the
rmal way to salvation.[1] William James' classic analysis
religious experience in the West divides religious
ople into two varieties, the second of which come to
ace through relatively sudden conversion. Consider the
llowing statement by John Wesley, which James cites:

> In London alone I found 654 members of our Society
> who were exceeding clear in their experience and
> whose testimony I could see no reason to doubt.
> And every one of these (without a single exception)
> has declared that his deliverance from sin was
> instantaneous, that the change was wrought in a
> moment. Had half of these, or one-third, or one
> in twenty, declared it was GRADUALLY wrought in
> THEM, I should have believed this, with regard
> to THEM, and thought that SOME were gradually
> sanctified and some instantaneously. But as I
> have not found, in so long a space of time, a
> single person speaking thus, I cannot but believe
> that santification is commonly, if not always an
> instantaneous work.[2]

ntemporary psychology likewise recognizes two paths to
alth, the latter being that cathartic experience whereby
patient suddenly "sees the light" or "puts it all to-
ther," sometimes after months of fruitless therapy.

Granted that the conversion experience is a phenomenon which has been accepted and advocated by many religious people, how are we to explain so sudden a reversal
of lifestyle? The early Christian Church explained it in
terms of possession by a new spirit. The Christian is
one who has been taken over by a Holy Spirit, so that he
sees, thinks and hears in a new way. In Paul's classic
description, it is Paul himself who is still living, but
in a sense it is no longer Paul but the Spirit of Christ
who directs his thoughts and actions. A more contemporar
(though not necessarily better) view is that the metanoia
is a change in consciousness. The thought categories by
which one perceives the world are realigned, so that one
sees in a new way, and *consequently* acts differently, in
accordance with that new vision.

The model of consciousness proposed by Henri Bergson
and later popularized by Aldous Huxley may be helpful in
our efforts to understand this latter explanation. This
model views the brain as a filter between the mind and th
outside world. The mind receives only the data from the
outside world which correspond to a limited number of cat
gories of the brain; these categories are determined and
formed by the upbringing and education of each person.
Thus the mind is always receiving a partial-- and therefore a distorted-- perception. There is an experiment
which provides a helpful analogy of the limiting/distorti
function of the brain. The eye of a frog is wired so tha
the experimenter can discern when objects passing before
the frog's eye cause an impulse to be sent to the brain.
Interestingly, the only objects so "noticed" are very sma

objects moving close to the frog's eye, and large objects
moving suddenly or directly toward the frog. It would
seem that such objects are related to food supply in the
first case, and to a would-be attacker in the second.[3] The
eye of the frog is "programmed" to allow entry of only
certain data -- data necessary for the frog's survival. To
put it another way, the eye of the frog is "programmed" to
ignore -- simply not to see--objects unessential to the
frog's survival. The frog sees in a partial and distorted
way.

In a similar manner, according to the Bergson-Huxley
model, the brain of each person is "programmed" by education, environment, and experiences to allow entry of only
certain aspects of reality.[4] This is what is meant by
one's consciousness: the categories by which one perceives
the world. There are many possible consciousnesses. While
one consciousness may be necessary and valuable at a certain stage of growth, it may prove a hindrance at another
stage when further development requires that the world be
seen and interpreted in another way. Continued maturation
is dependent upon an altering, reshaping or broadening of
consciousness.

Using this model, we could give the following account
for the religious conversion experience: an excessively
individualistic, ego-centered consciousness, one which has
been shaped largely in terms of individual survival in a
hostile world, cuts one off from that special perception
which is known by many names, but which seems common to so
many reports of religious experience. Abraham Maslow is
but one of our contemporary psychologists who calls upon

science to study this religious consciousness, arguing
persuasively for its importance because of the peace,
creativity and joy it generates.[5] This is not to deny
the importance of the more individualistic consciousness,
which may in fact be necessary in early stages of growth.
Rather it is to say that the individualistic consciousness
must, in later years, be replaced or at least modified by
a more "cosmic" consciousness (enlightenment, unitive consciousness, etc.) if one wishes to grow beyond the selfish
and ultimately unsatisfactory individualistic personality.
At least, so say those who advocate religious experience.[6]

The environment, experience, education, and reading
of some people are such that slowly and gradually their
consciousness is altered, and they increasingly discover
that new vision and new life of which religions speak.
But for others, the argument goes, the transition is not
nearly so smooth. For them, if it occurs at all, it is
traumatic and sudden. In either case, the process is essentially the same: a new series of categories is discovered and adopted, altering one's perception of the
world. As Joseph Pearce observes:

> We used to believe that our perceptions, our seeing,
> hearing, feeling, and so on, were reactions to ac-
> tive impingements on them by the "world out there".
> We thought our perceptions then sent these outside
> messages to the brain where we put together a rea-
> sonable facsimile of what was out there. We know
> now that our concepts, our notions or basic assump-
> tions, actively direct our percepts. We see, feel,
> and hear according to what Bruner calls a "selec-
> tive program of the mind".

> Metanoia is the Greek word for conversion; "a fun-
> damental transformation of mind." It is the pro-
> cess by which concepts are reorganized. Metanoia
> is a specialized, intensified adult form of the
> same worldview development found shaping the mind
> of the infant. Formerly associated with religion,
> metanoia proves to be the way by which all gen-
> uine education takes place... Metanoia is a sei-
> zure by the discipline given total attention, and
> a restructuring of the attending mind.[7]

Conversion, then, can be viewed as a method of re-
education whereby one seeks to "undo" the unbalanced or
unhealthy programming with which he or she has grown up.
The sudden conversion seems to be the only way in which
some people can enter into that broadening of consciousness which is the prerequisite of growth (which others
accomplish gradually under the influence of more gentle
proddings.) The list of men and women whose lives of
holiness and service have followed upon sudden and radical reversal is extensive--extensive enough to warrant a
benevolent view of the process. My point, in summary, is
that sudden conversion does seem to be a valid path in and
toward spiritual growth. The suddenness of the conversion
of many Unification Church members should not be used as a
criterion of inauthenticity. If one wants to consider sudden conversion as an inauthentic form of religious experience, he should at least realize that he does this in the
face of a long tradition of acceptance.

USE OF TECHNIQUES IN SUDDEN CONVERSION

It is not, however, the suddenness of the conversion
which disturbs many observers so much as the techniques by

which this is brought about. Apparently, many of these
conversions occur in the wake of rather strongly manipulative dynamics, which have occasioned the charges of
"brainwashing".   According to reports, the potential convert attends a workshop in some secluded retreat center,
where he or she is subjected to a rigid and exhausting
schedule with little time for privacy or reflection, and
where food and rest are kept at a minimum. Cut off from
contact with the outside world, the new member undergoes
six to eight hours of mind-numbing theology each day, all
of this in an atmosphere of communal love and acceptance.
Many an outsider concludes that the faith commitments made
under this kind of pressure and circumstance must be inher
ently inauthentic. We do well, then, to consider the matter in greater depth.

     Those responsible for spiritual growth have recog-
nized that the dawning of new consciousness is difficult
because it requires the partial breakdown of the former
consciousness. Because this does not occur easily for
some, spiritual teachers have developed methods which help
bring about the death/life process wherein the old consciousness is broken to make room for the new. For example, in the East, there are innumerable methods used by
the wise man, the guru, to help his disciples overcome
their misperception and to see the truth. Sleepless days
(kept sleepless by a cuff and beating when attention wan-
ders); insult and ridicule; weeks spent wrestling with
insoluble riddles; hours of labor at tasks with no purpose
--any or all of these are among the disciplines, hallowed
by centuries of experience, by which the master will aid

the student in his or her effort to find the light.   The
man or woman who senses that he or she is not living life
completely, whose actions have become counterproductive,
whose life has come to a dead end--such a person may *willingly* submit to these exercises and ordeals because he or
she knows how difficult it is to be "born again".

In American Christian history, the revivalist movement formed the backbone of American religion during the
awakenings of the eighteenth and nineteenth centuries.
Circuit-riding preachers traveled the country, finding
everywhere people willing to submit themselves to the
total emotional onslaught of the revival experience.   Participants traveled from their homes and towns to spots
cleared in forests, where they camped for several days,
enjoyed what was for some a rare opportunity to socialize,
engaged in hours of exhausting singing, praying, and witnessing, and submitted to the impassioned and terrifying
sermons of "hell fire" preachers.   And they did this in the
hope that, immersed in this believing experience, they
would find that vision which they believed to be essential
to salvation, but which many could not discover without
charismatic help.

Consider as well the methods used by some contemporary group therapies to bring their followers to new awareness.   For example, in the group-encounter movement, participants *willingly* commit themselves to sleepless "mara-
thon" sessions of probing, insult, nudity, attack, and
cajoling in the hope that the experience will free them
from emotional blocks and lead them to some new consciousness.   In the Erhard Seminar Training program, participants

subject themselves to a discipline of verbal assault, hyp-
notic exercises and repetitive lectures for sixteen hours
per day during which they can neither smoke, eat, or leave
the room for any reason, nor move or talk unless directed
to do so. (Some 35,000 Americans have paid $250 for this
experience.) *Willingly*--there is a waiting list--they
endure this ordeal because they recognize the need for
new vision and believe that Erhard has discovered methods
for releasing this.[10]

One might compare Erhard's structured methods for
altering consciousness with such traditional practices as
the thirty-day Spiritual Exercises of Ignatius Loyola,
the Russian practice of Poustinia (the hermit's life),
and the drug and alcoholic rehabilitation programs (which
usually depend for their effectiveness upon the *willingness* of the participants to be influenced). Behind these,
and so many other methods, is a truth which has been recognized throughout the history of religion:

a) Unhealthy behaviour is a sign that one perceives the
   world and his relation to it in a distorted way, and
   that new health is dependent upon restructuring that
   perception;

b) this new perception can be realized only after the
   old distorted consciousness has been broken down; but

c) because this old consciousness is not easily altered,
   there may be need to utilize some of the extraordinary methods which, when willingly embraced, act as
   catalysts in this process.

The use of manipulative techniques as catalysts in the conversion experience has a long and venerable history.[11] Effectiveness seems to depend largely upon the willingness of the participant to be affected. Therefore, even granting that the reports about Unification Church workshop tactics are accurate, we should not on that basis impugn the movement, unless we are prepared to reject as well the many forms of "methodism" which have characterized religious history. We must assume that those who attend the introductory workshops of the Unification Church are people (all of them old enough to vote) who are dissatisfied with their present lives and who are seeking a greater vision. They would not be present unless they were hoping to experience a personal transformation. In doing this, they line up with those men and women through out history who have sought a teacher, and who have willingly submitted to the methods by which he aids them in their search for meaning.

There is one final question to be asked with regard to the conversion process in the Unification Church, and that concerns the possibility of physical coercion. If physical coercion is involved in the conversion of Unification Church members, then that Church must be opposed for reasons too obvious and numerous to mention. Watchfulness over every new sect and movement in this regard is necessary and wise. However, a note of caution should be sounded to our would-be vigilante: in the Western world although there has often been suspicion of physical coercion in new religions, these suspicions have usually not been substantiated. The rumor--apparently believed--that

the first Christians sacrificed babies as part of their
rituals has not been without parallels in the attitudes
of Christians themselves towards later religious movements

Surely Catholics in America will be cautious in cre-
diting reports of coercion in the Unification Church.
They at least should remember how long the *Awful Disclo-
sures* of Maria Monk concerning her captivity in a Montreal
Convent continued to be circulated and believed by fellow
Americans--even after the report had been confessed a
hoax--and with what unfortunate results.[12] In the mid-
nineteenth century, the family and friends of a Rebecca
Newell stormed St. Xavier's Convent in Providence, Rhode
Island, in order to remove her by force, so sure were
they that she was being kept there against her will.
(They failed in their objective. Some years later, when
Rebecca decided not to pronounce final vows, she left the
convent without any noticeable difficulty.)

In fact, to my knowledge, there are no factual data
upon which to base a charge of coercion within the Unification Church. Free lance writers and reporters who have
attended the training session have reported no physical
coercion.[13] At present, the only unquestionable physical
coercion regarding the Church is that being practiced by
the professional kidnappers and deprogrammers working on
behalf of the parents.[14] There are reports of abductions
(in January, 1977, TV cameras videotaped the kidnapping
of Marie-Christine Amadeo in Lyons), enforced detention
for as long as two and one-half months, and a systematic
repudiation of the beliefs of the prisoner in sessions of
haranguing which may last for thirty hours without respite

Parents pay for these services in the belief that one must fight fire with fire. Believing that their children have been brainwashed, they feel justified in utilizing similar methods in order to rescue them. This too has its historical parallels, the most famous, perhaps, being the abduction, house arrest, and repeated admonitions suffered by Thomas Aquinas at the hands of his mother and brothers who were convinced that his decision to join the newly founded Order of Preachers was a mistake. From the vantage point of history, we can only be glad that they failed in their resolve.

Many observers conclude that there must be coercion within the Unification Church because of the reports they read about members in the movement being turned against their parents. Children, it is reported, refuse to visit or communicate with their families, and even are taught to regard them as the agents of the devil. In fact, the Unification Church urges its members to maintain contacts through phone calls, letters, visits to family and friends, when finances and the demands of the apostolate permit. Or rather, it should be said, the Unification Church would like to urge its members to do so. For when these visits or phone calls deteriorate into constant arguments--the parents pleading, cajoling, berating, or ridiculing the member's decision--then that member, especially if he is new, and therefore still shaky in his vocation, must for his own peace of mind limit this intercourse.

This is what any person, young or old, does when family and friends are unable to accept or at least tolerate a decision which he or she believes to be a vocation.

What marriage counselor would not advise a young man or
woman whose parents consistently berate or humiliate his
new wife or her new husband to limit these contacts, because one's first duty is to his or her new life, new partner, and new vocation? For centuries, the religious orders
of the Christian Church have acted in much the same way:
efforts are made to help family and friends to accept and
support the decision of the member involved to embrace the
communal vocation. But if parents' letters consist of
little more than pleas to the son or daughter to return
home, if the visits amount to little more than attacks by
the family upon the theology, lifestyle, or mission of the
novice, leaving him shaken and torn with grief, there is
not a novice master or mistress who would not discourage
any further communication, unless the family changes its
posture.

    The Unification Church, here, is simply following
tradional wisdom in helping a young person find his *own*
life and vocation.[15] One can view only with sadness the
distrust and anger which have arisen between members of
families in the wake of the conversion of one member to
the Unification Church. This in general would be far
bleaker were it not for the beneficial use that has been
made of the potentially dangerous process of conversion.
We probably do best, therefore, following the advice of
Jesus, to judge a movement by its *effect* rather than by
the *methods* it utilizes. By their fruits we must judge
them. With these observations, then, let us turn to an
examination of the nature and results of the commitment
which Unification Church members make in the wake of their
conversion.

COMMITMENT IN THE AGE OF PROTEAN MAN

At present, to be a fulltime member of the Unification
Church means that one enters into a communal form of life
and puts his or her whole life at the service of the
Church's mission. The person who joins the Church commits
himself or herself to the task of preparing the world for
the Second Coming of the Messiah. Many people outside of
the Church view a commitment of this kind as an impoverish-
ment. Such a commitment, they believe, prevents the person from "finding himself", from developing according to
his or her *own* vision and nature. It imprisons the person
in a narrow lifestyle, cutting him or her off from the
many opportunities for growth which life offers.

In this section, we will consider these objections by
analyzing the nature and effects of the total self-dedica-
tion made by members of the Unification Church. But, before we can do that, we must begin with an even more basic
consideration: that is the possibility and validity of
any commitment.

At present, ours is a culture which increasingly stands
wary of commitment. Robert Jay Lifton has coined the phrase
"Protean Man" to describe the contemporary person who, like
the Greek God, Proteus, can change shape at will. He can
embrace ideas and ideologies, modify them, let go of them
and then re-embrace them--all with an ease that stands in
sharp contrast to the faithfulness toward belief-structures
in the past.[16]   If Lifton is merely describing Protean man,
others are extolling him. William Kilpatrick has termed
the philosophy which reigns in contemporary America the

"cult of fluidity". The mature person, according to this
ethos, is one who remains ever-flexible, never allowing
himself or herself to be boxed in, always open to the many
life-experiences that evolve.[17]

Kilpatrick, whose work is essentially a critique of
this "cult", describes the way in which this faith is evi-
denced in everyday action. Contemporary man, he says,

> does not want to choose. He does not want to give
> up any of the possibilities. Indeed, he wants to
> taste all possibilities without ever having to
> choose among them. He looks about him at the many
> attractive identities from which to choose and
> fears that any exercise of choice will limit him
> to something less tham his appetite for variety
> demands... So he goes dashing about hoping to
> partake of all these possibilities, choosing none
> of them. He wishes to postpone commitment until
> a more convenient time--that is to say indefin-
> itely.[18]

There are many factors, both cultural and theoretical
responsible for the popularity of this "Protean" stance
toward life. Among these is the return, in contemporary
guise, of Rousseauian philosophy. A debate which has repeatedly marked the history of ideas centers on the question: Is mankind basically good or basically evil?
Rousseau believed mankind to be basically good. What evil
is found in human beings, Rousseau attributed to the distortions caused by the *constraints and influence of society*
That position, or a variation of it, can be heard again in
those contemporary psychological theories which understand
human nature as basically good, and which attribute whatever evil we find to the constraints of arbitrary and limiting decisions. People experience frustration and engage

in counter-productive behavior, the theory goes, because they fail to *be themselves,* to be authentic.   And that failure occurs because they allow themselves to be bound by the decisions and traditions made at an earlier stage in life.   It is because the "I" who exists today tries to live out the decisions of the "I" who existed yesterday that people experience conflict.

Unfortunately, the argument continues, our society tries to force us to live by the decisions made at an earlier date, by a self who was quite different from the self who exists today.   The truly "together" person is one who has learned to overcome these pressures.   This person is one who, being prepared to cast off any society-made shackles when necessary, listens to and corresponds to the inner self as it evolves in the face of a changing culture. Kilpatrick summarizes this understanding as follows:

> Health consists in flowing with this stream, being whatever thoughts and feelings are flowing through one now, and recognizing that these will be constantly changing...   It is not really necessary to do anything because one can trust one's self. Human nature is good, constructive, self-enhancing self-actualizing--if only it can be freed from the unnecessary boundaries we impose.   Lie back and float in the stream of it.   It may be scary but it's basically safe.   Trust yourself.
>
> The trouble with most of us, by [Carl] Rogers' account, is that over the years we build up a static self-definition which ignores the ebbing and flowing of our real self...   We buy somebody else's definition of what we should be and then spend our life trying to cram our unique experience into this procrustean bed.[19]

In these last sentences, then, we see the evil of commitments which are intended to be life-long. By them, we impoverish our lives, attempting to define at one point of time what we will be in a week, a year, or a decade. The average person has not read Carl Rogers, or any of the contemporary psychologists who advocate these positions. But through an amazing percolation process, these ideas (albeit in a distorted and unbalanced form) have become the stuff of common parlance among a large segment of our society. Another of the many factors involved in this stance is the growing popular belief that we *cannot* make and keep commitments, even if we wanted to do so.[20]

Perhaps we can now better understand why the contemporary student wants to exorcise from the catechisms of Christian doctrine statements about Hell. The Protean person with a fascination for fluidity, is uncomfortable with a doctrine which says that one is *capable of and responsible for* choices which affect the future. And a Protean person could only view the kind of commitment involved in the region of Rev. Moon, total and nearly irrevocable as it is, to be the height of masochism.

There is of course some truth to the insight underlying the principle of fluidity. But here, as is so often the case, there is need for a balancing principle--a principle which unfortunately is not often voiced of late. And that is the necessity of commitment in the mature personality. The attempt to keep every option open, never to choose, is just as destructive to human personality as is the effort of those with closed minds to permit no exceptions. Our culture today needs to hear this balancing principle. We need to be reminded that indecision can be a form of slavery and of evil.[21] As John C. Haughey has observed:

> Men have battled for centuries against slavery in
> the firm belief that its involuntary form of deter-
> minism is evil. The irony of our present age is
> that so many people, though free to do otherwise,
> allow themselves to become afflicted with the
> voluntary slavery of indetermination.[22]

There are studies which suggest that the lack of identity which follows from the cult of fluidity leads to un-
happiness.[23] Lifton recognizes the pain that accompanies
non-commitment, noting that Protean man

> indeed suffers from [guilt] considerably, but
> often without awareness of what is causing his
> suffering. For his is a form of hidden guilt,
> a vague but persistent kind of self-condemnation
> related to the symbolic disharmonies I have de-
> scribed, a sense of having no outlet for his
> loyalties and no symbolic structure for his
> achievements. [24]

THE NEED FOR COMMITMENT

In contrast to the philosophy of Protean fluidity
stands the existentialist emphasis upon choice and fidelity
to that choice. It is, existentialists say, in choosing
one option over another, and being willing to live out the
consequences of that choice, that one becomes a person and
develops a character. Without choice, one fails to emerge
into selfhood. And yet, unfortunately, it would now seem
that the contemporary man and woman avoid choices whenever
possible, and are led to believe that this is a sign of
maturity and wisdom. It is not easy to convince

contemporary men and women that real freedom consists in
the ability to make choices, choices that matter, and that
the freedom of non-choice is an illusion. What is more, a
choice is real only if there are consequences. The child
whose parents will right the result of anything it does
has no freedom of choice, because its choices make no difference. Isaac Asimov portrays this thesis powerfully in
his short story, *Multivac*,[25] about humans of a future time,
who live in a utopia created by a super-computer. The
genius of Asimov's story is that the reader is enabled to
feel the tragedy of a life where choices make no real difference. The reader enters into the experience of the
character and senses the shallowness--the inhumanness--that
a life without real choices would engender. In order to
become human, one must make choices--choices, let it be repeated, with consequences. John Haughey comments:

> Selfhood comes to be primarily by choosing. By
> failing to choose, by remaining in a constant
> state of indecision, a person's spirit is vaporous
> and, as it were, apart from him, hovering. In the
> act of choosing, most of all, the spirit of a per-
> son stands forth and is enfleshed. Our choices
> express self-understanding and at the same time
> make self-understanding possible.[26]

These observations on the necessity of commitment and
fidelity do not, however, belie the basic insight of those
contemporary writers who have argued for a more fluid concept of self. Anyone who has lived with the unbending personality, the person who makes absolutes of every detail
in his tradition, the person who is unable to distinguish
the essentials of his identity from accidentals knows

well how valid is the concept of flexibility. For, such
people tend to become ineffective with the changing of
times, and divisive and unhappy as well. But the correc-
tion to that position is not to become "like weeds blowing
in the wind". The goal requires a blending of flexibility
and commitment.   Hence, as Kilpatrick concludes,

> Fluidity and adaptability are necessary for people
> to deal with a changing future; and any theory of
> identity that emphasizes commitment must be tem-
> pered with an awareness of how difficult commitment
> has become under the new conditions. Still, there
> is a delicate balance at issue: the balance be-
> tween tentativeness and commitment, between fluidity
> and decision. No one wants to be confined in the
> wrong identity, but if we want any identity we do
> have to make choices. [27]

In his analysis of Norman Brown, one of the figures
whom he considers partially responsible for the present
cult of fluidity, Kilpatrick rightly observes that those
who write so persuasively in favor of this position are
usually men and women who have already established a sense
of identity through life commitments. What these writers
often forget is that they are being read by people who do
not share the luxury of an established identity. [28]

But to argue persuasively about the importance of commitment and to bemoan its absence in contemporary society
is futile if we fail to consider one last element. Com-
mitment--at least for most men and women--can be made only
where there is a meaningful objective in sight. If one
lives in a society which has relativized everything, commitment becomes difficult. Our society's knowledge of
history has made it difficult for many to hold our religions,

our nation, or any of our institutions as worthy of un-
swerving allegiance. Commitment presumes meaning. Victor
Frankl, in his psychiatric practice, found that the single
greatest cause of sickness in contemporary people is the
lack of meaning and purpose in life.[29] Toffler, in his
Future Shock, has chronicled with great insight the difficulty of commitment in a throw-away, mobile, and ever-
changing society.

This rather lengthy digression into the importance of
commitment and the lack of it in our contemporary ethos
puts us into a better position to understand the attraction
of, and the commitment made to, the Unification Church.
Quite simply, Unification Theology puts life into a meaningful context for its members, and therefore is able to
elicit the commitment which we have seen to be so important. In a recent survey of Church members, the most frequently listed reason given for memberhhip was the truth
of the Church's theology.[30]

Concerned pastors often ask themselves and others
about the attraction which the Unification Church holds.
Why, they ask, have people--especially those who were
raised in orthodox religious faiths--forsaken traditional
religions, traditional meaning systems, in favor of an
untried enthusiasm? A partial answer can be found in the
millenarian nature of Unification Theology.

Like all millenarian theologies, it provides a most
attractive meaning system, which in turn has the ability
to evoke and sustain an uncommon dedication. The person
who approaches the Church is presented with a theological
and historical perceptive which can, if he commits himself

to it, invest him with great value and importance: his
is the mission of preparing the world for the Second
Coming, for the fulfillment of Creation and Redemption.

Unification theology teaches that the Second Coming
of the Messiah is imminent, and that a world of peace and
prosperity is therefore possible in the very near future.
However, the success of that Messiah is dependent upon the
acceptance he will receive from mankind. He will fail if
the world does not *freely* accept his message and mission.
That is, according to Unification theology, God's way: to
respect the freedom of his creatures. This promise of a
relatively immediate reign of goodness and peace has the
power to call forth forces of dedication and energy which
are otherwise not easily touched.

True, traditional Christian theology also speaks of a
second coming of the Christ, at which time the world will
be renewed; but after two thousand years of waiting, that
promise about some unspecified future time cannot be expected to evoke the same enthusiasm and power as does the
millenarian promise of immediate possibilities. To be
sure, there are people who can and do work with untiring
zeal, without expecting any great transformation to take
place in their lifetimes. For them, the promise of the
ultimate victory of goodness, though rarely reflected upon,
acts as a horizon and ultimate source of hope. But their
number is few. Most people are able to exert that self-
less energy, which apparently lies within us all, but is
rarely tapped, only when the prospect of success is imminent.

The religious history of the Western world has witnessed the repeated emergence of religious sects which

claimed that the Second Coming was fast approaching and who pointed out signs to support their contentions. We might expect that anyone who is aware of this history, anyone who knows about the many millenarian precedents, would be unable to accept with enthusiasm the claims of this most recent theology of imminent renewal. Interestingly, Rev. Moon's followers are keen students of history and are not unaware of the many historical parallels to their movement. Because they believe that in God's plan of salvation the success of the Messiah depends upon the people's acceptance of him, the members of the Unification Church can account for the failure of previous promises and still maintain their hope about the present one.

In short, Unification theology provides an interpretation of life which enables men and women to commit themselves wholeheartedly. And if it provides an ideology, it is an ideology which just might escape the destructiveness of most ideologies: narrowness of vision and prejudice. The Unification Church, as its title suggests, is an attempt to create an ideology which unifies rather than divides, which integrates diverse ideas, peoples, movements, and spiritualities. The inter-racial communities and marriages are symbolic of the international and inter-cultural unification of insights, directions, and traditions which they seek to bring about. They hope to support and, where necessary, sponsor all efforts which bring about the restoration of human life, whether in the educational, aesthetic, or political field. If this is to be called an ideology, at least it is one which intends to be catholic, and which should lead its adherents to expansion and growth rather than narrowness of vision.

Enthusiasm and dedication are evident in the lives of
Church members. Whether their task be fundraising, witnessing, studying or organizational projects, they do it
with a generosity and zeal which none can deny, though
some would explain away. And contrary to the preconcep-
tions of outsiders, visits and interviews suggest that
there is joy and happiness and self-fulfillment as well.
This should surprise no one. For, ironically, one who
seeks joy and happiness and self-fulfillment directly
rarely finds them. As Frankl has observed, these "belong
to that class of phenomena which can only be obtained as
a side effect, and are thwarted precisely to the extent
to which they are made a matter of direct intention."[31]
In a similar vein, E. Pangborn has observed: "With all
due respect to one of the most human documents, ...the
pursuit of happiness is an occupation of fools."[32] Those
who rarely give a thought to themselves, but who dedicate
themselves to a cause outside their own needs, seem to be
the ones who find the joy and self-fulfillment which others
seek so diligently.

THE DANGERS OF RELIGIOUS CONVERSION

These reflections on the importance of commitment and
its reliance upon a meaning system would lend the concerned
observer to look upon the Unification Church's success with
appreciation. We should consider, however, several pitfalls
which may lie ahead for the new member as a result of his
commitment to the Unification Church. The first of these
is one which has always haunted and vitiated the religious
project, and especially those religions in which conversion
plays a major role.

The conversion experience introduces a person to a state of joy and peace, certainty and love, confidence and energy unlike anything known before. The problem is that some people expect that, once attained, this state should be permanent. This understandable expectation is encouraged by many religions which lead their members to view any doubts or confusions following conversion as moral weakness. A former member of the Unification Church is quoted as saying that "You had to make yourself love people when you didn't... You had to feel happy when you weren't."[33] This attitude inculcates the practice of externalism: people feel constrained to play out the role of absolute assuredness and moral uprightness long after certitude has begun to weaken. Or they interpret the fading of enthusiasm as an indication that the original experience of conversion was an illusion. Embarrassed, they give up the movement entirely. Both of these responses following conversion experiences are common, and both are unfortunate. Let us consider first the possibility of disaffection.

In so many areas of spirituality, one will find that an initial burst of insight and energy is followed by periods of doubt and dryness. Roman Catholic spirituality would have one interpret these "dark nights of the soul" as important and inevitable stages of growth, in fact as *anything but* signs that the religious experiences preceding them were inauthentic and to be disregarded. In my work, it has proved important to prepare young people for what seems to be the inevitable "coming down" which follow so often upon religious experience,[34] by helping them to see that this is a common pattern in the spiritual life.

I have tried to help them to view these experiences as God-
given glimpses into the way that life can be, a vision
which they should treasure, especially during the periods
of difficulty. Though the initial enthusiasm may pass, the
value of the experience remains, for, once having known
this other way of being, they have a goal and guide to
their lives. As William James says of the conversion experience:

> that it should for even a short time show a human
> being what the high-water mark of his spiritual
> capacity is, this is what constitutes its impor-
> tance--an importance which backsliding cannot di-
> minish, although persistence might increase it. [35]

The task is correctly to locate the value of these conversion experiences--peak experiences, Maslow would term them--
neither denying their value altogether, nor apotheosizing
them.

In introducing the second edition of his book, *Religion
Values and Peak Experiences,* Abraham Maslow reported that,
in the years that had passed since the first edition, he had
come to a greater appreciation for what he called the "plateau experience," a state of consciousness which shares
many of the characteristics of the peak experience, though
it is more serene and calm, always has a noetic and cogni-
tive element, is far more voluntary, and is the result of
hard work. He writes:

> A transient glimpse is certainly possible in the
> peak experiences which may, after all, come to any-
> one. But, so to speak, to take up residence on the
> high plateau of Unitive consciousness--that is
> another matter altogether. That tends to be a
> lifelong effort. It should not be confused with
> the Thursday-evening turn-on that many youngsters
> think of as THE path to transcendence. For that

> matter, it should not be confused with ANY single
> experience. The "spiritual disciplines," both
> the classical ones and the new ones that keep on
> being discovered these days, all take time, work,
> discipline, study, commitment. [36]

This, it seems to me, is a wise corrective to the
emphasis Maslow placed in his original edition on the sudden, peak experience and to the implicit denigration of
the spiritualities of duty, perseverance, effort, and as-
ceticism. But to come away with the impression that those
moments of sudden insight are useless would be an equally
distorted position. Many people would never begin the
slow and laborious path toward the "plateau experience,"
were it not for a momentary glimpse, a moment of insight,
into the way things could be. Conversion experiences can
be the "doors of perception" without which many would
never be introduced into the spiritual life. Their value,
however, may be lost if people are not prepared for the
days of doubt and darkness which often follow.

The Unification Church seems to understand this dynamic. They immediately follow up the conversion experience
with a series of workshops during which an intensive study
of the theology of the movement is pursued, thus allowing
a firm intellectual faith to support the insight of the
first moments. Spiritual directors within the Church advise the younger member who is having problems to pray
more, work harder, and study more deeply. This director
knows that there is a tendency for one to lose his new
vision, especially in the beginning years, unless it is
reinforced by prayer, work, and action. The loss of enthusiasm and the appearance of doubts are not signs of a
mistaken vocation, but the inevitable lapses of vision

which are to be expected. The person is urged to pray
even when prayer does not come easily, to be joyful even
when there are feelings of disease, to be externally con-
fident, dismissing the tactics of the devil.

And that is not bad spiritual direction. But it
brings with it the other danger mentioned above which pla-
gues religions, and that is the danger of externalism.
The person can begin to identify external righteousness
with internal wholeness...to be satisfied with the externally upright life. Such a person, identified with his
new image, acts it out in everyday life, and withstands
the attacks of the devil by effectively repressing anything within himself which contradicts this image.

The problem is complex. For,in fact, one way to
achieve a spiritual ideal is to *act* as a holy person does,
in the hope that what is at first only an external obser-
vance will in time affect one's inner consciousness. "Putting on the new man" is a tried method of spirituality.
But there is the inherent danger in this method that the
person will confuse his external behavior with internal
renewal, and will thus assume that he or she has *reached*
stages of holiness which correspond to the external actions.
After that, any internal suggestion of relapse--any wayward
desire or feeling--must be subconsciously denied and repressed. In healthy spirituality, a person suppresses (a
term used in contradistinction to represses), at the price
of sacrifice and pain, those desires and feelings which
contradict his ideal. This is far different from the person who has been taught to *deny* that such feelings even
exist, since such feelings are unworthy and, in fact, impossible for one who has been called to a special vocation.
This latter dynamic can lead to real sickness. Erich

Neumann has written insightfully about these dynamics and
the consequent evils of projection and anger which repression engenders.

> Suppression is a conscious achievement of the ego,
> and it is usually practiced and cultivated in a
> systematic way. It is important to notice that in
> suppression a sacrifice is made which leads to suf-
> fering. This suffering is accepted, and for that
> reason the rejected contents and components of the
> personality still retain their connection with the
> ego... In repression, the excluded contents and
> components of the personality which run counter to
> the dominant ethical value lose their connection
> with the conscious system and become unconscious
> or forgotten--that is to say, the ego is entirely
> unaware of their existence. Repressed contents,
> unlike those suppressed, are withdrawn from the
> control of consciousness and function independently
> of it; in fact, as depth psychology has shown, they
> lead an active underground life of their own with
> disastrous results for both the individual and the
> collective.[37]

It is these "disastrous results for both individuals
and the collective" that have caused spiritual directors
to be wary of the "idealistic" approach to spirituality.
The reaction of many is to regard all spiritualities which
propose *imitation* (such as the "imitation of Christ") as
sickness-engendering. "Be yourself" seems to the contemporary spiritual director a more valid form of spirituality.[38] Neumann, on the other hand, while recognizing the
dangers of an "idealistic" approach to spirituality, does
not deny its value. Rather he calls for a complementary
approach.

What is needed is a spirituality which encourages beginners to strive for the highest goals, pointing out to
them that a holiness or wholeness beyond their most san-
guine expectations is possible if they but strive for it.

In this approach, the initial enthusiasm and fervor will
be treated as valid insights and religious experience,
valuable as visions of what can be. But, at the same time,
this spirituality must be balanced by one which teaches
beginners to recognize their fallen human nature and to
accept patiently rather than repress the weakness of that
nature.

In a religion like that of the Unification Church,
there may be a tendency to ignore this second aspect of
spirituality. Members believe that the salvation of the
world is dependent upon the witness they give to all they
meet. They may be so intent upon giving "good example",
being at every moment witnesses to the joy and integrity
of Unification Religion, that they will have no time to
listen to, and to deal with, that side of them which remains unrenewed. Ronald Knox's thumbnail sketch of enthusiastic religionists may apply to a possible tendency
within the Unification Church. Members of such groups,
says Knox,

> will have no "almost Christians," no weaker bre-
> thren who plod and stumble, who...would like to
> have a foot in either world... Poor human nature!
> Every lapse that follows is marked by pitiless
> watchers outside the fold, creates a harvest of
> scandal within.[39]

A further danger of which the Unification Church must
be aware is the attraction their lifestyle will hold for
frightened people, for whom the commitment to religion represents a refuge from the task of creating an identity.
Religion has always appealed to those who do not want to
accept the responsibility for their lives. Such people
adopt willingly the ready-made identity provided by the
Church and thus escape the difficult project of creating

their own identity. This is a particular danger for reli
gions which practice a communal lifestyle, as does the ma
body of the Unification Church at present. Every communa
attempt inevitably--and unfortunately--tends to enforce
uniformity rather than unanimity. The strong personality
can undergo this without any damaging effect. For this
person, communal life will be a valuable asset, providing
as it does, helpful structure, valuable freedom, and a
strong sense of support. But, for the passive personalit
the tendency toward uniformity within communal life can
destroy whatever tender shoots of self-definition might b
growing within. For this person, membership in the Unifi
cation Church could be most unhealthy.

Another danger from the viewpoint of spirituality,
and one particularly likely in the Unification Church is
the possibility of an obsession with duty. A man or woma
who understands the present time to be of crucial signifi
cance, who thinks that the future of the world is in a
sense dependent upon the fidelity of a small group to its
vocation, can understandably begin to see life in terms o
duty, and to judge every occurrence in terms of its effec
tiveness. Every action, every relation, every decision
must be judged in terms of its "productivity" in spreadin
the message and mission of the Church. There are personalities for whom this kind of spirituality is not healthy.
They feel guilty for wasted time; they regard any relaxation as indulgent, unless it can be justified in terms o
the work; they become what has been half-seriously labele
"workaholics". In turn, they gradually lose the ability
to enjoy life and its beauties, and, at least in my understanding of a whole spirituality, that is an unfortunate
distortion.

There is within Unification theology a factor which may prevent this distortion from occurring: its healthy materialism. The *Divine Principle*, the major work of Unification theology, states that there can be no spiritual happiness apart from true physical happiness. According to the same text, the fact that religion has until now de-emphasized the value of everyday reality, of physical happiness, in order to stress the attainment of spiritual happiness is one cause for its relative failure.[40] In taking this position, however, the Unification Church stands squarely in the tradition of orthodox Christianity, which has rejected as heretical those sects--Gnostics, Albigensians, Jansenists--which would regard the material world as evil. This recognition of the validity of physical pleasure by Unification Church theology would require that its members balance their sense of duty with times of relaxation, celebration, and enjoyment. The danger, let it be repeated, is that certain personalities who might be attracted to the Church will be unable to live within the tension of this theology and will consciously or unconsciously allow the duty principle to dominate their lives.

SEXUAL ATTITUDES AND PRACTICES

The priest-psychologist, Eugene Kennedy, has suggested that in sexuality we find a reflection of a person's attitudes and well-being.[41] This principle, one may surmise, would also apply to a group. Thus, it may be worthwhile to conclude our considerations of the commitment involved in Unification Church membership by considering briefly

the Church's practices concerning sexuality. Though the
theory and practice of marriage within the Unification
Church is still in a developmental stage, the basic directions can be discerned.

The new member of the Church begins by spending a
period of preparation in the state of celibacy; even couples who enter the Church after marriage live temporarily
in abstinence. When the time of preparation is completed
-- a judgment which is made by the person in conjunction
with Church authorities, but never before three years of
membership have been completed--the person attends the
next gathering of the Church for the blessing of marriages,
at which time Rev. Moon recommends a marriage partner. The
two members recommended for one another may never have met
before; they may be of different nationalities. The two
are given a short time to meet and to decide whether they
can accept one another (they may refuse without loss of
standing in the Church). Should they accept his recom-
mendation, they participate soon after in a marriage ceremony, after which they begin their life together.

This emphasis on communal control of sex and marriage
is not unique to the Unification Church. In his analysis
of communal attempts in America, John H. Noyes pointed out
that one factor common to all the communities which succeeded in America was that they brought sexuality and marriage under the aegis of community control. For example,
the Shakers suppressed every expression of sexuality,
living lives of complete celibacy; the Perfectionists of
Oneida forbade marriage of exclusive relationships, while
allowing the practice of communal sexuality; and the communists of Amana, although allowing marriage, discouraged
the practice, relegating the married to lower echelons

of influence.[42] Thus they prevented divided loyalties between the needs and demands of the family, for such a division of loyalties weakens seriously the strength of the communal undertaking. One is tempted to interpret the marriage practice of the Unification Church in this context: as an attempt to control the potentially divisive influence of the smaller family unity within a communal setting.

According to Thomas Driver, almost every religion has made sexuality a principal concern, either seeing it as a form of divine worship or as a source of human degradation.[43] We might do well to consider Unification Church marriage practice by placing it in the context of those religious groups which have understood sexuality as a basically religious act, which can be appreciated only when performed in a sacred and sacramental context.[44] To place marriage in a religious context, we might briefly sketch the theology of sexuality advocated by one such group, the Perfectionists of Oneida, who lived a communal life-form in upper New York during the mid-nineteenth century.

Underlying their practice of sexuality, the Oneida Perfectionists held to a theology which understood the masculine-feminine principle to be characteristic of all reality, and integral to the divine plan of salvation.[45] They practiced and wrote about a kind of love which they realized would appear sterile and joyless to those uninitiated in its ways, but which, they assured their audience, introduced one into the most delightful and enduring of experiences. This love, always under the control of the will, was directed toward those whose attraction was based on their spiritual gifts. Through it, the grace of God

was passed from person to person, the more spiritual of
the two acting as the "masculine" inspirator to the less
advanced "feminine" receiver. Love was thus a sacrament
through which one came into touch with the Divine.

> The great question for the whole nation...to study
> is the question of the relation of man and woman...
> Settle this...and everything else will be settled;
> ...people...will be called to study the great con-
> stitution of the universe which is imaged in the
> two-fold relation of man and woman.[46]

In addition, because the Oneida Perfectionists believed
that spiritual strengths could be passed from generation
to generation, much as physical attributes are, they
thought it was essential that only those who had achieved
a high degree of holiness should parent children. What is
more, they believed that parents should be paired so as to
complement one another in a healthy way. Thus, the child
born of this union should begin life in a state of spiritual strength.[47] But this economy of salvation would be
frustrated so long as people continued to pursue relationships which were not based on these principles.

    According to the Oneida Perfectionists, the relation-
ships carried on by most people were based on anything but
an understanding of the role sexuality has to play in the
world's salvation. Though called by the name "love," the
relationship which was advocated by the world was anything
but true, Christian love. The Perfectionists referred to
this idolatrous relationship as "romance." By romantic
love, they meant that all-consuming passion, based on external attractions, and characterized by jealousy, envy,
and conflict. This they considered to be comparable to th
bondage of slavery, the degradation of narcotics, and the

sinfulness of idolatry. No intelligent observer could
deny, they maintained, that the passion of sex and romance
as practiced in the world and portrayed in popular writings was an enemy of God and a fountain of corruption and
misery for the human race.[48]

Though dissimilar in many important respects, the
theory of the Oneida Perfectionists provides a context in
which to understand the practices of the Unification Church
For it too has a theology which understands the masculine-
feminine principle to be a reflection of the Godhead, and
to be integral to God's plan for the salvation of the
world.[49] For it, too, the world will be renewed only when
men and women, who have first perfected themselves, enter
into relationships which are blessed by God, and based
upon the spiritual attractions of the parties. It too
believes that the children born of these unions will from
their birth be free of the hereditary effects of original
sin.[50]

Consequently, one can understand that a member of the
Unification Church might consider marriage to be so crucial
to individual and world salvation that it cannot be con-
tracted on the basis of mere attraction. One can see why
they might assume that no one has enough self-knowledge to
choose wisely the person suited to complement his or her
own personality. Therefore, it makes sense to leave the
choice of partners to another, especially if one believes
that one has access to the direction of a man specially
inspired by God.

No doubt the idea of "arranged" marriages will repel
many an American observer. It should be pointed out, however, that until relatively recent times, the practice of

"arranged" marriages was common in the Western world, especially among those who held positions of importance. The
experiment (for it is just that) of marriage based solely
upon romantic attraction with little account being given
to the advice of family, has been underway for too short
a period to be evaluated. This much can be said: at present there are no convincing data to suggest that the arranged marriages of the past were any less successful than
those based on romantic attraction. The partners entered
their wedded state with a sense of vocation; theirs was
the responsibility to care for the other in good times and
in bad. In many a case, this dedicated service gave way
in time to a deep love. There is more than a moment of
good theatre behind the song Tevia sings to Heidl in
Fiddler on the Roof. Having watched his daughters, one
by one, set out on marriages of their own choosing, Tevia,
whose marriage was arranged for him, asks his wife if she
loves him. And she assures him that if twenty-five years
of service and sharing and worrying is not love, then she
does not know what it is.

Though only time will tell, there is reason to believe that Unification Church marriages--based on the objective judgments of the trusted leader, who presumably
knows his people well, and entered into only after a
period of preparation with a sense of vocation and an
openness to the transcendental element of the sexual ex-
perience--contain the elements of healthy and lasting
relationships.

CONCLUSION

These are my initial thoughts regarding the Unification Church, intended for those who feel responsibility
for one involved in or attracted to membership in that
Church. We have seen that the methods of conversion used
and the commitment evoked by the Unification Church are
ones which, while permeated with dangers, have been utilized throughout the history of religion, especially at
times when the general interest in religion was at a low
point. Not only is this path common, but it also seems
capable of leading the person to a deep and balanced faith.

There are dangers: the danger of anxiety in the face
of doubt, an anxiety which may give rise to hypocrisy or
to externalism with the consequent practices of repression
and projective bigotry. Or consequent doubt may give way
to a disaffection by which the person eschews all religious values as illusions. There is the very real possibility of a passive, non-questioning acceptance, whereby
the person allows his or her critical faculties to fall
into disuse. There is the very real possibility that all
this enthusiasm will be channeled into a cause and projects which are not that valuable to a world which cannot
afford to see its limited resources of human idealism
squandered. There is the possibility that the Reverend
Moon will use the power which he holds over his devoted
followers to further his own interests or even to create
a totalitarian movement.

But balancing these possibilities are the positive
ones which could arise out of this movement. This movement may give to people a purpose, a goal, and a vision
which they would never have found otherwise. This

movement may lead people from lives of "quiet desperation"
to lives filled with purpose. This movement may nurture
people fully alive, straining the limits of human goodness, human energy, and human ability. This movement may
be one of those which revitalizes not only a particular
group but religion and society in general. If the world
had destroyed every enthusiastic movement, simply because
of its inherent dangers and possibilities, the world today
would be very much impoverished.

I know of no better way to conclude this study than
with Ronald Knox's conclusion to his study of enthusiastic
sects. Having chronicled in great detail the unpredictabl
paths along which enthusiasm has led its followers through
out history, having lamented the distortions these groups
have introduced into the Christian religion, Knox neverthe
less concludes:

> Men will not live without vision; that moral we do
> well to carry away with us from contemplating, in
> so many strange forms, the record of the vision-
> aries. If we are content with the humdrum, the
> second best, the hand-over-hand, it will not be
> forgiven us. All through the writing of this book
> I have been haunted by a long-remembered echo of
> *La Princesse Lointaine:*
>
> Brother Trophus: Inactivity is the only vice, master
>   Erasmus; and the only virtue is ...
>
> Erasmus: What?
>
> Brother Trophus: Enthusiasm! [51]

[1] For example, in colonial America, one was not "saved," one could not be a member of the Congregational Church, until he had experienced a moment of conversion. Though a man and a woman accepted the truths of the faith, attended and supported the parish functions, observed the morality of the Christian life, he or she was refused Church membership if there were no signs of conversion. For these practices were considered but external conformities--no substitute for the profound change of heart and mind by which one knew without doubt that one was in grace. Wesleyan Methodism, American Perfectionism, and the religions which found nurture in the revivals of the eighteenth and nineteenth centuries are other examples of Christian groups which have accepted and even expected the sudden conversion as the work of God. Christian preachers are found speaking on street corners and in the haunts of the wicked because again and again such chance exhortation has triggered the conversion of the most hardened cynic.

[2] The following is but one of the many extracts which William James includes to illustrate the religious experience of a large number of people:

> After I sat down, being all in confusion, like a drowning man that was just giving up to sink and almost in agony, I turned very suddenly around in my chair, and seeing part of an old Bible lying in one of the chairs, I caught hold of it in great haste; and opening it without any premeditation, cast my eyes on the 38th Psalm, which was the first time I ever saw the Word of God;it took hold of me with such power that it seemed to go through my whole soul, so that it seemed as if God was praying in, with and for me... At that instant of time... redeeming love broke into my soul with repeated scriptures, with such power that my whole soul seemed to be melted down with love; the burden of guilt and condemnation was gone, darkness was expelled, my heart humbled and filled with gratitude, and my whole soul, that was a few minutes ago groaning under mountains of death, and crying to an unknown God for help, was now filled with immortal love, soaring on the wings of faith,

> freed from the chains of death and darkness... I
> so longed to be useful in the cause of Christ in
> preaching the gospel, that it seemed as if I could
> not rest any longer, but go I must and tell the
> wonders of redeeming love.

The Varieties of Religious Experience, (New York, 1958)
pp. 178f, 184.

3 J.Y. Lettvin, H.R. Maturana, W.S. McCulloch, and
W.H. Pitts, "What the Frog's Eye Tells the Frog's Brain,"
in *Embodiments of the Mind,* Warren S. McCulloch, ed.,
(Cambridge, Mass., 1965) pp. 230-255.

4 See: Robert E. Ornstein, *On the Psychology of Medi-
tation,* (New York, 1971) pp. 171f. and Aldous Huxley, *The
Doors of Perception* and *Heaven and Hell,* (Harmondsworth,
Eng., 1959) p. 21f.

5 See A. Maslow, *Religion, Values and Peak Experiences,*
(New York, 1970) pp. 59-68; 91-96. See also Andrew Greeley
and William McCready, "Are We a Nation of Mystics?" *New
York Times Mazazine,* Jan.26, 1975, pp. 12ff. This last
article cites the unusually high correlation found between
those who reported such experiences of altered consciousness and the high scores obtained on the Psychological
Well-Being Scale developed by Norman Bradburn--the highest
correlation, according to Bradburn, that had ever been
observed with this scale.

6 The Bergson-Huxley model of consciousness is but one of
many which are utilized by contemporary thinkers in their
efforts to account for religious experiences and for conversion. Others use a model which posits different parts
of the brain, each responsible for differing modes of perception. Religious conversion occurs when the part of the
brain which perceives in unitive or religious categories
has been inoperative and is suddenly brought into operation
For example, Robert Ornstein works with a two-hemispheric
model. He suggests that in our society the analytical, in-
dividuating consciousness of the left hemisphere tends to
dominate the more intuitive, religious consciousness of
the right hemisphere--a dominance which must be broken down

if one is to perceive in a whole way. *The Psychology of Consciousness,* (San Francisco, 1972) pp. 138f.

7 J.C. Pearce, *The Crack in the Cosmic Egg,* (New York, 1973) pp. 2,7.

8 Robert Jay Lifton, in opening his study on brainwashing in China [*Thought Reform and the Psychology of Totalism,* (New York, 1961) p. 3f.] makes the following observation which serves to put the accusation of brainwashing in an historical perspective:

> Originally used to describe Chinese indoctrination techniques, it was quickly applied to Russian and Eastern European approaches, and then to just about anything which the Communists did anywhere (as illustrated by the statement of a prominent American lady who, upon returning from a trip to Moscow, claimed that the Russians were "brainwashing" prospective mothers in order to prepare them for natural childbirth.) Inevitably, the word made its appearance closer to home, sometimes with the saving grace of humor...but on other occasions with a more vindictive tone--as when Southern segregationalists accused all who favor racial equality (including the Supreme Court) of having been influenced by "left-wing brainwashing;" or equally irresponsible usages by anti-fluoridation, anti-mental-health legislation, or anti- almost anything groups leveled against their real or fancied opponents.

9 See, for example, Berkeley Rice, "Honor Thy Father Moon," *Psychology Today,* January, 1976, p.40.

10 Mark Brewer, "We're Gonna Tear You Down and Put You Back Together," *Psychology Today,* August, 1975, pp. 35ff. In a companion article Richard P. Marsh, of San Francisco State University, concludes his remarks about the Erhard System as follows:

> Thus, EST is not brainwashing. Nor is it hypnosis. What is it then? De-hypnosis, perhaps. An attempt to release the individual from the cultural trance, the systematic self-delusion, to which most of us surrender our aliveness. An effort to rescue free

> will and personal responsibility from the decline
> into which they have fallen and place them again
> at the center of human regard. But, whatever EST
> is, if my experience is to be trusted, it takes
> its place alongside the other major disciplines by
> which people can hope to find their way to personal
> fulfillment. ("I am the Cause of My World,"
> *Psychology Today,* August, 1975, p. 38.)

[11] See Huxley, pp. 113-122.

[12] See John Cogley, *Catholic America,* (New York, 1974)
pp. 38-39. "The Awful Disclosures of the Hotel Dieu
Nunnery of Montreal" (1836) described in detail, with
illustrations, a "nest of debauchery" in which infanti-
cide, murder, and rape were to be found.

[13] E.g., Berkeley Rice, p.47.

[14] In *Newsweek,* June 14, 1974, International Edition,
Pam Fanshier, who was abducted and transported from Kansas
to Ohio for deprogramming, reports that it was "the most
hellish and terrifying" incident of her life, in which she
was mocked and degraded, kept in a state of exhaustion and
forced to watch her possessions burnt.

[15] The attribution of the parents' efforts to the work of
the devil is the inevitable conclusion to be expected in a
theology which views life as a confrontation between the
forces of good and evil.

[16] Lifton cites *Time* magazine's characterization of
Marcello Mastroianni as a man with a spine made of plastic
napkin rings as applicable to modern man, who realizes
that there are advantages to a backbone (representing
strength, courage, and will) rendered flimsy and malleable
See *Boundaries,* (New York, 1967) p. 50ff.

[17]
> Our current inability to sustain relationships or
> responsibilities is the result of a largely unno-
> ticed but nevertheless remarkable transformation

> in our sense of self stemming from...philosophy.
> The prevailing theme of this confrontation is a
> reverent faith in what we may call the fluid
> self. It has become the dominant cultural ortho-
> doxy of our day. [Kilpatrick, *Identity and
> Intimacy*, (New York, 1976) p. 3.]

18
    Kilpatrick, p. 43.

19
    Kilpatrick, pp. 46-47.

20
    John Haughey attributes belief that commitments are
impossible to the massive influence of Charles Darwin
and Sigmund Freud. Quoting Silvan Tompkins, he
says of the latter: "Psychoanalysis is a systematic
training in indecision." [*Should Anyone Say Forever?*
(New York, 1975) p. 26.]

21
    See M. Buber, *Good and Evil*, (New York, 1953) pp. 99ff.

22
    Haughey, p. 23.

23
    See, e.g., Kenneth Keniston's study of *The Uncommitted*,
(New York, 1965) and George Gilder's recent study of
"Swinging Singles" in *Naked Nomads*, (New York, 1974).

24
    Lifton, *Boundaries*, p. 59.

25
    New York Times Magazine, January, 5, 1975, pp. 12ff.

26
    Haughey, p. 22.

27
    Kilpatrick, p. 63.

28
    Ibid., p. 143.

29
    See *Man's Search for Meaning*, (New York, 1969) and
Psychotherapy and Existentialism, (New York, 1968).

[30] Nora Spurgin, "A Sociological/Psychological Profile of Unification Church Members," Unpublished Manuscript.

[31] *Psycholotherapy and Existentialism,* (New York, 1968) p. 8.

[32] *Mirror for Observers,* (London, 1955) p. 138.

[33] *Newsweek,* June 14, 1976, International Edition, p.45.

[34] See William James, p. 206, who refers to the work of E.D. Starbuck in his *Psychology of Religion.*

[35] James, p. 205.

[36] New York, 1970, xv-xvi.

[37] *Depth Psychology and a New Ethic,*(New York, 1973) pp. 34-35. See also, p. 68.

[38] Many religious orders within the Roman Catholic Church have in recent years dropped the practice of having new members take a new name upon their entrance, precisely because they fear that this practice will encourage the tendency of young religious to regard entrance into a new vocation as the obliteration of the old person with his problems and difficulties.

[39] *Enthusiasm, A Chapter in the History of Religion,* (New York, 1950) p. 2.

[40] *Divine Principle,* 2nd edition, (Washington, D.C., 1973) p. 8.

[41] "It Shows up in Sex," *Critic,* July-August, 1970, p. 3.

[42] Charles Nordhoff, *The Communistic Societies of the United States,* (New York, 1966) pp. 36, 117, 275ff.

[43] "Sexuality and Jesus," in *Sex, Thoughts for Contemporary Christians,* Michael J. Taylor, ed., (New York, 1972) p. 59f.

[44] That there is a relationship between religion and sexuality has long been advocated. The fertility cults of many ancient primitives, the practice of temple "prostitutes," and the ancient disciplines of tantric yoga are examples of the actualization of this theory. Freud recognized this recurring association and interpreted it as a sign that religion is nothing but a sublimation of healthy sexual instincts. Jung accepted Freud's data, but inverted its significance, much as Hegel was turned upside down by Marx. Jung saw sexuality as a symbol, as a form, of something much bigger than itself: the search of the finite for the infinite. In this context, the thesis of Denis de Rougemont in his *Love in the Western World,* [New York, 1974] is fascinating, for he argues that the romantic poetry of the middle ages was in fact disguised mystical theory. Alan Watts observes:

> ...a sexually self-conscious culture such as our
> own must beware of its natural tendency to see reli-
> gion as a symbolizing of sex, for to sexually un-
> complicated people it has always been obvious that
> sex is a symbol of religion; that is to say, the
> ecstatic self-abandonment of nuptial love is the
> average man's nearest approach to the selfless
> state of mystical or metaphysical experience. For
> this reason the act of love is the easiest and
> most readily intelligible illustration of what it
> is like to be in "union with God," to live the
> eternal life, free from self and time.

Myth and Ritual in Christianity, (Boston, 1968) p. 164ff.

[45] See *Circular,* 26 March 1853, p. 149. An analysis of this dynamic in Oneida's theology can be found in my own unpublished thesis "The Oneida Community's Concept of Christian Love, " University of St. Michael's College, Toronto, 1973.

[46] *Circular,* 30 May, 1864, p. 82.

47 *Oneida Circular,* 12 July, 1875, p. 218.

48 *Ibid.*

49 See *Divine Principle,* pp. 31, 38-39.

50 The members of the Unification Church can live for a generation of "new" beings. Unlike others, who inherit by a process of osmosis the frustrations and anxieties of their parents, these children will be born of unions formed by parents who have first established their union with God, and will be raised in homes where peace and love are the inheritance. Young Oon Kim, a theologian of the Unification Church, explains their viewpoint:

> Where do we learn conflict? In the family. Our
> personalities are highly determined within the
> family at an early age. Therefore, if we would
> see a world of harmony and peace, we must have men
> of harmony and peace; to produce men of harmony
> and peace we need families of harmony and peace.
> That is the key to world peace, the key to univer-
> sal unity; the key to God's kingdom on earth lies
> within the Family.

Unification Theology and Christian Thought, (New York, 1975) p. 19.

51 Ronald Knox, *Enthusiasm,* (New York, 1950) p. 591.

THEOLOGICAL ANALYSES

MARRIAGE, FAMILY AND SUN MYUNG MOON

JOSEPH H. FICHTER

By some odd coincidence the majority of young
Moonies with whom I have spoken used to be Roman Catholics. I met them here and there, but mainly at the annual conferences of the International Cultural Foundation, and I always asked them where they came from and
why they joined the Unification Church. The young women
and men who told me their religious beliefs did not pre-
tend to represent a cross section of the membership, but
they were chosen to meet and host the conference participants. They are alert, articulate, enthusiastic and,
above all, they have a strong sense of vocation.

The comments I present here are limited to a central aspect of their spiritual calling: their vocation to
godly marriage and family. For a deeper understanding of
their religious commitment I searched the "revealed
scripture," *Divine Principle*. In the fast-growing literature about the movement, I studied Young Oon Kim's comparison of *Unification Theology and Christian Thought*,
Frederick Sontag's sympathetic book *Sun Myung Moon and
the Unification Church* and the dire warnings of Irving
Louis Horowitz in *Science, Sin and Salvation*.

There is also a "bad press" on the Rev. Sun Myung
Moon's influence over young Americans, which began even

An earlier version of this essay appeared in *America*,
Oct. 27, 1979, pp. 226-228. Reprinted with the permission of the editor.

before the Jonestown tragedy triggered hysteria about religious cults. The main criticism centered around the
"brainwashing" of the conversion process, based on the
assumption that people willingly join other churches but
have to be tricked and coerced into membership in the
Unification Church. Barbara Hargrove says that parents
and ministers tend to suspect "sinister means" at work
among those who succeed (where they have failed) to in-
still filial piety and religious zeal among young people.

The process of becoming a full-fledged member of
the Unification Church is in some ways similar to that
which a Catholic experiences on entering the novitiate
of a religious order. Life there is regulated, disci-
plined and goal-oriented. You give up your worldly aspirations and your worldly goods and commit yourself to
the ideals of the organization. No drugs, no alcohol,
no sex, no money, few decisions and few worries. You put
yourself under spiritual direction and you develop a
loyalty to the religious congregation, its philosophy,
its program, its leaders.

In both cases the individuals feel a call to a
deeper spirituality, a closer union with God and a more
meaningful prayer life than they had previously experienced. They also develop an enthusiasm for the church's
teachings that encourages them to share the good news of
salvation with others. Catholics who have converted to
the Unification Church feel that their new religion has
a universal concern, a program for embracing the whole
mass of humanity, while they think that Catholicism tends
to focus its spirituality on a predominantly personal relationship with God. One of them, who likes ecumenical
jargon, said that the Catholic Church is "culture-bound"
and doesn't make much progress with non-Europeans and
non-Westerners.

From the point of view of a prospective lifelong vocation, the big difference is that the Catholic religious
orde₁ is guiding you to a career of permanent celibacy.
Personal holiness lies in that direction. In contrast,
the totally committed member of the Unification community
is being prepared for marriage and family. The individual is spiritually incomplete until joined to a spouse in
holy matrimony, and is participating in a blessed family.
Single persons who are converted to the church—most of
them are in their mid-20's—soon learn the theological
and spiritual importance of family life, for which they
are destined. With rare exceptions, there is not much
future for a celibate in the Unification Church.

Young people who "join the family" take up residence
in a Unification center with other male or female members,
strictly segregated by sex. Frederick Sontag calls it a
"coed monasticism." They develop a family relationship
looking across sex lines at brothers and sisters and not
at potential marriage partners. There is spiritual kin-
ship, close-knit comaraderie and group support within the
residence. Selfishness is a serious personal fault. Christian love is the key word, and this collective relationship
can be harmonious only if it is God-centered.

One of the more inflammatory charges against the Unification community is that the membership is disruptive of
family life. The new convert leaves home and family,
brothers and sisters, to dedicate himself entirely to the
religious calling. Parents sometimes charge that their
children have been "brainwashed." Similar charges have
been made about Catholic religious orders that lured a
daughter to a convent or a son to a seminary. God's call
must be obeyed even if parents are in opposition. Some
Catholic parents have forbidden their teenage children to

attend charismatic prayer meetings lest they be drawn too
frequently out of the family circle. The fact is that the
great majority of Moonies continue to maintain cordial relations with their parents and family.

The marriage chances for a Moonie are limited in one
direction and expanded in another. The member is not per-
mitted to marry outside the family, that is, the spouse
must be a fellow member of the movement. This is the same
strict rule that governs the marriage of Salvation Army
officers and the mate selection of Israeli Jews. It was
the same rule against mixed marriages which has gradually
lost its effectiveness in the Catholic Church. Any member
who wants to marry outside the Unification community has
obviously misunderstood the central significance of sharing religious values in lifelong fidelity.

On the other hand, there is a broadening of marriage
opportunities in the Unification approval of "mixed" marriages across ethnic and racial lines. The conventional
American pattern of marrying someone of your nationality,
and especially of your own race, is widely disregarded in
this movement. At the most recent engagement ceremony,
about one-third of the couples were interracial. The
large Oriental membership, especially of Japanese and Ko-
reans, makes available to Caucasians a prospect of marriage partners that they would not ordinarily have.
Sharing the same religious convictions and practices provides a value that transcends racial preferences.

The Unification Church does not allow teenage marriages among its members and thus avoids what seems to be
one of the main stumbling blocks to marriage stability.
Members must wait until they are 25 years old to marry,
and the preference is that they delay even longer. The
stages of formation and growth precede the stage of

perfection. It is clear that Moonies do not rush into
marriage, but then there is no need to hurry. The female
members do not have to be anxious and nervous if they are
not engaged before they are 30. Their religious calling
is marriage, and Mr. Moon will find a spouse for them and
preserve them from living out their lives as old maids.

·Marriage is a serious and holy sacrament for which
lengthy preparation is required, and one of the notable
aspects is the willingness of the members to have Mr. Moon
pick their life partners for them. The concept of "arranged" marriages is alien to young Americans although it
has been an accepted pattern for most of humanity during
most of history. This is not a compulsory arrangement.
Members are urged to express their preferences, but they
do have a deep trust in Mr. Moon as the voice of God for
them. One recently engaged man remarked: "You try to have
confidence in your prayer life that God knows what is best
for you, that He will work through Reverend Moon to suggest the proper match for you."

Preoccupation with the dating game, the hazards of
flirty infatuation and the excitement of romantic love are
avoided in the custom of arranged marriages. The attraction to each other is spiritually motivated and spiritually sustained. They are putting God's will, as expressed
to them by their religious leader, before their own. As
in everything else they do, the primary motive in preparing for marriage is to follow the will of God. "We
both love God more than we love each other; and that's
the way it ought to be, and it's the only way we can hope
to have a God-centered family."

The secular and contemporary way of "getting engaged" is a very private agreement in which parents, rela-
tives and friends must not dare to interfere. There may

be a party celebrated, and even some gift-garnering "show-
ers" after the announcement has been made. The custom of
a religious and solemn engagement before friends and in
the presence of a priest was in vogue among Catholics for
a while when the liturgical movement was young. The engagement ceremony for members of the Unification Church
is a sacred and public event, and it is celebrated by numerous couples simultaneously. When the couple shares a
cup of wine on that occasion they are establishing a spiritual lineage.

        The engagement that is blessed by God and approved
by the church is not primarily of the flesh. It allows
no liberties of a sexual nature; premarital intercourse
is completely prohibited. The whole notion of "living together" before marriage is abhorred as sinful, lascivious
conduct. Even after marriage the couple may abstain from
sex for some period of time. They may be sent on separate
missions to different parts of the world before settling
down to the consummation of their marriage.

        The primary purpose of marriage is to give joy and
glory to God, and the primary purpose of sexual coition
is the procreation of children. The biblical injunction
to increase and multiply is taken seriously by members of
the church. Spiritual perfection cannot be achieved in
self-centered and lonely celibacy. It comes through ex-
periencing the three stages of love in the God-centered
family: the mutual love of wife and husband, the love of
parents for children and love of children for parents.
The family is the foundation for understanding the love
of God. To become "true parents" and to populate the
earth with spiritually perfect individuals is to help create the kingdom of God and to bring salvation to a sinful
world.

Unification theology provides the rationale for the
emphasis on family life. God created Adam and Eve with a
potential to both spiritual and physical perfection. "The
purpose of creation is to give joy to God," writes the
theologian Herbert Richardson. The first great joy for
our original parents was meant to be the experience of
God's love and the attainment of individual perfection.
The establishment of a saintly family meant that God's
love would be shared in the second great joy. Ultimately,
then, the sharing of God's love with the whole universe
fulfills God's plan for His kingdom on earth.

According to the theology of *Divine Principle,* the
revealed scripture of the Unification Church, God intended Adam and Eve to marry and have perfect children who
would populate His physical and spiritual kingdom. This
intention was frustrated when Eve was sexually seduced by
the archangel Lucifer, committing the original sin of
adultery and causing the spiritual fall of mankind. Her
impurity was passed on in premature and illicit intercourse with Adam, causing the physical fall of man. Later,
God sent Jesus to redeem mankind from sin. He accomplished His spiritual mission, but He was killed before
He could marry and father a new race of perfect children.
Our first parents threw away God's love; Jesus was prevented from completing the redemptive mission on which
His heavenly Father had sent Him.

The time has now come for the members of the Unification Church to establish perfect families in love and
justice and unity, which in turn will unify all races,
all nations, all religions. The divine scheme of love
and family is laid out in the "four-position foundation,"
which appears to be a cumbersome theological and relational formula. The four positions are: God, husband,

wife, and child. The pure and perfect relationship with
God helps to establish the perfect relationship between
husband and wife, and then between parents and children.
The spiritual and physical kingdom of God, the total salvation that God intended in sending the Messiah, will be
achieved by the ever expanding network of such God-centered families.

Conventional Christian theologians find these teachings rampant with heresy, but a pragmatic sociologist is
likely to say that the Moonies have come upon a family
program that works. While marriage counselors and parish
priests are wringing their hands over the breakdown of
family life, the Unification Church is doing something
about it. The God-centered family is not merely a nice
slogan or a spiritual ideal suggested by the church leaders. It is the essential core of community among the
faithful of the church. It is also a deeply motivated
system for restoring marital fidelity and family stability to modern society.

One need not be expert moral theologian to recognize
the notable shift that has been occurring in the marital
and family values of American society. Many secularists
see this change as an expression of personal freedom, an
opportunity for self-actualization. Spiritually sensitive
people see it as a decline in personal morality as well as
a disregard for community needs and values. In either
case, these changing patterns of behavior reflect a significant restructuring of the family system that has long
been integral to Western civilization.

Some families are in trouble because of social factors that call for collective attention: inflation, poverty and discrimination in housing and employment. These
social causes may combine with personal causes in influ-

encing the shifting values in marriage and family. The
evidence is drawn from fairly reliable statistics on human behavior and attitudes: premarital sex, venereal disease, teenage pregnancies, pornography, infidelity, divorce. These are all symptoms of the strain and stress
that affect the home life of many Americans.

The religious values of the Judeo-Christian tradition have generally been supportive of marital fidelity
and family stability. Church leaders, pastors and preachers often express concern that these values are being destroyed. Yet in some instances, the churches have "re-
laxed" their values and doctrines to accommodate the behavior patterns and preferences of their adherents. Moral
concessions have been made in the matter of divorce, birth
prevention and even abortion. Organized religion in the
mainline churches has been relatively unsuccessful in
stemming the downward curve.

Whatever else one may say in criticism of the Unification Church as a social and religious movement, one has
to   recognize   its systematic program for the restoration of "old-fashioned" morality, its emphasis on chasti-
ty before marriage, prayerful preparation for marriage, a
readiness to accept guidance in the choice of a partner,
marital love reflective of love of God, transmission of
spiritual perfection to children. There has been much
comment and criticism of the theological, political and
economic aspects of the Unification Church, but very little has been said about the positive value implications
in regard to marriage and family.

When Catholics talked about "having a vocation"
they almost always meant the kind of life that required
permanent celibacy, whether in the diocesan or religious
priesthood, as well as among religious sisters and

brothers. This was the "more perfect" spiritual path to one's own salvation and also in the ministry to all other people. There was always room, of course, for the vocation of marriage, but it was at best a second-level and risky pathway to God. The Moon people have turned this around. If you really want to do God's will; if you want the higher vocation; if you want the life of spiritual perfection, you marry and have children.

It is commonplace observation that the family is the moral basis of society, and that religion constitutes the moral bond of family solidarity. Slogans abound in praise of family life. The family that prays together stays together. The moral level of a community reflects the moral level of its families. The Unification ideology emphasizes the centrality of the family in maintaining a religious culture and in transmitting a spiritual tradition. We may well conclude here with the remark by Harvey Cox: "Here is a movement which manages to combine religious universalism, pentecostal immediacy, a warmly supportive family and a program for allegedly building the kingdom of God on earth. Such a potent admixture cannot be dismissed lightly."

CHRISTIAN HERMENEUTICS AND UNIFICATION THEOLOGY

FRANK K. FLINN

If someone were to ask me "What is the most important passage in the *Divine Principle*?" I would reply unhesitatingly "The section called *Our Attitude Toward the Bible*."[1] In this passage, Sun Myung Moon makes a telling statement: "Since the time of Jesus, no one has been able to reveal this heavenly secret. This is because we have hitherto read the Bible from the standpoint that John the Baptist was the greatest prophet of all."[2] The implications of this passage are far reaching and give us a clue as to Rev. Moon's own standpoint toward biblical hermeneutics. What is new about his understanding of the Bible and what does this new understanding entail?

According to the *Divine Principle*, the most important problem of our time is the reconciliation of religion and science.[3] The problem is not simply a matter of reconciling two academic disciplines. Rather, the problem points to the need for the restoration of the original unity of body and mind, the external and the internal, subject and object, the male and the female, and the vertical and horizontal dimensions of human existence.[4] The original purpose of God in the Creation was not simply to establish a kingdom, dominion, or sovereignty in inner hope but to establish them outwardly on earth, in time and space. Up until now science has dealt with the truth in its inner and spiritual aspect.[5] The result has been

disastrous. While we have come to know God on a spiritual
plane, we have not yet known him on a physical level.
Therefore, we have *failed* to know God in the fullness of
His creation which is both spiritual and physical. The
lack of relation between modern science and modern religion attests to this failure.

The *Divine Principle* teaches that the separation of
religion and science in the modern world has caused un-
told harm to the development of humanity. Who among us
could disagree with this statement? At the same time, the
reconciliation of religion and science is no easy achievement. In the last century the theologian Franz von Baader
diagnosed the illness of our age: we fail to see the
spiritual implications of the physical world and the physical implications of the spiritual world. Hence we tend
to fall into an unscientific Pietism or an irreligious
Rationalism.[7] As a result we suffer from a cultural
schizophrenia, which means simply that we go through life
with a split mind. We embrace scientific achievements as
the latest and best for mankind without being aware of
their spiritual implications. We perceive the dangerous
aspects of modern technology without having the spiritual
wherewithall to counter its ill effects. Upon the *reconciliation* of religion and science, according to the *Divine
Principle*, depends the *restoration* of humanity's original
mind before the Fall. As a spiritual heir to Baader, I
personally have difficulty in disagreeing with Rev. Moon.

Let me return to the crucial passage from the *Divine
Principle* which I quoted above. Like the gospeller St.
Luke, Sun Myung Moon paints a diptych between Jesus and
John the Baptist. Unlike St. Luke, who may seem to

harmonize the missions of the Baptist and Jesus, Rev.
Moon uncovers a fundamental discrepancy in the role of
John the Baptist. John represents the Jews in their disbelief of Jesus' mission. According to Rev. Moon, the
Jewish authorities were ready and eager to accept John as
the Prophet to Come, i.e., as the reincarnation of the
spirit of the prophet Elijah and predecessor to the Messiah. However, the Baptist replies to them that he is not
that Prophet (Jn 1:21). Thereby he contradicts the tes-
timony of Jesus himself.[8] John's *failure* (and failure is
a theological concept in the *Divine Principle*) to recognize *his own identity and mission* as the forerunner of the
Messiah lay in his inability to reconcile the spiritual
and the physical.

Spiritually, John the Baptist received the revelation
that Jesus was the Anointed One. But, physically, he
failed to put his body where his spirit was, i.e., he
failed to minister as a disciple to Jesus. John's failure
to minister to Jesus created a wall of doubt among the
Jewish people. Because of John's blindness, the Jews were
led to disbelieve in Jesus as the Messiah. The Jews would
accept John as Elijah, but they would not accept Jesus because he violated not only the Sabbath itself, but the
proscriptions of the Law, by associating with harlots,
tax-collectors, poor people and fishermen.[10]

John initially succeeded spiritually, but he failed
physically. Jesus succeeded spiritually and physically as
the Incarnate Word. However, the disbelief of the Jews
caused him to choose to be crucified at the very stage in
his life when he should have chosen a "bride" who would
generate with him the true children of God according to

the original purpose of Creation. Therefore the mission
of Jesus, while complete in principle, remains unfulfilled
in historical reality. Says the *Divine Principle*,

> From the time of Jesus through the present, all
> Christians have thought that Jesus came into the
> world to die. This is because they did not know
> the fundamental purpose of Jesus' coming as Messiah,
> and entertained the wrong idea that *spiritual* sal-
> vation was the only mission for which Jesus came to
> the world. Jesus came to accomplish the will of
> God in his lifetime, but had to die a reluctant
> death due to the disbelief of the people. There
> must first appear on earth the bride who can re-
> lieve the humiliated and grieving heart of Jesus
> before Christ as the bridegroom can come again--
> this time to complete his mission with his bride.[11]

Without doubt, the above interpretation of the Bible,
illustrated in the respective roles of John the Baptist and
Jesus, will strike many establishment Christians as somewhat alien to their own ideas. Therefore, while recognizing
that there is something new about Rev. Moon's hermeneutics,
and he often makes claims of discovering something new in
the Bible,[12] what I now hope to do in this essay is to show
that the fundamental aspects of the hermeneutic in the
Divine Principle are not as novel as establishment Christians
would like to believe.

In order to discover the aspects of the *Divine Principle* which are not new, but which have a foundation in the
tradition, it is necessary that we go back and re-examine
the *principles* of interpretation which have prevailed in
Christian hermeneutics. The reaction of establishment
Christians that there is something odd, and therefore wrong
about Rev. Moon's hermeneutics could be based on an authentic perception. On the other hand, their perception could

originate in their failure to remember the principles of
interpretation which belong to the long history of Christianity itself. In this situation it behooves the theologian to be careful and caring. Carefulness and caring-
ness are, I suggest, the proper ways to approach the hermeneutics of the *Divine Principle*.

PRINCIPLES OF CHRISTIAN HERMENEUTICS

A distinction should be made between the principles
of Christian hermeneutics and the history thereof. We are
all aware that these principles have emerged in the stress
of particular historical situations. However, I must leave
historical questions to those who are far more skilled in
this discipline than I. By the term "principle" I mean the
mode and *motive* which undergirds a given interpretation of
how the Scriptures *ought* to be appropriated for living out
one's Christian existence. Let us now examine these modes
and motives from a systematic point of view.

In the Middle Ages there appeared a Latin ditty which,
though it seems trivial, summarized the modes and motives
of biblical interpretation. The ditty is far from being
comprehensive, but it is a convenient starting point:

> Litera gesta docet
>   Quid credas allegoria
> Moralis quid agas
>   Quo tendas anagogia.

There have been many translations of this oft-quoted qua-
train. Most of them have been in error.[13] At the risk of
enriching this history of error, I will now attempt a translation of my own.

> The *Letter* teaches feats done in the past;
>   What you are to believe – *Allegory*;
> The *Moral* – what you are to do;
>   Whither you are to direct yourself – *Anagogy*.

Although this ditty seems to refer to a fourfold distinction, there is more subtle and more basic distinction
underlying it. This is indicated by the use of the indicative (*gesta*) as opposed to the present subjunctive
(*credas, agas, tendas*). The present subjunctive in Latin
has the peculiar quality of conveying a double sense. It
refers to both the notion of the future and the notion of
what is imperative. In the Middle Ages, this distinction
between what is and what ought to be (in the future) was
what people at that time meant by interpreting the Scriptures literally or spiritually.[14] In the translation
above I try to indicate this difference by using the past
indicative (feats done) and the subjunctive imperative
(are to...).

The relation between the literal and spiritual senses
of the Scriptures has always been the central problem of
Christian hermeneutics. Indeed, the history of Christian
hermeneutics often looks like a see-saw between an emphasis on the spiritual sense and an emphasis on the literal.
This see-saw first occurs in the conflict between the Alexandrine and the Antiochian schools of interpretation; it
reappears in the conflict between Medieval Catholicism
and Protestantism. I suggest that the conflict between
the hermeneutics of establishment Christianity and that of
the Unification Church is a continuation of the very same
debate which has always been present in Christianity: in
what way and for what reasons are the teachings of the
Scriptures to be appropriated for Christian life? Thus

there is a question of modes and a question of motives. My
perception tells me that the modes depend upon the motives
and not vice-versa. These motives, in turn, depend upon
certain emphasis placed upon a given sense or a combination
of senses of Scripture.

In general, there have been four basic modes for the
interpretation of the Bible. For the sake of convenience
I will divide them into the Catholic (Orthodox and Roman)
modes and the Protestant (Lutheran and Calvinistic) modes.
The Catholic modes have always stressed the spiritual sense
of the Scripture. The Protestant modes have always
stressed the literal sense. However, there have been important differentiations within these two basic modes.

Orthodox Catholicism stresses the allegorical mode of
interpreting the Bible. This emphasis is true not only for
the past but also the present. In itself, this mode of
interpretation does not differ from that of Roman Catholicism. (For example, we see the allegorical mode in the
many western commentaries on the *Canticle of Canticles*.)
What is different between the orthodox and the Roman modes
is this: the orthodox mode is collegial and communal; the
Roman mode is individual and particular. This does not
mean that the orthodox mode neglects the individual nor
that the Roman mode shuns the collective. The orthodox
appropriates the individual on behalf of collective man
and the Roman appropriates the collective on behalf of
individual man. But it follows from this that the spiritual hermeneutic of the East tends toward what is called
mystagogy-- the leading of the individual soul toward the
universal vision of God. Roman Catholicism, on the other
hand, tends to appropriate the *moral* and typological side

of spiritual hermeneutics by applying the universal vision
to the practical conduct of life.[15]

The difference between orthodox and Roman hermeneutics
explains, I believe, the failure of mysticism to take
anchor in Western spirituality -- even though mysticism has
always flourished and still flourishes in the East. Orthodox Catholicism is rooted in *vision* and its mode of biblical interpretation is to see in the Bible indication of the
journey toward God. Roman Catholicism, in contrast, is
rooted in *hearing* and finding one's place and position in the
world.[16] The difference between these two modes of appro-
priating the Bible is much like possessing a guide book to
a country as opposed to having a map.

The allegorical and typological modes of exegesis had
the virtue of being able to integrate both the Old and New
Testaments, the Old Testament being the shadow or antitype
of the New. But there was a weakness in this strength.
As the content of the Christian Scripture gradually lost
its eschatological edge, the idea of spiritual Eternity
replaced the expectation of the imminent temporal arrival
of the Kingdom of God on earth.[17] In this way, the historical implications of the spiritual sense of Scripture
became obscured. The imminent eruption of God's spirit
into time was reinterpreted as a never-historical Eternity
This can be seen in almost any Medieval painting in which
the material and temporal aspects of human existence are
depicted in a state of suspended animation. As the orthodox mystagogical hermeneutic of Journey/Vision and the
Western typological hermeneutic of Shadow/Type became more
and more verticalized, the meaning of the historical process as the continuum of God's providential restoration of

our humanity and the meaning of the world as the *theatrum glorea Dei* tended to lose their theological validity.

The Protestant return to the normativity of the Scriptures (*scriptura sui ipsius interpres* = "Scripture interprets itself") came on the heels of mediaeval allegorizations and ecclesiastical sacramentalizations of the primitive Christian message. In Luther's hermeneutic we witness a rediscovery of the literal and historical dimension of the Bible's primitive eschatology. Luther gradually shifts from the fourfold hermeneutic (i.e. the four modes described above) to a hermeneutic of Law/Gospel and Promise/Hope. Luther says that the believing Christian is reconfronted with the *adventus Christi* in promise (Old Testament) and final coming in Judgment.[18] Luther's hermeneutic of Law/Gospel tends to break down the mediaeval distinctions between eternity and history and it frees the believer to discover the historical implications of the eternal. Under this new hermeneutic both Church and State, priest and layman, are subject to the model of waiting for the coming of the Reign of Christ.

There were ambiguities in Luther's Law/Gospel approach. Eschatological urgency could lead to the total dissolution of the distinction between the spiritual and the "carnal" dimensions of Christian existence. In the furious fervor of the moment, the great distinction between what is attainable and what ought to be hoped for could disappear. The Peasant's War was a prime example of this confusion, which might be called *eschatologia disordinata*.[19] The peasants believed that the kingdom of God had already arrived.

Calvinism, the other protestant approach, is the
attempt to correct the ambiguity in Luther's theory. If
Luther may be said to have restored the eschatological
sense of time, Calvin can be said to have restored the
eschatological sense of space. The difference between
Luther and Calvin can best be seen in the relative stress
the former places on the doctrine of Redemption and the
relative stress the latter places on the doctrine of Creation. For Calvin, the grace which comes to the believer
through redemption in Christ is not simply the restitu-
tion of fallen humanity toward the hope of fulfillment;
it is also the restoration of God's original purpose for
creation itself.[20] Calvin's awareness of the importance
of the doctrine of Creation, with its subsidiary notions
of the *imago Dei* and angelology, led him to subordinate
the Lutheran hermeneutic of Law/Gospel within a broader
hermeneutic based on Creation/Restoration. Like Luther,
Calvin maintains that human nature is totally corrupted
by the Fall. Implicit in Calvin's hermeneutic, however,
is a tentative claim that the original created image of
the original Adam can be restored in time and space -- if
only because the original image still remains imprinted
on man's soul in some dark glimmering.

With his hermeneutic of the Law and the Gospel,
Luther freed himself from the fourfold sense of Scripture.
Calvin, concerned as he was about the order of Christian
existence, could not wholly abandon the idea of Scriptural
modes. In particular, he could not accede to the identification of the literal sense with the historical. For
Calvin, the literal sense could no longer be identified

with the historical sense because the origin of history
is creation. Calvin believed that creation was more than
history, for it included all the ontological structures
of existence in space and time. For Calvin, therefore,
the real question was not whether or not one was forgiven
(in Luther's sense), but to whose Kingdom one belonged in
time and space. Before forgiveness lay the creation (God
and world and the Fall, Adam, Eve and Satan). After forgiveness there awaited the awesome choice between the
true Kingdom of God and the pseudo-Kingdom of Satan.

For Calvin, salvation meant not so much man's forgiveness from *sin* but man's restoration to serve the *glory
of God* as it is revealed in the original purpose of creation. Luther was willing to live *in via,* i.e., on the way
to the future glory, not knowing the cosmic meaning of historical events. "Our life," Luther said, "is a beginning
and a going forward, not a fulfillment."[21] But Calvin
calls men to participate in the cosmic struggle between
forces of Good and forces of Evil. Those forces impinge
on man from the outside, and they equally call upon him
from within. We must struggle with them. This is why,
for Calvin, the chief issue is not sin and forgiveness
(as it was with Luther), but it is for man to be a participant in the restoration of God's glory upon earth.

Earlier I made a distinction between mode and
motive, and proceeded to discuss the modes without reference to the motives. The motives are just as important
as the modes, but they are much more difficult to talk
about. Nevertheless, there is this much that can be said.
The hermeneutics of orthodox Catholicism and Calvinistic
Protestantism have something in common: they tend to see

the spiritual freedom of the individual in terms of the
restoration of the whole. Roman Catholicism and Lutheran
Protestantism, on the other hand, tend to see the freedom
of the whole in terms of the restoration of the individual
Yet, clearly, behind the motives of Christian hermeneutics
is a fundamental dilemma: there can be no restoration of
individuality without a sense of the purpose of the whole,
nor any restoration of the whole without a sense of the
purpose of the individual. Calvinism, the latest religiou
embodiment of this insight, has been subject to distortion
from both polarities: on the one hand it has been subject
to intolerant Covenantalism, and, on the other, to capital-
istic individualism. This is why its symbolic role in the
modern world has been so great.[22] (Perhaps Rev. Moon's
impact can be traced in part to his Calvinist roots.)[*]
Unless we all become aware of this dilemma, we will not
know how to wait for the Kingdom of God; we will find ourselves in the same boat as John the Baptist, not knowing
to which sovereignty we truly belong.

THE HERMANEUTICS OF THE *Divine Principle*

If the earliest Calvinistic principle of hermeneutics
contained a stress on the literal sense of the Scripture,
it also contained a sense of expectation. This is because
early Calvinists identified with the history of Israel
and Israel's hope for a Messiah. Because early Calvinists

---

[*] For a discussion of Moon's Calvinism, see Herbert
Richardson's, *A Brief Outline of Unification Theology* in
this volume.

focussed on the Old Testament Messianic vision of a
Kingdom of God on earth, they reinterpreted the Catholic
theory of Jesus' work in a new way. Their idea was no
less radical in their time than Rev. Moon's in ours.
Calvinism interpreted Jesus in Old Testament categories.
For Calvin, Jesus was preeminently prophet, priest, and
king rather than God-man. This Old-Testamentalizing of
Jesus gave to early Calvinism its world reforming vision:
the restoration of creation to the image of God. But as
that reforming work faltered before the immensity of the
task, and was countered by the Enlightenment stress on
human autonomy, Calvinism tended increasingly to accommodate to the world as a kingdom ruled by necessary evil.
It gave up its earlier vision.

It is my contention that the hermeneutic of the
Divine Principle attempts to restore the full meaning of
creation and the Kingdom of God not only to Calvinistic
theology but to Christian theology as such. In the following pages, I outline the ways in which it attempts to
do this.

1. *Allegory*. When the Protestants at the time of
the Reformation, abandoned the allegorical mode of exegesis, a vacuum was left in the heart of Christendom. Up
to the time of the Reformation, allegory was the way in
which most people could express the meaning of their own
existence. Allegory was the Medieval way of telling
one's own story. However, to use figures and tropes of
allegory to interpret Scripture could also obscure its
simplicity and commonness.[23] In an attempt to recover
the allegorical spiritual meaning of Creation for the
Reformation tradition, John Milton sought to translate

its structure into the *dramatic epic*: *Paradise Lost* and
Paradise Regained. While Milton's theological epic may
have had too many Homeric tropes to suit the tastes of
the average Puritan, it still achieved its intended purpose of justifying and making plain to Puritans the ways
of God toward men. The *Divine Principle* shares with
Paradise Lost and *Paradise Regained* the same qualities
of attempting to convey the *epical urgency* of our place
in time and space as well as attempting to make plain the
figures of the Scriptures in the Last Days.[24]

One way the *Divine Principle* affects its epical dra-
matization is by reintegrating Old Testament creation history with the New Testament proclamations of the Last Days.
In this way the *Divine Principle* identifies the eschatological apocalyptic with the restoration of creation. The
method of apocalyptic becomes in this way, the repetition
of the history in Scripture (Heils-geschichte). Just as
New England Convenanters conceived their experience as
Exile, Wandering in the Wilderness (the flight from
England), and a new Crossing of the Jordan (the Atlantic
Ocean), so the *Divine Principle* allegorically interprets
the conflict between democracy and communism as the eschatological encounter of the Kingdom of God with the Kingdom of Satan. (Those who do not understand allegory think
he is calling for a *literal* world war.) Seen from this
perspective, Rev. Moon's seemingly new allegorization of
the type of Abel (democracy) as opposed to the type of
Cain (communism) is not as strange as it may look.[25]
From this perspective, it might be most appropriate to
describe the *Divine Principle* as a dramatic Biblical epic,
whose closest analogue is Milton's *Paradise Lost* and

Paradise Regained.

2. *Angelology.* One of the amazing phenomena in modern Western theology is the disappearance of the doctrine of the Angels. That disappearance is not without theological importance. According to Calvin, the doctrine of Angels manifests to man not only God's original plan of Creation but also the spiritual destiny of man himself.[26] In other words, without a theology of Angels, Christian humanity would be hard put to articulate its spiritual mission in a physical world. This is precisely the argument of the *Divine Principle*. Rev. Moon sees the hermeneutical importance of a theology of Angels to be a way of understanding our eschatological position in time and space. Here, again, there is an amazing congruence with *Paradise Lost* and *Paradise Regained,* particularly Milton's conceptions of the relations among Adam, Eve, and Satan. Moreover, it is precisely by virtue of his doctrine of angels and his distinction between the two kinds of creation (spiritual and material) that Rev. Moon's theology is most closely related to Catholic Christianity.

3. *Marriage.* The *Divine Principle* sees adultery as the eschatological final sin. The argument is as follows: Adam and Eve fell when they were immature, i.e. they fell when they failed to complete the full growth process intended by God for them. This full growth process involved their fulfilling the commands to "Be fruitful and multiply". Rev. Moon understands their fulfillment of these commands to be their perfecting of the image of God in themselves. But before they could perfect this image and fulfill the command to multiply (and marry), Adam and Eve fell into sin. The work of the Christ must be, then, to restore

the integrity of this 'growth' process to the human race
so that people may grow to personal maturity and form
mature God-oriented marriages.[27] Thus the restoration of
marriage is understood by Rev. Moon to be the beginning
of the restoration of mankind in the last days. It is
precisely because the essence of the perfected image of
God in creation and restoration involves married love
that adultery (rather than pride or some other sin) is
the eschatological final sin.

    While there are other aspects to Rev. Moon's theo-
logy of marriage, I can say at least this much: Moon's
understanding of marriage derives from his Covenantal
theology.* We see a very similar conception in both the
prophecies of Hosea and the Book of Judges (the history
of Israel's infidelity towards God, i.e., Israel's adultery). Secondly, the Medieval tradition retained this
understanding of eschatological love as marital love in
its symbolic interpretations of the most sensual of the
Old Testament books: the *Song of Songs*. Finally, the
Divine Principle's conception of the primary *spiritual*
goal of marriage (*personal relation,* not sex) is exactly
what Milton thought on his.

THE DOCTRINE AND DISCIPLINE OF DIVORCE

    While Catholicism may have sacramentalized marriage,
it gave marriage neither spiritual nor eschatological

---

    * For a fuller discussion of the Unification Church
doctrine of marriage see Prof. Warren Lewis's *Is Rev.
Moon a Heretic?* in this volume.

value. Protestantism, on the other hand, had the tendency
of desacramentalizing marriage, thereby casting it to the
wolves of "the latest psychological insight" and "the needs
of capitalism". Neither Catholicism nor Protestantism
taught that marriage is primarily the spiritual consent and
communion of two souls. Marriage in the *Divine Principle*
is not the full *eschatological reality*. Rather Rev. Moon
wants to restore the meaning of marriage as an *eschatological type* which corresponds to the creator's original
purpose in creation. In this way, Rev. Moon strikes between the classical Protestant and Catholic theologies of
marriage. Like Milton, he places marriage at the center
of our salvation.

    4. *Numerology*. Little needs to be said about the
symbolic numerology in the *Divine Principle* (e.g. the
importance of "1981").[28]* This is because I think it is
secondary to the essential foundation of Rev. Moon's hermeneutic. That foundation rests on a belief that *Biblical
history* is the *type* of all *history*. Without this realization, readers of the *Divine Principle* might fall into the
mistaken notion that Rev. Moon applies numbers to the
understanding of universal history much in the same way
that an astrologer applies the movements of the stars to
the individual states of the soul. To read the *Divine
Principle* in this way would be a failure to sense the
grand conception Rev. Moon has of the Bible as the key to
the interpretation of the drama which Christians call

---

    * For an explanation of the symbolic importance of
"1981" see Lewis's *Is Rev. Moon a Heretic?* in this volume.

salvation.   Rev. Moon thinks that what God has done with
Israel is paradigmatic for all other peoples, places and
times in this world.

        Throughout the *Divine Principle* there are numerous
references to theological conceptions which, on the surface, look as though they belong to the religions of the
East.   I am thinking, for example, of the references to
the notions of Yin and Yang,[29] transmigration of the soul[30]
and reincarnation.[31]   Furthermore, Rev. Moon's conception
of the Prophet's task shares many affinities with the
understanding of the Prophet in Islamic theology and the
avatar in Hinduism.[32]

CONCEPTS FROM EASTERN RELIGIONS

        How shall we interpret these concepts that are found
in non-Christian religions?   Do they mean that the Unification Church is not a *Christian* movement but rather, an
oriental syncretism that has picked up Christian ideas
and in that process distorted their "true" meaning?   This
is not a matter that can be easily decided for it involves
more than individual concepts, but the general framework
in which they appear.   It could just as easily be the case
that rather than interpreting Biblical doctrines in
light of an Eastern mode of hermeneutics, Rev. Moon is
doing just the reverse.   He could be "Christianizing the
religions of the East".   He could have created the
"indigenous Christianity" Christian theologians have been
calling for since the early 1900's.   Now that it appears,
what did they expect?   Nicea, all over again?

I do not here claim this question is clearly or easily settled. But I do think the universality of Rev. Moon's hermeneutical approach to the Bible allows him to illuminate the meaning, strengths and deficiencies of the chief doctrines of Eastern religions.[33] Also I think his hermeneutic is grounded in a thorough-going adherence to a Coventantal doctrine of time and space which is fundamentally different from anything found in Eastern religion and which is also the overarching structure of the Bible. But all these questions deserve further study and such study should prove helpful to better understand the relation of the Bible to other religions.

CRITICISM AND EVALUATION

Earlier I mentioned that Calvin's hermeneutic of the Old and New Dispensations made spiritual (eschatological) symbols for the historical and political process. He identified God's Kingdom with the spatio-temporal-physical world. He believed the gospel meant *both* forgiveness and a *new*, transformed human life. Calvin did not believe that a perfected transformation of humanity would occur in time and space, nor did he believe that people could establish the perfect Kingdom of God on earth. While he stressed the need to strive for perfection, he also stressed the power of sin to persist until the end of history. In this way, his stress on the ineradicability of sin kept him from asserting the realizability of perfection.[34]

The *Divine Principle*, on the other hand, offers the realizability of perfection by stressing that sin can

be overcome in historical time. It de-emphasizes Protestantism's preoccupation with "forgiveness" and "looking
backward". Rather, Rev. Moon gives centrality to *archetypes of expectation,* the paradigm of which is John the
Baptist. New wine cannot be put into old wineskins.
Those in a state of eschatological expectancy must be
prepared not only for the heady new wine of the New Age,
but also for the new bodies that must go along with it.
But how do we become *new?* Enter again into our mother's
wombs?

The *Divine Principle* seems to imply that we can prepare ourselves for the newness of the kingdom by recapi-
tulating the formative stages of growth intended for the
original Adam and Eve. At the same time, this doctrine
of recapitulation which is intended to put man in a state
of eschatological readiness, also makes Rev. Moon eager
and willing to use "scientific metaphors" from the modern
technological world.[35] Are these scientific metaphors
the new element in Rev. Moon's theology? If so, is
scientific mastery over nature and mankind an original
purpose of God for man? Rev. Moon seems to think so. In
his interpretation of God's command to Adam to "Be Fruitfu
Multiply and inherit the Earth", Rev. Moon discerns "Three
Blessings". The first is the individual's relation to God
which alone makes him "fruitful". The second is marriage
("multiply") which we have already discussed. The third
and crowning blessing is that man shall have dominion over
all creation. This means that man's spiritual life finds
its fulfillment within the physical world.

Rev. Moon's belief that man's fulfillment is within

the *physical world* means that he cannot follow Calvin in
finally dehistoricizing the Scriptural promises of the
Kingdom. For Calvin, the Kingdom was only realized in
life after physical death. For Rev. Moon, on the other
hand, the fulfillment must take place in the physical
world. This is why perfection must be a realizable possibility *here*. Rev. Moon, at this point, is a genuine
humanist. He will not use the escape hatch of "heaven"
to save the truth that God will establish His Kingdom.
He believes that if these Biblical teachings are true,
Kingdom must be established here. The problems is:
how?

We have already noted above that the "how" seems to
involve for Rev. Moon the recognition of the value of
science as a means to transform life for the better.   (Of
course the worse is possible too, for Satan is always
active.) Here are the *Divine Principle's* metaphors from
science and the "third blessing". But even more noteworthy
are Rev. Moon's international Science Conferences where he
brings together renowned professors from all disciplines
and nations to discuss how science can serve "absolute
values", i.e., God's purpose to transform the world into
a perfect society. These science conferences are not public relations ploys (as some detractors suggest) nor
frosting on the theological cake. They are the expression
of Moon's conviction that genuine theology must bring
together both the *spiritual* and the *physical* worlds, both
religion and science. Only as religion and science
work together as a unity, can spiritual values find physical embodiment and eschatology become history.   When that

occurs, the Kingdom of God is established politically and physically on earth.

At this point we should return to the topic of this essay and explain how these reflections on science give the decisive key to the hermeneutics of the *Divine Principle*. What we have seen is that Christian hermeneutics has stressed either the allegorical-spiritual meaning of Scripture (Catholic) or the literal history meaning (Protestant). The opposition between these two traditions has led to controversy about the meaning of salvation. The Catholic tradition, stressing allegorical interpretation of the Bible, locates salvation in the *spiritual* order. The Protestant tradition, stressing the literal interpretation of the Bible, locates salvation in the *historical* order. The Calvinist attempt to *unite* the two orders and modes of meaning by eschatologizing spiritual doctrines, making them *ideals* and *goals* whose realization we should seek *in time,* failed because Calvinism did not find a way to *transform people*. The "new birth" was preached but neither Puritan moral athleticism, nor pietistic emotionalism, nor social gospel politicism changed the heart of man. The colonists found *no spiritual means to transform the physical world*. Today, their courage weakened, they drift between the Scylla of "Realism" and the Charybdis of "Resignation".

What the *Divine Principle* teaches, however, is that there is a means to "transform" the physical heart and physical world, but it is not a spiritual one. It is rather, a "physical one" -- not theology or evangelism but science and technology. Physical means to transform physical things. Spiritual means to transform spiritual.

What is needed therefore is to use science where science has competence, religion where religion has competence *and work for a unity between them*. When this is done, when science and religion work together in perfect unity, then there could be established a *perfect world*.

Rev. Moon's concern for a "full" hermeneutics, a hermeneutics which gives equal value to all four modes (spiritual, physical, individual, communal) is exemplified in the way he reads the Bible and in the form of mission to the world which he is undertaking. His science conferences are no less essential to his vision than his Unification Church. Only if science and religion can work together in unity towards God's purpose can the Kingdom on Earth ever come.

In all cases hermeneutics have systematic implications for all aspects of life. That is what we have seen, no more and no less, in the *Divine Principle*. What might be surprising to many is that it is not esoteric, but very common sense. That, too, is part of Moon's appeal.

[1] *Divine Principle,* p. 163.

[2] *Ibid.,* p. 163.

[3] *Ibid.,* p. 10.

[4] *Ibid.,* p. 22.

[5] *Ibid.,* p. 4ff.

[6] *Ibid.,* p. 10.

[7] See Baader's essay "Ueber durch unsere Zeit herbeige-führte Bedurdnis einer innigeren Vereinungen der Wissenschaft und der Religion" in *Franz von Baader: vom Sinn der Gesellschaft,* ed. Hans A. Fischer-Barnicol (Koln, 1966) pp. 131-145.

[8] *Divine Principle,* pp. 157-159.

[9] *Ibid.,* p. 162.

[10] Rev. Moon is careful to note that Jesus went first to the chief priests and scribes. He eventually called the beggars in the streets only after those invited did not come. (*Divine Principle,* pp. 160-161.)

[11] *Divine Principle,* p. 152.   [emphasis mine.]

[12] In the *Divine Principle* the newness of interpretation is invariably called a "new truth." See, e.g., pp. 16, 131, 163, etc. Rev. Moon, however, always refers these "new truths" to the rediscovery of the Principle in the Last Days, i.e., to the awareness that the Last Days is all important for one's interpretation of the Scriptures. Failure to attend to the urgency of the End-time can lead to a response like that of John the Baptist.

[13] These errors arise from a failure to perceive the particular nuance of a term in medieval thought or from a

failure to be attentive to persons and tenses. J.R.
McNeill's rendering of this verse suffers from two of
these defects: "History tells what happened; allegory
teaches what is to be understood; anagogy, what is to
be sought after; tropology, what is to be done"
(*Interpreter's Bible* I; 121).

[14] See St. Thomas Aquinas, *Summa Theologica,* Pt. I, q.1,
art. 10.

[15] Lest the reader be dismayed, I ought to explain my
terms. In Alexandrine Christianity, the mystagogical
sense (which embraces the allegorical and anagogical
senses) looks toward how one ought to *see* the world.   In
Antiochian Christianity, the typological sense (which embraces the literal and moral senses) looks toward how one
ought to *act* in the world.

[16] The difference in the Eastern and Western hermeneutics
explains in great part the East's ability to absorb Platonic and neo-Platonic elements into its biblical interpretation.   In the West there have always been strands of
distrust for philosophical speculation (e.g., St. Bernard,
Luther, etc.).

[17] See Martin Werner, *The Formation of Christian Dogma,*
(New York, 1957) pp. 71-119.

[18] See James S. Preuss, "Old Testament *Promissio* and
Luther's New Hermaneutic," *Harvard Theological Review,*
v. 60, #2, (April, 1967) pp. 156-161.

[19] See Norman Cohn, *The Pursuit of the Millenium,* (New York,
1961) pp. 25-271.

[20] For a clear and concise understanding of Calvin's doctrine of Creation, see Francois Wendel, *Calvin,* tr. by
Philip Mairet (London, 1963) pp. 169-177.

[21] *Werke,* (Weimar, 1892) v. 23.

[22] From this statement it should be clear that I do not accept Max Weber's thesis about the intimate connection between Puritanism and capitalism; this, however is not the time or place to refute such a detailed thesis.

[23] Cf. *Divine Principle*, p. 132.

[24] On the theological significance of the "plain style," see Perry Miller's "Introduction to Jonathan Edwards,"in *Images or Shadows of Divine Things,* (New Haven, 1948) pp. 1-41 and *The New England Mind,* vol. 1, (Boston, 1961) pp. 331-332.

[25] *Divine Principle*, pp. 241-251.

[26] Cf. Calvin, *Institutes of the Christian Religion I,* 14, 3ff.

[27] *Divine Principle,* p. 172ff.

[28] This type of symbolism is not without precedent in Christian hermeneutics. See Emile Male, *The Gothic Image,* (New York, 1958) pp. 5-14.

[29] *Divine Principle,* p. 26ff.

[30] *Ibid.,* p. 167ff.

[31] *Ibid.,* p. 188ff.

[32] *Ibid.,* p. 188.

[33] *Ibid.,* pp. 26, 188.

[34] See Calvin, *Institutes of the Christian Religion III,* 1.1; 20, 4-12.

[35] See, for example, *Divine Principle,* pp. 28-30.

IS THE REVEREND SUN MYUNG MOON A HERETIC?
LOCATING THE UNIFICATION CHURCH
ON THE MAP OF CHURCH HISTORY

WARREN LEWIS

One doctrinal pattern evident in church history
is damn the heretic and adopt the heresy. This process
can be observed in the development of theological orthodoxy. The Council of Nicaea, A.D. 325, proclaimed that
the Second Person of the Godhead (Jesus Christ) is of
the same substance as the First Person (God the Father).
But, the term "homo-ousios" (same substance), finally
drafted into the creed under the influence of Athanasius
of Alexandria and Ossius of Cordoba, is not found in the
New Testament. It was originally coined in Christian
Gnostic circles in the second century.[1] The language
of heresy had become the definition of orthodoxy.
     The case of the Nestorian heresy is similar. The
opinion of church councils swung back and forth from
Ephesus (431) to Chalcedon (451), to II Constantinople
(553), and back again to III Constantinople (680/681)
over the Christiological issues raised by Nestorius.
At one council, his ideas-- with modification, but without
apology to Nestorius-- had become orthodoxy. So the
pendulum swings. Ecclesiastical climates change.
Issues are seen in a different light until the perspective or truth which lies at the heart of every heresy
becomes more evident.

Etymologically, "heresy" in Greek means "choice, selection." A heretic is one who chooses, though, in the opinion of the orthodox, chooses wrongly. Frequently, a heretic picks up older ideas or ways of life that have been carried within the Christian traditions but are currently unfashionable. Christians are perennially preoccupied with the past, with an alleged historical golden age of the church when the canon of scripture was produced, when the apostles and their colleagues were alive, and when the church is said to have been one. Hence, appeals to the past--picking up neglected ideas and using them for church reform--are characteristic of heresy.

Backward looking choices may be deemed heretical by the orthodox for various reasons. The heretic frequently acts upon the new-found old truths in a schismatic way, claiming them to be the whole truth. Sometimes the new heresy is the natural, but no longer wanted, child of the older orthodoxy. For example, the convenors of the Council of Constance (1414-1417) executed the heretic, John Hus, for believing a variant of their own anti-papal doctrine. The Council deposed the first Pope John XXII for an impressive list of papal crimes, accepted the resignation of Pope Gregory XII, and took action against Pope Benedict XIII, who refused to submit graciously. On April 6, 1415 the Council declared its dogma that an ecumenical council has authority over the Pope ("Sacrosancta"). But, on July 6 of the same year, these same orthodox, conciliar reformers burned John Hus at the stake because, among other charges, he was insufficiently obedient to the Pope.

A second source of Christian heresy is new

scientific and cultural ideas. Theologians seek to
relate religious beliefs to other human concerns. The
early Christian Gnostics were the first to try to make
the Gospel relevant to a pagan world. They wedded their
faith in the heavenly Redeemer to the world view of
their Hellenistic culture. In this way the Gnostics
produced, with the same stroke, both the first theology and the first heresy. Another example is the deist
theologians of eighteenth-century England, who defended
the reasonableness of their faith in terms of Newtonian
scientific conceptions, thereby producing air-tight
eternal proofs which managed to be convincing for a
few short years. When the Newtonian world view changed,
thanks to Darwin in the nineteenth century and Einstein
in the twentieth, the scientific rug was pulled out
from under their Queen Anne faith.

The issues at the heart of the orthodoxy/heresy
debate continue. Nicaea is still with us, but so is
the unitarianism it opposes. Anti-Nicene Unitarianism
has been a powerful theological and ecclesiastical movement since the middle ages. It is, in fact, the *orthodoxy* of today's Harvard and New England as well as the
unspoken presupposition of much of the historical study
of the New Testament done in our time. Another example
of the staying power of heresy is the renewal of the
Gnostic/Deist apologetic in our time by theologians
like Teilhard de Chardin and Karl Heim.

Let us, from the above, suggest a first law of
heresy/orthodoxy. These two terms exist in historical
symbiosis. They are mutually dependent; one produces
the other. Theology is a man with two feet. He steps
off on the left foot of heresy, the right foot of

orthodoxy lagging behind. Progress is made when the
right foot gains the ground already pioneered by the
left and overpasses it.

THE HERESY/ORTHODOXY GAME

The ferment of new and heretical ideas in Christian
Europe from the eleventh to the sixteenth century destroyed the presumptions of those who saw themselves as
upholders of a unitary, monolithic orthodoxy. Theological, social, economic, and personal diversity increased during this time. There was a heretic at every
level of social reality: the individual heretic (Eon
of Stella, Tanchelm); disorganized popular movements
(the Mad Ship of Saint Truiden); small organized groups
of pietists or intellectualists (Brethren of the Free
Spirit, Brethren of the Common Life, Beghards and Beguines); new churches and mass movements (Waldenses,
Albigenses); philosophical heretics (Averroists); nat-
ionalist heretics (Jean d'Arc, John Hus); tamed heretics
within the Church (Francis of Assisi); the emperor as
heretic (Frederick II); the Pope as heretic (Boniface
VIII, John XXII); the Church as heretic (Councils of
Constance and Basel); Europe as heretic (German, Swiss,
British, Bohemian, Scandinavian, and Dutch reformations).
During this time, there was never an orthodoxy of the
majority on any current issue.

It may be true that medieval people felt they
had a heritage. Social reality for them was constructed
in terms of theological legitimations which came,
they believed, from antiquity: *"quod semper, quod
ubique, et quod ab omnibus"* (Vincent of Lerins). But

their sense of antiquity was often historically wrong.
What seemed to them to be as eternal as Rome might,
in historical fact, be no more than a century or two
old.   The notion of an imperial papacy provides one
example.   After the eleventh century, the papacy dominated both the temporal and religious spheres of European
life, claiming to be as old as the bishopric of Rome
itself.   The imperial papacy was, however, a recent
political creation which emerged because of the persistent assertiveness of the Popes and canon lawyers
of the Gregorian Reform tradition who based their arguments on a recently forged document which was pur-
portedly written at the time of Constantine.   This
recently forged *Donation of Constantine* gave imperial
authority to the Popes, and they used this document
to claim that they had had such authority since the
time of Constantine.   In this way, the strongman papacy
arose as an innovative novelty after centuries of mud-
dled relationships between church and state in which,
often as not, local bishops and the Roman Pope were pawns
in the hands of the emperor and the kings.   But, by 1122,
this new "ancient" Roman invention had become an orthodoxy which would remain in force until the fifteenth
century and, in theory, forever.

A more strictly theological movement provides
another example.   Augustinianism was a development of
the early theology of Augustine combined with the later
monastic reform movement (Bernard), the spirituality
of the Victorine movement, and the humanism of Chartres.
It was systematized and defended in the thirteenth
century by the Franciscans   (Alexander of Hales,
Bonaventure, Peter John Olivi, and a host of others).

This eight-century long development gave that feeling
of permanency which is the byproduct of all orthodoxy.
However, because of this developed uniformity of the
western tradition, it was unable to cope with the new
intellectual and political ideas coming from the Arabic
world.

When, in the mid-thirteenth century, scholars and
theologians began to deal with the new ideas, they were
condemned by the Augustinians for heresy. Italian scientific thinkers (Averroists), Dominican theologians
(Albertus Magnus, Thomas Aquinas) and others attempted
to evaluate and integrate the new science. The Augustinians organized formal condemnations of these new
theological developments in 1270, 1277 and 1284. Then,
in a surprising turnabout, Thomas Aquinas was installed
as the great canonical theologian of the Catholic church
("doctor communis"). His heresy now became the orthodoxy
of the Roman Church and, from this time forth, it was
the Augustinians who were in danger of being judged as
heretical. In fact, this is exactly what happened when
Luther and Calvin took up the older Augustinian tradition
in the sixteenth century and used it to reform the church.
The chief opponents of these Protestant Augustinians
were not only the Thomists but, more especially, the
Jesuit Thomists who represented a *still* more recent
ecclesiastical novelty.

Our first law of heresy/orthodoxy was that the two
exist in historical symbiosis. We can now suggest a
corollary to this law, namely, that neither heresy nor
orthodoxy is the sole religious truth. Rather the religious truth arises out of the continuing struggle
between them as each seeks to surpass the other. If

each plays its role well, the game of heresy/orthodoxy
can result in a win for all, as a new symbolic reality
emerges and people choose sides to begin the new game.

TRUE BELIEVER/TOLERANT PLURALIST

In twelfth century Europe, issues which had been
settled generations before were no longer thought to be
pressing questions. These were felt to have been se-
curely nailed down. But when the shingles of orthodoxy
began to be loosened by the winds from the new science
and from new social experiences, they began to blow away.
People thought that the whole house might fall down,
and they reacted in a spasm of intolerance and persecution. We moderns are horrified at the Inquisition
which burned thousands at the stake for confessions of
religious deviation, confessions extracted by enforced
deprogramming and torture. Yet, the Inquisition was
generally supported by all levels of society from kings
down to the simple people who were ready to pitch their
handful of twigs on the heretic's pyre. Heretics were
viewed as threatening the existing structures of society,
so had to be converted from their error, one way or
another. Otherwise, it was thought, society itself
was liable to be destroyed. It was argued that the order
of society needs theological legitimation. The Inquisition was the socially approved legal process which
brought these "criminals" to their just punishment.

But the tide of heresy still flooded over Europe,
destroying ancient landmarks, removing barriers, wearing
away the boundaries of orthodoxy. When the tide had
ebbed, the land was still there, but its contours were

changed. Rills had become rivers, valleys had been
exalted, rough places had been made plane. Moreover,
heresy itself had become a habit. From the eleventh
century on, Europe simmered in an alphabet soup of
tangy religious heresies: ordinary Catholics floated
alongside Amalricians, Beguines, Cathari, Dunkards,
Eastern Orthodox Schismatics, Fraticelli, Gallicans,
Humanists, Inquisitors, Jansenists, Knights Templars,
Lollards, Mennonites, Nominalists, Orebites, Petrobru-
sians, Quietists, Ranters, Socinians, Taborites, Utra-
quists, Vaudois, Witches, X, Y, and Z. From the one
came the many. Christianity underwent a process of
pluralization and democratization. Orthodoxy knew
heresy and begat religious pluralism, which has itself
become the new orthodoxy which we in America believe.
But, ironically too, it is America's tolerant pluralism
which itself generates so many true believers groups.

     In America, anyone can try to be a reformer or the
founder of a new faith. Whoever disagrees may split
from his church and start a new one of his own. Rome
no longer fulminates against heresy; in fact, those
whom Rome once would have branded for the heretics
they are, now are embraced as "separated brethren".
Today it is liberal pluralism which is the common truth.
But there can be no pluralism unless there are also
some true believers. However, true believers are
often attacked for being "totalitarian" or not plural-
istically tolerant. The true believers are persecuted
today as "heretics" by the orthodoxy of pluralistic
tolerance.

     Heretics and orthodox exist in symbiosis. Jehovah's
Witnesses, the Amish, and India-export gurus continue to

exist because the Methodists, Presbyterians, Catholics, and Baptists need them to prove how tolerant their new orthodoxy is. True believer/tolerant pluralist is the form of the symbiotic heresy/orthodoxy struggle today.

A METAPHYSICS OF HERESY/ORTHODOXY

As one ponders these configurations, one conclusion seems unavoidable. Both "orthodoxy" and "heresy" are meaningless words. If heresy becomes orthodoxy and orthodoxy becomes heresy, if the one produces the other and the other by adaptation yields the former, what sense is there in making a distinction? We need a new set of semantic tools with which to work on heresy/orthodoxy. Hitherto, because the very theologians who discussed the problem of heresy/orthodoxy themselves also were believers of one or the other, they tended to see the matter in terms of either/or. If "A" were true, then "not-A" could not be true. This way of thinking is seen not only in the dogmatic arguments of theologians but also in modern science. For example, $E = mc^2$. We think in terms of opposites and identities. So we argue that if man is at work, God cannot be. If God is active, then man is not. If the laws of cause and effect are operative, then there can be no miracle. If there is a miracle, then natural laws have been violated. Either one or the other. But never both at once.

But could we not think about these things another way? It has been suggested that reality is both waves and particles at one and the same time. When we must look at things from two points of view at once, it

could mean that there is a duality at the heart of
reality itself. Reality could be "this" and "not this"
at the same time. As one philosophical tradition expresses it, reality is yin and yang.

If we consider the yin-yang diagram (above), it does
not symbolize dualism: two terms. There is both the
white and the black, but there is also the interstitial
S-shape between them. The S is not a line, but rather
an optical illusion caused by the interlocking of the
two colored shapes in a unity-of-affinity. This unity-
of-affinity is a *third* thing which unites the other
two. Wherever there are two terms that are *related*,
there are three terms: yang (positivity), yin (passiv-
ity) and their unity-of-affinity (mutuality). There
are two's that do not go together and two's that go
together. Those that go together are two and *more*.

   This model of reality could suggest to us something about heresy/orthodoxy. It suggests that heretics and orthodox might relate to each other on the
basis of a unity-of-affinity. They seem to interlock.
Each continues to exist only so long as each maintains
an active give-and-take with the other term. Though
each is different, both are united. Therefore, they
are simultaneous: orthodoxy does not begin to exist
when heresy is phased out. Each keeps the other alive.

   Without heresy's creative quest for tuth, orthodoxy becomes pat answers and unimaginative old wives'
tales. Without orthodoxy's bequest of truth, heresy

becomes madness. If one does not exist, neither does
the other. Taken together, they produce both the
conservation of tradition and revolutionary reaction
against it. To persecute one is to put the other on
trial; to burn one at the stake is to cremate the other.
This is the law of the symbiosis of heresy/orthodoxy.

Not papal and/or conciliar pronouncement, nor
return to biblical primitivism however verbally inspired,
nor implementation of vague ecumenical union can put
an end to the give-and-take of heresy/orthodoxy. But
since history has taught us about this symbiosis, we
can now make creative use of the tension between the two
terms. Having seen the unity-of-affinity of heresy/
orthodoxy, we can use this insight better to understand
religious disagreements and to avoid certain mistakes
of the past: theological myopia, acrimonious heresy
trials, defensive reaction by both parties, and the
promotion of hatred and fear.

IS THE REVEREND SUN MYUNG MOON A HERETIC?

The Reverend Sun Myung Moon, with his book *Divine
Principle* and his Holy Spirit Association for the Unification of World Christianity (*alias* the Unification
Church), offers himself, his book, and his movement
as the way to the unification not only of splintered
Christianity but of all world religions. Whether or
not Reverend Moon provides a unified basis for the
future world-wide culture which he hopes to establish
is a question which I, as a church historian, would
prefer to answer after the fact. That Rev. Moon's
theology is best understood neither as orthodoxy nor

as heresy, but as an attempt to *unify* both by employing
the tension between them to create a new symbolic field
is my thesis.   It is not surprising that in a time
when we have come to see the necessity for both orthodoxy and heresy there should emerge a conscious
effort to *unite* both so that the give-and-take between
them could be used for creative social purposes.   That
is exactly what Rev. Moon and the Unification Church
are seeking to do.   The law of the symbiosis of heresy/
orthodoxy has produced a predictable result: a self-
conscious attempt at the unification of historical
heresies and orthodoxies in what is designed to be the
metaorthodoxy for the next millenium.

   In Rev. Moon, the yin/yang of heresy/orthodoxy
has created a new Christian-philosophic world view.
There are many previous examples of what he is doing.
The Hellenization of the Hebrew-Christian Gospel within
the Late-Roman Empire produced the hybrid of Medieval
Christian culture.   Similarly, the Unification Movement
is a social field where Oriental philosophical and social concerns are cross-fertilized with Western Christian
religious and cultural concerns creating a new hybrid.
Like the Christian Gnostics of the second and third
centuries, or the medieval Christian Aristotelians,
Rev. Moon calls for the "unification of science and
religion".   Like Emperor Constantine and his court
theologian, Eusebius of Caesarea, Moon calls for the
"unification of politics and religion".   Like Origen,
the Cappadocians, and Augustine, who presided at the wedding of Greek Neoplatonism with the Christian Gospel,
Moon has made a wedding between his version of Korean
Christianity and his sampling of Oriental thought.

Rev. Moon's Christianity is a composite of the
results of Presbyterian missionary preaching, Methodist
holiness, and Pentecostal charisma. To this he adds
his own reading of the Bible and his mystical experiences
with Jesus Christ. According to Moon, Jesus first appeared to him on a Korean mountainside on Easter Morning
in 1936, when he was sixteen years old. Jesus told
Moon that he was to complete the messianic task of bringing about the Kingdom of Heaven on earth. Moon's Christian experience has been tested in the historical trag-
edies and spiritual sacrifices of his people:
the *suffering nation of pray-ers, Korea*.

There are also oriental elements in Rev. Moon's
experience and thought. These include ideas and practices from Buddhism, Hinduism, Taoism, Confucianism,
and Korean Shamanism. But all these oriental elements
in the Unification system have undergone the same sort
of alchemical transformations which the Christian
elements also undergo. Taoist yin/yang metaphysics,
Confucian filial piety and ancestor worship, Buddhist
metempsychosis and expectation of the Maitreya Buddha,
and Shinto public, political faith all are taken into
the systems by being resymbolized within the furnace
of Moon's Christian eschatology. The resymbolization
occurs by mating two or more traditional terms together
until they fuse into a third new thing. This process
is controlled by Moon's sense of the *new* possibilities
for everything. It is this which marks Moon as a new
kind of heretic, a meta-orthodox theologian who understands far better than his orthodox detractors, the real
eschatological possibilities within the Christian faith.

DIVINE PRINCIPLE -- Orthodox Heresy or Heretical
                    Orthodoxy?

In the *Wizard of Oz,* after Dorothy Gale's tornado-
tossed house has fallen upon the Wicked Witch of the
East thereby liberating the little green Munchkins,
it is patent to one and all that Dorothy is a witch.
Otherwise she could not have killed the wicked witch
with her wonderful flying house. The question is
therefore put to Dorothy: "Are you a good witch or a
bad witch, which?" It never occurs to the Munchkins
that Dorothy may be neither a good witch nor a bad witch,
but only a farm girl from Kansas who got caught up in
a flying house.

In the same spirit, many theologians read the
Divine Principle with the growing awareness that it is
a congery of heresies and orthodoxies, and they wonder:
Is this orthodox heresy or heretical orthodoxy, which?
The *Divine Principle* is translated from Korean into a
too literal English and published in a black book which
looks like a King James Bible. The teaching it contains
is an *omnium-gatherum* of the theological debates of
history, here put through the strainer of Rev. Moon's
oriental Christian mind. It is ideological theology,
a theology which already has an answer and so culls
the Christian tradition to find biblical and historical
confirmations of its initial insights. The *Divine
Principle* is, in other words, a systematic theology
like that of Thomas or Barth, though in a thorough-
going eschatological mode.

There is even an eschatological theory about
the *Divine Principle* itself. Unificationists talk about

a future "golden version" of the *Divine Principle*
which will represent a "perfection stage" of the present
"black book." Within the Unification Church, members
read the *Divine Principle* as an inspired Third or
Completed Testament (after the Old and the New Testaments). But loyalty to the *Divine Principle* is not
confused by them with a literal interpretation of its
contents. The church's theologian, Dr. Young Oon Kim,
agrees that some portions of the present edition are
more edifying than instructive and therefore not to be
taken literally. Paralleling the experience of other
churches, the better-educated Unification seminarians
are fully capable of discussing the "contradictions"
in the *Divine Principle,* whereas rank-in-file Unificationists tend to be more fundamentalistic. It remains
to be seen whether a split within the Unification Church
will develop along the seismic lines of "biblical"
faults.

THE FOUR POSITION FOUNDATION

Rev. Moon's teaching about God evidences the international and scientific character of his theology. God,
according to the *Divine Principle,* is the Ground-of-
Energy/Matter of the dual reality of energy/matter.
God has both internal and external aspects, both male-
ness and femaleness, both "spirit" and "matter". Everything that exists reflects this dual nature. Everything contains its own "sung sang" (a Korean term meaning "internal character") and "hyung sang" (a Korean
term meaning "external form" or "external shape"),
its own thetic/arnitic polarity, its own relativity

of matter/energy. These polarities show that every
created thing manifests "the image and the likeness"
of God, its creator.

According to the *Divine Principle,* not only is
everything polar in itself, but it *also* has a polar
relation to God. The polar relation between God and
a thing is paralleled (doubled) by the polarity *within*
that thing itself. This double polarity is called
"the Four Position Foundation". This "Four Position
Foundation" is the divine principle. The book, the
Divine Principle, derives its name from its exposition
of this theory of reality.

The *Divine Principle's* theory of polarities is presented theologically as an explanation of God's act of
creation. God Himself creates a second thing, the creation. The creation is itself internally polar, or
two more things. The interaction or give-and-take of
these two created terms *with each other and with God,*
is itself a *fourth* term. In this way the four terms
of the Four-Position-Foundation come into existence.

While this may sound impossibly abstract, it is
actually very simple to understand and to apply. The
reason is because the theory is presented as an explanation of a concrete human experience which also stands
at the beginning of the Bible itself: the story of
human parenthood. This story tells how *God* created
Adam and *Eve.* (These symbolize the first three terms
of the Four-Position-Foundation.) In principle what
should have happened is that Adam and Eve would have
loved each other and each would also have loved God
as God loved them. Such a three-way love would have
generated children and these children would have been

a fourth term which also expresses the love of the
other three. In fact, because Adam and Eve did not
express love for God in their love for each other, but
used their love to separate themselves from God, the
divinely intended Four Position Foundation did not become actualized at the beginning of human history.
Hence, according to the *Divine Principle*, God's work
of salvation must aim at restoring and actualizing the
Four Position Foundation; that is, it must seek to
create a human family whose love (and children) are
centered on God. We can diagram these ideas as follows:

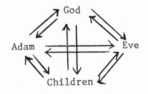

In this diagram, God comes first and expresses Him/
Herself in a reciprocal action with man-Adam (second)
and woman-Eve (third), resulting in the procreation
of children (fourth). Throughout this Four-Position-
Foundation, each of the four parties is said to maintain give-and-take action with each of the other three.
Hence, all four terms have give-and-take at the same time.
In the case of God-Adam-Eve-children (all four terms)
God maintains give-and-take action with both of the
parents while the parents have give-and-take with each
other; the parents have give-and-take with the children,
and the children have give-and-take with their parents
and with God. In this way, God would get to be the
grandfather of Cain, Abel, Seth, and eventually the
entire human race--to the delight of his Fatherly heart.
The Four-Position-Foundation repeats itself infinitely

throughout nature and all existence.[2]

This theory aims at the moral result of establishing
a metaphysical basis for proper cosmic and familial
"li" of Confucian ethics. It is also a rehabilitation
of the Neoplatonic, medieval Christian fascination
with the "great chain of being". Here the tamed Gnosticism or Greek-speaking Christianity in the tradition
or Origen, the Cappadocians, Dionysius, the Areopagite,
and John Scotus (Eriugena) speaks again. God is the
highest being whose very nature flows outward and downward into all subsequent being in an interconnectedness
of all that is. Nothing is essentially evil, since all
has come from and will return to God. The eschatology
of this metaphysics is Origen of Alexandria's heretical
teaching, the *apokatastasis panton*. It is an idea which
Karl Barth has revived in our time, an idea with which
Nicholas Berdyaev agrees, and one which Einstein would
support. It teaches that nothing is lost ultimately.
All will return to God, the giver of all. As Saint
Paul says, God will be "all in all" (I Cor. 15:28).
Even Satan will be converted at last. There is no
eternal hell.

THE WAY OF SALVATION

Rev. Moon's rejection of the doctrine of hell
arises out of his understanding of the personal qualities of God according to which He is not an external
Creator, but a Father whose heart is intimately involved
with his children. Adam and Eve are the children
of their Father who loves them with the love of a true
Father. When Cain killed Abel, God's grandfatherly

heart suffered infinite pain. When Jesus died on the
cross, Jesus' Abba in heaven covered His face with
horrified sorrow. The crucifixion was no part of the
divine plan of a loving heavenly Father. Nor was the
Fall. God was disappointed and hurt when Eve ruined
her Father's Garden. The Father was forced to revise
the providential plan when his daughter, seduced by the
Archangel, upended her proper relationship with Adam.

The *Divine Principle* teaches that God is a suffering
Father whose own emotional well-being is intimately
bound up in how His children behave. This passionate
insight into the heart of God leads Rev. Moon to qualify
God's omniscience in order to preserve his total love.
Within the chosen limits of his totally loving nature,
God stood broken-heartedly by and watched Eve and the
Archangel commit the first sin, restricted by His own
love of their freedom. God could not possibly have
foreknown that Eve would in fact use her freedom to sin.
He could only have foreknown that she might. According
to the *Divine Principle,* God neither foreknows future
contingencies and future events nor is He the Absolute
Sovereign of Isaiah 45:7 who "forms the light and creates
darkness, makes peace and creates evil". Moon's limited
God has not chosen from before all ages the means which
will ultimately restore the creation. He is a process-
God with an original intention for His creation which
has had to be revised as a result of the Fall. According to this interpretation (and contrary to the Apostle
Peter's sermon in Acts 2), God did not by His "deter-
minate counsel and foreknowledge deliver up" Jesus to
be crucified by the "hands of men outside the law."
God intended Jesus Christ's message and life to be

received. Jesus' death on the cross is the most awful
accident in history. It was brought about by the failure of Jesus' contemporaries to receive him. It was
not God's will, but man's sin.

The *Divine Principle* does teach that Jesus, in his
obedience to God's will, did accomplish "spiritual
salvation" in his self-sacrificial and supremely loving
death. Nevertheless, the work of Jesus was left incomplete because of his crucifixion. Jesus had prayed:
"Thy kingdom come...on earth, as it is in heaven". It
was God's plan (and Jesus was about to carry it out
before he was crucified) that Jesus marry a perfected
bride, give birth to perfect children and establish
the Kingdom of Heaven on Earth. This would have restored the Four-Position-Foundation. Because he was
crucified, Jesus could not carry out this plan.

The *Divine Principle* theologizes the "Messiahship"
of Jesus in terms of his work and spiritual purpose
rather than in terms of the specialness of his person.
Jesus is not regarded as possessing powers greater than
any other perfected human being. The *Divine Principle*
defines the sonship of Jesus to his Father in terms of
Jesus' loving obedience; it does not affirm that Jesus
is a person who existed before the world was created
(the Trinitarian dogma). Moreover, because it regards
Messiahship as a work and not a person, the *Divine Principle* teaches that the messianic task of "being a Christ"
can be taken up by others, even by *all*. Luther said
"Be a Christ to your neighbor." That is exactly the
teaching of Moon.

According to the *Divine Principle,* great saints
throughout the centuries have sacrificed themselves

in a messianic striving to redeem human history.   In
our day, however, Jesus has caused the office of Messiahship to be transferred from himself to the Lord of
the Second Advent.   The spirit world of angels, saints,
and the "spirits of just persons made perfect" is working
mightily in cooperation with the earthly plane to
restore, recreate, and resurrect the entirety of the
human race in a Kingdom of Heaven on Earth.   The Unification Church believes that when all the conditions
have been met, it will be Sun Myung Moon whom Jesus
has chosen to "come again" and establish the divine-
human family where God and humankind can dwell together
in mutual delight.   "But," Rev. Moon told me just recently, "If someone assassinates me, God has someone
else to do the job."

One can spot several points of heresy/orthodoxy
in the foregoing.   God is traditionally held to be a
God of love and fatherly feeling, but this has usually
been asserted with the reservation that God the Father
does not Himself suffer.   It is also usually considered
heretical to say that God does not know everything
before it takes place or that God can be thwarted in
what He proposes.   It is orthodox to try to maintain
both God's total sovereign power and God's total love,
however mutually contradictory these ideas may seem
to be.   The *Divine Principle* sets forth a heretical
orthodoxy when it affirms God's total love at the expense of limiting His foreknowledge, but it also redeems
God's sovereignty by extending His will into a now bright-
ening future when He will have another chance to work
out His deepest purposes.

For some Christians, it would seem that the

Divine Principle denies centrality and exclusive saving
value to Jesus' death and propitiatory blood atonement.
Again, the idea that the work of Messiahship can be
transferred by Jesus to someone else is claimed by some
to be a remythologized Buddhist transmigration of souls.
However, in the *Divine Principle,* the focus is on
Messiahship as a task rather than on a Christological
definition of a "divine person". In the *Divine Principle,* there is no suggestion of reincarnation of the
soul of Jesus in Rev. Moon nor is there any belief
in Moon's "divinity". Moon is believed to be, rather,
one who may be able to renew and unite mankind in the
task of ordering life in terms of the primary of love
and service of God.

PREDESTINATION AND FREE WILL

The *Divine Principle* agrees in part with Augustine and
Calvin on predestination and election, but holds to freedom of will with the Armenians and Methodists. This
results in a redefinition of predestination in a semi-
Pelagian way. Election is God's general will that all
be saved. God intervenes in particular ways to call
individuals to specific missions within the general
providence. Therefore, the *Divine Principle's* basic
understanding of grace is that humans are free to choose
for or against God, who constantly floods mankind with
blessings and gifts of many kinds, but never overpowering
human freedom of choice.

     In the *Divine Principle,* the created divine image
in humanity is understood primarily in terms of our
godlike ability to make free choices. For example,

it was precisely in Eve's refusal to choose freely to
obey God (which was also the only way she could have
retained her freedom) that she lost her power to choose
freely and thereby injured her original relationship
with God, Adam, and the created world.   Precocious
Eve committed adultery with the Archangel in her spirit-
body, then involved Adam in her sin by seducing him into
sexual intercourse before the two of them had reached
the point of maturity intended by God for them.

The *Divine Principle's* concept of the first sin
of the human race as an act of concupiscential love is
close to the ideas of many Catholic writers.   More interestingly, the *Divine Principle's* notion that Eve first
sinned through being seduced by Satan and then she led
Adam into sin through an act of sexual intercourse
parallels in some respects Milton's interpretations of
Genesis in *Paradise Lost*.*

According to the *Divine Principle,* the sin of Adam
and Eve led to the domination over the human family
by Satan, but did not cause a change in the physical
being of the human race.   The *Divine Principle* denies
that physical death is the consequence of sin.   Adam
and Eve were physically mortal in the first place;
thus physical death was not a result of their fall.
After the original sin, they retained their freedom,
their intelligence, and their ability to obey God,
but they died spiritually.   Their spiritual redemption
would have to wait until the Lord of the First Advent

---

*For many resemblances between the *Divine Principle*
and *Paradise Lost,* see the essay by Professor Frank Flinn
which also appears in this volume.

(i.e. Jesus) would come to redeem them from spiritual
death. The Lord of the Second Advent then has the task
of restoring the human family to its original stage of
God-centered physical-social life. This physical and
social restoration of the human family comes about as
the result of an eschatological-moral effort to eliminate
bad conditioning, habitual sinning, and those social
conditions which force "moral man" to behave badly within
"immoral society". The Messiah and the unified family
gathered around him are to act as models and exemplary
influences.

        According to the *Divine Principle,* since the first
sin of Adam and Eve involved a disordering of family
relationships, it follows that salvation from such sin
requires membership in the restored family of the Lord
of the Second Advent. This spiritual-social family is
seeking to be that group of people whose relationships
are being perfected. Consistent with this view, the
sacramental life of Unification Church members is
focussed entirely upon the process of unifying with the
family of the Lord of the Second Advent. For Unificationists, the traditional sacraments of baptism, eucharist,
and holy matrimony happen all at once one time only, on
the glorious occasion of their "Blessing", when they
are married within their church and thereby are united
permanently with their new family.

        Westerners tend to think that marriage is the way a
person gets a husband or a wife, but overlook the fact
that a person also gets a new family: a new mother, a
new father, new sisters and brothers. But, becoming
part of a new family and getting new parents and sib-
lings is regarded as the deepest meaning of marriage

in other parts of the world. (This partly explains
why it is common in the orient for parents to propose
spouses to their children. After all, the *whole family*
is taking in a new member.) When, therefore, Rev. Moon
proposes to someone that he or she marry one of his
"spiritual children", he is inviting that person to
become a member of his own spiritual family. This
is how a Unificationist becomes a member of Rev. Moon's
spiritual family. This is how a person enters, fully
and permanently, into the restored human family and
leaves behind the fallen human family which is dominated
by Satan. Such considerations explain why, for Unificationists, marriage is a "Blessing" which is equivalent to Christian baptism, eucharist, and marriage,
all at once.

So we see that the *Divine Principle* combines many
traditional teachings in a new way.[3] The *Divine Principle's* teaching that sin is a concupiscence specially
manifest in sexual disorder would be agreeable to Augustine and to Milton. The *Divine Principle's* teaching
on human freedom would be acceptable to John Wesley,
and Wesley would also agree with the Unification ideal
of perfecting oneself in life. The humanism of the
Divine Principle is close to Unitarian-Universalism,
although these traditional heresies do not have the
added interest of a thorough-going eschatological moti-
vation. The *Divine Principle's* teaching that marriage
is a sacrament and that the church is a spiritual
family presided over by a spiritual father (pope =
papa) is Catholic.[4] The strength of Unification theology
is not in creating new ideas, but in combining old ideas
in a new and persuasive way.

THE MEASURE OF THE MAN

In our time, we Westerners are witnessing the missionary inroads of a herd of Indian gurus and a pride of Zen masters, just as the Orientals, in their time, endured the foolishness of the preaching of the Christian missionary's gospel. But Rev. Moon should not be classed as one of these typical missionaries from the East. He is an original Christian thinker and believer who is at once as Western and Christian as he is Oriental.

Rev. Moon is like Tertullian. Tertullian was a Christian first and a Montanist second. Tertullian was a believing theologian and also a Roman legal mind which translated everything passing through it into the useful, precise terminology of Roman jurisprudence. Tertullian was a heretic, but a heretic whose Latin neologisms became the basic concepts of Western Christianity. These same things could be said of Thomas, who was both an Augustinian and an Aristotelian. They could be said of Teilhard, who was both a Jesuit and a Darwinian. Moon is like these men. All of them-- Tertullian, Thomas, Teilhard, and Moon--are heresy-risking minds with orthodox hearts who are able to function creatively within the tension of orthodoxy/ heresy.

Nevertheless, there is opposition in America, as elsewhere, to Rev. Moon. He is a non-professional, i.e., a non-academic theologian. In an era when Christian theology is done almost exclusively by German professors or their students, what validity can there be in the theology of a Korean electrical engineer?

Moreover, Moon is not ordained by any establishment church, yet is called "Reverend." His explanation-- "God ordained me"--seems boastfully impertinent to ecclesiastical bureaucrats. The fact that he is a master administrator and a successful fundraiser causes unrest among those who think that the new messiah ought to resemble the homeless Jesus or the poor Francis of Assisi. In addition, it should be acknowledged that Americans might be just racist enough not to want to be taught "their" Christianity by an Oriental inter- loper.

Perhaps most unsettling is Rev. Moon's current public image. He gives some people the impression of being a quasi-political, pulpit-pounding, arm-waving revivalist. At worst he seems to them to be a political demagogue; at best he seems to them to be still another soul saver. Yet, when one has the rare opportunity to know him personally, he turns out to be a thoughtful, expressive, loving man with a charming wife and several normal boisterous children. I myself know him to be a praying man and I have witnessed his discernment of spirits. I am convinced, however mistaken he might be in his aspirations to save the whole world, that he is no charlatan. I am convinced that he is a significant theologian. He is eccentric and full of surprises, he is a do-it-yourself systematizer who writes theology out of autobiography and fun.[5] He does come from the other side of the world; but this makes his theology interesting too.

Rev. and Mrs. Moon are the parents of ten children. Rev. Moon himself had a previous wife and Mrs. Moon is twenty years younger than him. Moon's life experience has made of him the image of father and grandfather,

one who has tasted the joy and bitterness of marital
failure and success, one who has learned by experience
how to be a true parent. Rev. Moon is called "True
Father" especially by those who have found in him a
strong, personal, fatherly figure. Mrs. Moon is similarly called "True Mother".

These titles are not only emotional ones but are
understood as theologically significant. According to
Rev. Moon's theology, God is triune. In God, the Word
(Logos) and Wisdom (Holy Spirit) are the perfect expres-
sions of the Father's mind and heart. Word and Wisdom
are conceived to be the internal masculine and feminine
(yang and yin) duality within God. Hence, God's Word
and Wisdom are our "True Heavenly Parents." In turn,
Rev. and Mrs. Moon seek to be an image of God thus
conceived. They seek to be "True Parents" in whose
loving and parenting the heavenly marriage *(hieros gamos)*
is enacted. Within the Unification Church Rev. and Mrs.
Moon are loved as "True Parents" and this love often
(though not always) takes the form of an Oriental familial deference. Unification Church members bow to the
Moons as Catholics bow to the Pope or as High Anglicans
bow to the Archbishop. But theirs is the respectful
bow of youngers towards elders --and there is no au-
thoritarianism in this familial relationship.

As True Parents, it is the work of Rev. and Mrs.
Moon to set an example of true parenting so they can
be imitated by their "children". In so doing, they are
trying to do something Jesus would have done had his
life not been cut short by his untimely crucifixion.
Jesus was able, during his short lifetime, to give a
perfect example of a single but not a married life.

The example of Jesus' "single life" has been followed
by countless holy celibates. But where can we find an
incarnate example of perfected divine-human marriage?
The disasterous stage of marriage and family life in
our time is understood by the *Divine Principle* to be
partial proof of the incompleteness of Jesus' proposed
ministry. As Second Adam, Jesus should have married his
perfect Eve; they should have procreated perfect children;
then the world would have had an incarnate example of
perfect parenthood through His life. Following Jesus'
example, the Moons seek to become the "Third Adam and
Eve" in an attempt to finish his Messianic work. As
this is done, God brings down His blest abode from
heaven to earth in order, through the True Parents and
their family, to dwell among men and women.

NEAR, BUT NOT YET

There is, nevertheless, a "not yet" within Unification eschatology. Though it has a Messianic vision
and hope, it does not proclaim Moon as Messiah. (He
could not yet be the Messiah because to be so requires
the completion of the Messianic task). Hence, there
is a notable modesty in talking about Rev. Moon. Dr.
Young Oon Kim, Professor of Unification Theology at
Moon's three year old Unification Theological Seminary
in Barrytown (New York), almost invariably refers to
Moon as "our Leader" or "our Master". Similarly, Mr.
David S. C. Kim (no relation to Dr. Kim), acting President of the Seminary and one who refers to himself as
"Rev. Moon's left-hand man" (Rev. Moon's right-hand man
lives in Seoul), calls Moon "a prophet", one sent by

God to proclaim God's will. I do not imply that either
President Kim or Dr. Kim would hesitate to theologize
on the role of Rev. and Mrs. Moon as the earthly True
Parents (for it is essential to the theological system).
But that these less highly-charged titles come more
easily to the lips of Moon's oldest and closest associ-
ates is indicative of the range of theological interpretations of Rev. Moon's role in history.

Such modesty of speech could also be understood
theologically. The Unification Church is one of the
many apocalyptic movements which is convinced that it
can tell you the dates of God's plans for the end of the
world. According to the Unification timetable, we have
just completed Rev. Moon's struggle to establish the
necessary conditions for the Kingdom of Heaven on Earth
in America. In 1978, Moon began his European re-enact-
ment of this same mission. A significant stage in this
development shall have been reached by 1980/81. At
this time, Mrs. Moon shall also have completed her
twenty-one year period of preparation to assume her full
dignity as True Mother. Although it is no official
doctrine of the Unification Church, I presume that
ideally she will, by that time, have given birth to her
twelfth child. (This is her symbolic restoration of
the original college of twelve apostles.) All these
things are stages and conditions for the inauguration
of the Messianic Age.

Until the Messianic Age begins, Rev. Moon continues
to function in a "John-the-Baptist role." But if Moon
proves successful in establishing the necessary providential conditions for the kingdom, he might then also
be anointed by God to be the "Father" in that kingdom.

According to exact Unification timing, Moon at this
point is only proleptically the "Lord of the Second
Advent." At the present moment (1978), he is in a state
of becoming. Dean Therese Stewart of the Unification
Seminary describes his present role as "Messiah-desig-
nate." Though he may already function emotionally and
religiously as True Father for many church members, he
is not actually nor technically the Lord of the Second
Advent at this time.

Rev. Moon himself is well-aware of this distinction.
He is a charismatic seer and visionary who has, report-
edly, not only visited the spirit world but has won
cosmically significant victories there. He is, in the
language of comparative religions, a shaman of large
proportions: one who has suffered, who has experienced
"soul-loss," who has overcome the spirits of the nether
and upper worlds, and who can now command the coming of
spirit and power. As such, Moon is revered as an infallible seer, revelator, and prophet.

When Rev. Moon himself is asked -- as I once asked
him -- whether he is the Lord of the Second Advent, he
keeps the "Messianic secret" as carefully as Jesus
kept it. But Moon's reticence about giving a clear
"yes" or "no" to this question should not be dismissed
as dissimulation. He knows that his time -- if it ever
is to come -- is not yet. At this moment, he is still
functioning as harbinger of the new age. One might say
that he is acting as his own forerunner. For when I
put this question to him, he replied: "Dr. Lewis,
you may be the Lord of the Second Advent. There are
now alive one hundred and twenty persons who may be
the Lord of the Second Advent." Intensely aware of the

implications of his own theology, Rev. Moon acknowledges
that neither he nor even God yet knows with exactitude
how future history will unfold.

Rev. Moon absolutely trusts that God will attain
His historic victory in the establishment of the messianic kingdom before the end of this century. However,
Rev. Moon knows that his role in God's future is entirely
dependent upon his own and his Church's faithfulness,
hard work, and cooperation with the spirit world. Once,
at an early Sunday morning meeting at Belvedere Estate
(Tarrytown, New York), Rev. Moon was preaching about
the importance of the year 1980/81 on God's timetable.
He was urging the 500 people present to greater and
greater work. Then he suddenly slipped from Japanese,
which he had been speaking, into the charming but
broken English which he occasionally employs:

"Will we make it?" he asked
"Yes!" roared the young and enthusiastic audience.
"Will we make it?" he cried a second time.
"Yes!!" came the antiphon, twice as loud.
But then he asked: "*How* will we make it?"

Ordinarily, the dynamics of group action like this do
not call for hard questions at the emotionally crucial
moment. The audience was confounded. Gung-ho-ism could
not produce the right answer. They faltered. Then,
from the back of the crowd, one member, more devout
than the others, erupted:

"With you!"

There was an uncertain cheer, interrupted by Rev. Moon

himself as he raised a quizzical finger:

"With me?"

Moon's eyes disappeared behind his smile wrinkles as
he embraced them with the shining grin of his Oriental
countenance. Then pointing heavenward, he gently cor-
rected them and said,

"With God!"

The building shuddered with the roar of hearty approval
and relieved devotion.

THE HOLY SPIRIT ASSOCIATION FOR THE
UNIFICATION OF WORLD CHRISTIANITY

There is as yet no official "Gospel" which tells
stories of Rev. Moon's personal suffering at the hands
of the North Korean Communists, and other stories presenting parallels between his life and Jesus Christ's.
Neither is there an official "Acts of the Apostles"
to describe the beginnings of the Unification Church
in its early, more pentecostal-charismatic days in Korea
An adequate historical study of the Unification Church
would include a description of the current condition
of Christianity in Korea and Japan, and especially a
sociological analysis of the proliferation of Messianic
and other new sectarian religions in the Orient. I
am convinced that those elements which usually seem
inspired to the uncritical insider (and usually very
strange to the critical outsider) would not seem so
exceptional if the Unification Church were assessed
within its original context: the psychosociological
background of contemporary Far-Eastern Christian
existence.

The present name, "Unification Church", has come
to replace an older name for the movement. (This development in nomenclature resembles the way that "Christian" seems to have displaced "the Way" as a primitive
denomination of one of the earliest Jesus-movements.)[6]
The original and proper name for the Unification Church
is "Holy Spirit Association for the Unification of World
Christianity." It would be appropriate, however, to
make this title even more inclusive and add "and for
the Unification of World Religions," since this is the
ultimate goal.

The reason for the name "Holy Spirit Association"
is clear neither from the theology nor from the activity
of the American Church. Aside from the highly significant identification of the Holy Spirit as the female
dimension within Godhead, whose earthly image is mir-
rored in Mrs. Moon, there is no particular preoccupation
with defining the nature or charismatically experienced
presence of the Holy Spirit. Moreover, although within
the church there is reference to the mystical experiences
of Rev. Moon and other leaders, and although the spirit
world is understood to participate in the work of the
church, Unification in America today is very different
from the special charismatic orientation of the earlier
Holy Spirit Association in Korea. In Korea, in the
1950's, there was miracle-working and visionary communication. But today this has either been suppressed or
taken a back seat to the more institutional and typically
American style of the church. Even Mr. David Kim, President of the Unification Seminary in New York, says that
"Holy Spirit" in the name does not refer to the Holy
Spirit as the third person of God, but means the holy

and spiritual nature of the church. Already within the
lifetime of its founder, that "cooling-off period"
which typically belongs to the second generation of
charismatic movements seems well advanced.

OTHER ORGANIZATIONS

The American Unification Church is the institutional
expression of Rev. Moon's expansive personality. There
are several groups related to the Church (often called
"front organizations" by critics, to lend an aroma of
subversiveness) which are concrete manifestations of
Moon's many concerns. Among these are the International
Federation for Victory over Communism (VOC) and the
Freedom Leadership Foundation (FLF). These are independent but ideologically related organizations which seek
to combat Marxist-Leninist-Maoist Communism. The
FLF publishes *The Rising Tide,* an anti-communist pro-
paganda newspaper, and arranges other kinds of public
activity.

Another area of concern is work with professors,
students and clergy. The Collegiate Association for
Research of Principles (CARP) instructs ministers and
intellectuals in the insights of the *Divine Principle.*
It frequently seeks to organize chapters on campuses
and to do student work. The International Cultural
Foundation (among its other activities) hosts an annual
International Conference on the Unity of the Sciences
(ICUS) to foster the unification of science and religion.
Tong-Il Pharmaceutical Company advertises the health-
bringing properties of Korean ginseng tea and merchan-
dizes the product. The Korean National Folk Ballet

was founded by Rev. Moon to bring to the West the delightful grace and dignified charm of ancient Korean folk
dance. The *News World* is a daily New York newspaper,
independent from the church, but supported by it (like
the *Christian Science Monitor*). There is also a seminary in New York, a large fishing business in Virginia
and Alabama, and a program on behalf of International
Children's Year. Already there are more than forty of
these para-ecclesiastical organizations worldwide.

Such external evidences of the Church's concerns
bear a direct relationship to its internal, spiritual
design. This notion is best expressed in two Korean
Phrases mentioned earlier, which are frequently used
to describe the pattern of dualities which runs throughout Unification theology: *sung sang* (internal form)
and *hyung sang* (external shape). According to the
Divine Principle, everything is composed of *sung sang*
and *hyung sang*. The external shape *(hyung sang)* of
the Unification Church is these myriad projects and
programs for the incarnation of the Kingdom of Heaven
in the cultural flesh of the earth. The internal form
(sung sang) of the Unification Church is its spiritual
purpose to be the holy ground upon which God can build
His Kingdom.

In one sense, the Unification Church is something
less than a model for future society. Moon envisions
that the Unification Church itself is destined for
annihilation as an ecclesiastical body politic. Even
it must be subsumed into the culture of the coming world.
During a faculty dinner at Tarrytown, Rev. Moon, who
uses these occasions as a time of informal "table talks",
gesticulated grandly (as is his wont) and urged us, the

professors of the Seminary: "Do not speak of the
Unification Church! The Unification Church is nothing;
it must die! Speak only of God and of one world under
God!" Moon's intention is that the present organizational
Church function as a bridge to the future, as a means to
reach the goal of the one-world culture.

It is not uncommon for visionary leaders, who entertain grander schemes for the future than their followers are able to carry out, to relegate even the
institutions which they have founded to a transitional
role. But the drag of sociology is against them; movements of this nature tend to die a slow death. The
Unification Church will pass away only if the kingdom
actually comes.

One aspect of the Unification Church, usually judged
negatively by some parents of youthful recruits, is
its high demands on their children. Being a Moonie
is not easy. The Unification Church lives in the
belief that there is only a short time to accomplish
a great thing; hence, it appeals to the heroic in
young people. It calls them to intense study of the
Divine Principle, exhausting fundraising activities,
night-long prayer struggles, and aggressive evangeliza-
tion as prophets of the Kingdom who storm the bastions
of this Satan-dominated world in a spiritual Battle of
Armageddon. Of course, when you join the army--whether
the Lord's or Uncle Sam's--you have to leave home. But
when Mom and Dad are not in agreement with your new
direction, family conflict is the result.

Disagreement with their parents over ideals and
life style is acute for some members of the Unification
Church. Their parents believe that 1981 is not a

specially eschatological year. But Unification Church
members quote the words of Jesus that "one's enemies
shall be they of his own household." Such total commitment sometimes sets father and son, mother and daughter
at odds with one another. Here one is reminded of the
youthful Francis of Assisi who desired chaste espousal
to Lady Poverty. When his father tried to force him
home, claiming that he himself had given Francis the
clothes on his back, Francis returned the clothes to
his father and set about naked to follow the naked
Christ. So such parent-member conflicts are not totally
without precedent. Moreover, Unification Church members do not see these separations as destructive, but
rather as laying the foundation for more solid family
structures in the future.

IF PROPHECY FAILS

The Unification Church belongs to the continuous
line of lonesome prophets and Messianic movements which
have existed in every century: Papias, Justin Martyr,
the Montanists, the Irenaeus in the second century;
Joachim of Fiore in the twelfth; the Flagellants,
Franciscans, Bohemians, and Anabaptists in the High and
Late Middle Ages; right up to the latest utopian social-
political-cultural dreamers of a Third World Age of the
Holy Spirit/Consciousness III/Noosphere/Age of Aquarius.
All these have kept us believing that "there's a new
world comin'." In our own time, theological forces
as diverse as the Jehovah's Witnesses, the "theologians
of hope" (Juergen Moltmann and his school), and the
Evangelical Fundamentalists (Hal Lindsey, David Wilkerson,

et al.) all move in this heady atmosphere.

In every previous case, the conductor in charge
of God's railroad train read the timetable wrongly.
From Jesus' apostles gazing into heaven right down to
today's latest cloud-watcher, they have all been wrong.
Embarrassed by "delays" they then readjust the schedule.
Luke substituted a "second coming" of Pentecostal fire
in place of the more apocalyptic fire of final judgment.
William Miller honorably returned to his ploughing when
his Adventist prophecies for the years 1843 and 1844
(adjusted) remained unfulfilled. The Jehovah's Witnesses
still carry on undaunted, after having spiritualized
their predictions concerning 1914.

One may view the failure of all these eschatological
groups as evidence of their idiocy and use this judgment as sufficient reason to suppress or persecute them.
But one may also note that, even in the failure of
their kingdom dreams, the eschatological groups have
been a major creative force in history. They have
opposed outdated forms and overturned established powers.
They may be credited as a ferment towards a better,
even if not a perfect, tomorrow. Without medieval
Joachism, the early-modern peasant would never have
found the courage to revolt against his feudal lord.
Not unfairly, contemporary Marxist philosophers of
history cite John Hus, Thomas Muntzer, and Jan van
Leyden as spiritual forerunners of the rise of the
proletariat today.

Spiritual hopes have produced secular results.
New forms of political government and new styles of
economic organization are the creations of sectarian
enclaves of communitarians, whether they be the

Anabaptists in the hidden valleys of Upper Austria,
or the experimenters at New Harmony, or the Mormons
on the American Frontier. Quaker ranting brought
slavery to an end in England. Methodist "enthusiasm"
moved the British heart to enact child-labor laws and
reform the industrial revolution. Other kinds of progress which have come about as a direct result of eschatological striving may be less glorious, but no less
substantial. Amana builds deep freezers and Oneida is
famous for silverware. The Shakers invented the washing
machine, the Adventists invented the cornflake, the
Campbellites invented the ecumenical movement. Rev.
Moon has started the long desired "other morning newspaper" in New York.

In his recent speech at Yankee Stadium, Rev. Moon
recapitulated the history of America under the providence of God. He then described our present immorality,
loss of faith, and lack of direction as things which
might cause God to forsake America. "Soneone has got
to do something about it!" he said. This social activism which aims at *saving the world* distinguishes the
Unification Church from most previous apocalyptic sects.
Previous apocalyptic groups stayed back in their valleys
or out on the frontier, waiting for the Lord to come; or
they emphasized preaching missions to a fallen world.
The Unification Church, however, enflamed by the same
eschatological vision, has self-consciously taken up
social responsibility for the entire globe.

The ultimate goal of the Church, in the words of
Seminary President Mr. David Kim, is to bring about a
"world-wide theocratic socialism for the whole world."
In a private conversation with Mr. Kim, I was once

told that whereas the Marxists use the wrong methods
(force, violence) for the wrong ideology (atheistic,
dialectical materialism), nevertheless their dream of
a global society of socialized equality is also the
economic aim of the Unification Church. "We will do
what the Marxists are trying to do," said Mr. Kim, "but
for the right reasons and in the right ways." Dr. Young
Kim describes the Church's vision of the future by speaking of a World brotherhood which will work to fulfill
the goals of socialism (or capitalism) but with the
methods and inspiration of God."[7]

        Here I am inclined to ask: what difference will
it make should time prove the Unification Church wrong
in its date-setting? Some embarrassment would be suffered by the Church. Internally, it would have to adjust. Some members would lose faith. Others would
reinterpret. Perhaps Rev. Moon would be redefined as
having always been providentially destined to remain
in his John-the-Baptist role. The mantle of Messiah-
designate might pass to one of his children, or to an
outstanding disciple, or to the Unification Church as
a whole. But none of these adjustments of God's timetable would be essentially different from those adjustments that have taken place in apocolyptic movements
numberless times before. The heretical thrust of the
Unification Church into the future would then be reab-
sorbed into the orthodoxy of the ongoing church.

SOME POLITICAL QUESTIONS

        Many contemporary Christians have given up the
expectation that Jesus will appear on the clouds of glory

either to take the faithful home to heaven or to set up
a millennial reign.   Rev. Moon and the Unification Church
agree with this assessment, arguing that the images
used in this biblical version of the parousia are
prescientific metaphors rather than a literal description
of future historical reality. That this Unificationist
position is hateful to the biblical literalist is clear
enough. But, for most people, the question is not this
at all. It is rather the political implications of his
organization. Could not Rev. Moon be a religious Adolph
Hitler who might make his youthful brigades into an
American version of the Nazi Youth? Might not external
conditions allow the secular results of spiritual hopes
to produce not a messianic kingdom of peace but a totalitarian religious regime?

First, it can be said that such frightening phrases
are not new. Rather, they are the typical accusations
that have been thrown at many new groups as justification
for persecuting them. When theological debate proves
ineffective in vanquishing the social heretic, modern
upholders of orthodoxy, like their medieval counterparts, have often resorted to violence. The Salem
Puritans were stampeded by their fears of unorthodoxy
into witch hunting. Innocent people died. A century
later, Mother Ann Lee, Foundress of the Shakers, was
beaten and sexually maltreated near Boston and Albany.
Joseph Smith, the first Mormon, was lynched by a religious mob in Carthage, Illinois.

The current tactics of religious opponents of the
Unification Church like Rabbi Maurice Davis of White
Plains and Rev. Jorge Lara-Braud of the National Council
of Churches are not essentially different from what

representatives of orthodoxy did during medieval in-
quisitions. Yet these inquisitors are more subtle
than to send Moonies to the rack and the stake. They
urge tax-fraud investigations, suggest deportation of
undesirable foreigners, and impugn the integrity of
Unification conversions by describing them as "brainwashing." For example, some professional psychologists
recently testified before the Vermont Senate to support
the allocation of State funds for the "psychiatric care"
of anyone who experiences an immediate conversion to
anything at all. The game of heretic hunting is the
same today as it was five hundred years ago. Only we
now call the game not "heresy-hunting," but "helping
the people remain free to make their own choices."

In response to the accusations of potential totalitarianism, a Unification Church member replies as
follows: Rev. Moon is not a would-be religious Hitler
because Rev. Moon is acting under the direction of Jesus.
Therefore, he believes in heart and love, and he preaches
pacifism as the only ultimately effective way of overcoming hostile Communism. Rev. Moon describes the Battle
of Armageddon as the Third World War, but says that it
is *already* being fought. It is *already* being fought
because it is an ideological struggle between Christianity and Communism which can only be won with spiritual
weapons. (This ideological warfare does not preclude,
admits the Unificationist, the possibility of peace-
keeping military intervention by the "free" powers.)
A Unification member would further argue that Rev.
Moon has never yet used force or unethical tactics
to accomplish his purposes; therefore, he would not
resort to these "fallen" methods even if he were in a

position to wield considerably more power than he now
does.

It is surely true that the Unification Church
believes in and lives for the day when there will be
a one-world culture, under the one God as taught in
the *Divine Principle*. Such an international theocratic
socialism would embody the economic implications of
heavenly relationships in an earthly governmental structure. Rev. Moon's message is that God is offering
America first choice to become the political model for
such an international Kingdom of Heaven on Earth. For
America to reject this offer, say the Unificationists,
is to reject God and deny America's own providential
history and prophetic promise.[8] If America rejects
this possibility, then she will have rejected God's
blessing--with all the consequences that loss of blessing
entails. For America to accept this offer, say the
Unificationists, is for America to realize her own dream
of being one nation under God, with life, liberty, and
the pursuit of happiness for all.

This is the point at which we modern, liberal,
democratic intellectuals feel most uncomfortable with
Rev. Sun Myung Moon. He is at liberty to be a harmless
religious freak; there are certainly enough of those
around--Billy Graham, Oral Roberts, the whole Sunday
morning religious T.V. crowd. But when Moon appeals
to our American patriotism, our nineteenth century American optimism, and our recurring dreams of manifest destiny, then he is troubling our national conscience and
exposing our agnosticism. "There's no special providence
for America," say the realistic among us. But, the
idealistic among us still feel the call of providence

to democratize the globe. Within living memory, Americans have waged successful warfare against both Oriental
and European totalitarianism. We think of the Jews
and know we were not wrong. So, we are susceptible to
a new, even heretical, vision of the old hope. This
explains why American resistance to Rev. Moon is most
angry when it protects its own susceptibility to his
special appeals.*

The Unification Church preaches a "Civil Religion"
which resembles that proposed by the distinguished
sociologist, Robert Bellah.[9] Yet, the Unification
viewpoint differs from Bellah's in one essential:
whereas Bellah's vision begins and ends with typically
American realities (though he is aware of influences
from the East), the Unification Church is internation-
alist and gives symbolic importance to non-American
places, people, and events. Whereas Bellah's approach
might yield an American version of National Socialism
with religious roots, the Unification Church is growing
an International Socialism with those same roots.
Whereas Bellah speaks of American Civil Religion, the
Unification Church seeks to create a future Global Civil
Religion.

As the Unification Church sees it, a world-wide
theocratic socialism could be attained with America
as its political base and Korea as its spiritual base.
This would involve the awakening of America to its
political religious destiny by the target date 1980/81;

---

*For further discussion of this theme see the essay
in this volume by Professor M. D. Bryant, *Unification
Eschatology and American Millennial Traditions.*

the exertion around the world of a *pax Americana* in fulfillment of America's providential role as the vanguard of political freedom; the continuing protection of the "divine" nation of South Korea against possible "satanic" invasion from the Communist North; and the ever-widening spiritual influence of the Lord-elect of the Second Advent.

To many Americans, Rev. Moon's ideal seems arrogant. He seems to be harkening back to our ideological golden age when we read our own history as biblical. We would like him to go away. But even when he does (he is now in England), we cannot ignore him. Even the *New York Times* continues to give him space four days a week! He seems to stick in our conscience and to touch our heart. What are we to do? In the main we have responded by vilifying the man and caricaturizing the message. Why does he upset us so?

WHAT TO DO WITH A NEW MESSIAH?

What should we do with a new religious movement which makes a messianic claim upon us? The phrase from James Russell Lowell's hymn "Once To Every Man and Nation" haunts us at a moment like this:

> "...Some great cause, God's new Messiah,
> offering each the bloom or blight..."

Is the great cause of Reverend Sun Myung Moon a bloom or a blight? We could wait, as Rabbi Gamaliel advised, to see whether Moon and his movement be of God. History, surely, will have its say. Yet public opinion again

and again damns the heretic, and then is conquered by
his message. The change in public opinion is often
very sudden. Jesus, Augustine, Thomas, Luther, Wesley,
Abraham Lincoln--they were all acclaimed soon after by
the very people who called them names. If Moon is also
prophet and theologian, the same thing will happen to
him.

What can we do with this new Church?

(1) We could oppose it. In 1976 a publication of
the Korean Joint Action Committee of the National Council of Churches of Christ in the U.S.A., wrote:

> The Council of Churches of the City
> of New York has twice turned down, on
> doctrinal grounds, the Unification
> Church's application for membership.
> Some notable Korean and Japanese
> Christian theologians have labelled
> Unification doctrine "heresy."

This medieval pronouncement refers to the results of
an inquisition which I attended as an observer. The
ecumenical committee which considered whether the
Unification Church was "Christian" included a Mennonite, a Czech Evangelical, a Campbellite, a Lutheran,
a Presbyterian, some Black Methodists and Baptists,
and one or two others. It was a "cage of unclean
birds" (Jer. 5:27), the representatives of previously
schismatic movements, who ecumenically voted that Rev.
Moon is no Christian and that his theology is heretical.
Rev. Moon later laughingly told us that in this way,

at least one of his goals had been accomplished: he
had caused all Christians (and Jews!) finally to unite--
against him!

The decision of the New York Council is even more
astonishing when one remembers that it had previously
admitted Swedenborgian anti-trinitarian clairvoyants,
Universalist humanists and Roman Catholic papists and
mariolaters to its club. If the Unification Church
were excluded from Councils of Christian Churches on
grounds of heresy, then one wonders how any other church
ever got in. What Christian church is sufficiently
orthodox to call another a "heretic" without having
the epithet thrown back at it? But it is a matter of
church-historical record that the holy synods have not
always concluded their decisions on the basis of rational
consistency. Political motivations were as much a part
of the decision this time as they were at Nicaea or at
the Robber's Synod.

Even more alarming is the fact that the author
of the report on which the National Council of Churches
based their condemnation of the Unification Church had
not met with even a single member or theologian from
the Church. Moreover, when invited to visit the Church's
Seminary and at least meet some of the people condemned
in the report, the reply was that the author is too
busy to accept such an invitation until 1981.

(2) A second possible response to the Unification
Church might be to accept the presence among us of a
new tradition, one which is not itself yet tainted
by narrowmindedness. Rev. Moon's Unification Seminary,
for example, demonstrates a policy of theological openness implicit in the word "unification" itself. The

faculty now includes a Polish Catholic priest, a Dutch
Reformed Minister, a Texas Pentecostalist, an Eastern
Orthodox layman, a Hungarian Jewish Rabbi, a Canadian
Presbyterian, a Chinese Confucianist, an Irish Catholic
layman, and a lady theologian from Korea who is also
a member of the Unification Church. The student body
similarly represents the wide world of racial, national,
and confessional distinctions. Such an institution
embodies, in its organization, the faith of the Church.
Surely, we might allow their peculiarity within the large
Christian fold.

(3) As a third response, we might even approve and
encourage Rev. Moon's most outstanding accomplishment
to date and its implications for the cultural community.
The International Cultural Foundation is preparing for
its Seventh Annual International Conference on the Unity
of the Sciences (ICUS) to take place at Thanksgiving,
1978, in Boston, Massachusetts. Its roster of past
and present participants is a list of Nobel laureates
and their closest colleagues. The conferences have
provided the world's most renowned scientists an opportunity to think together about their fields and to
address, especially, the question of values in relation
to science. The ICUS conferences are under the general
direction of one of Rev. Moon's brightest lieutenants,
Mr. Michael Young Warder. Their spirit flows directly
from the inspiration of Rev. Moon's concern to unify
religion and science.* One could only hope that Moon's

---

*For a discussion of the organic relation of science
and religion in Unification theology see the essay by
Professor Flinn in this volume.

concerns for the unification of other fields, such
as politics and religion, economics and religion,
Christianity and other world religions, could be as
successful as these.*

(4)   A fourth alternative would be for the theological
community to undertake a fair-minded investigation of
the Unification Church. This would involve meeting
with Unification theologians and members to engage in
thorough and critical discussions of the *Divine Principle*
and its implications. Such a fair-minded investigation
is the least we owe Rev. Moon; it would also restore
the dynamic of orthodox/heresy to its proper context,
namely, on-going theological discussion. Perhaps a
church-historical observation is to the point: outstanding heretics in the past have very often applied
for eschatological orthodoxy by appealing their case
to a future general council when they cannot get along
with their contemporaries in the church.

---

*Since this paper was written, the Unification Church
has established a conference and collaborative program
working towards the unification of world religions. In
1977/78, there have been three major meetings in San
Francisco, New York, and England.

[1] Hippolytus, *Refutation of all Heresies*, 7:21:7.

[2] To stress the love relation between God and human
beings in this way raises the question whether God is independent from the creation at all. Christian theology
which in this way stresses that God is love usually goes
on to argue that God is also independent from the creation and yet *still* can be love because God contains within Himself His own eternal object of love and also His
love for that eternal object. The doctrine of the
Trinity arises in precisely this way: as a solution to
the question how God can be *love* and yet be independent
from creation. This doctrine says that in God there are
three principles: Lover, Beloved and Love (Father, Son
and Spirit). The creation is not needed for God to love
but the *overflow* of God's prior existing love. This
orthodox Christian view is precisely that of the *Divine
Principle*. Diagrammatically the *Divine Principle* teaches
that God (1st) expresses Himself in Christ (2nd) and in
the Holy Spirit (3rd) and this *results* in creation (4th).

God Father

Word/Christ   Wisdom/Holy Spirit
(male principle;   (female principle;
positive polarity)   negative polarity)

Creation

The *Divine Principle's* trinitarianism is closer to
Eastern Orthodoxy than to St. Augustine.

[3] Young Oon Kim, *Unification Theology and Christian
Thought,* (New York, 1975), *passim,* which presents a careful restatement of the contents of the *Divine Principle,*
annotating it from the perspective of the spectrum of the
several Christian traditions. Dr. Kim is professor of
systematic theology at the Unification Theological Seminary.

[4] Allegations of impropriety have been leveled against
the Blessing Ceremony, see, for example, Jane Day Mook,
"New Growth on Burnt-over Ground," *A.D.,* (May 1974) p. 34,

which alludes to a "pikarume", a rite of "blood separation," a secret initiation accomplished through sexual
intercourse practiced by some religious groups in the
Orient. Ms. Mook asserts that "in the early days of the
Unification Church, this was with Moon who, through the
act, made pure the initiates." Unfortunately, Ms. Mook
provides neither evidence to support her assertion regarding the Unification Church nor bibliographical reference to the Korean and Japanese sources which she
claims.

5   Asked by one overly serious follower what the Holy
Spirit looked like, Rev. Moon replied "A feminine green
mist!" When I wanted him to explain a theological difficulty to me, he seemed stumped. Then he advised, "Use
your own imagination, Professor Lewis. That's what I do."

6   cf. Acts 19:9, 23, 11:26.

7   Young Oon Kim, *op. cit.*, p. 158.

8   America has been chosen as the nation to receive
                the Messiah for ultimate world salvation in our
                century. America's 200 year history has served
                as indemnity to pay for the 2,000 years of his-
                tory since the crucifixion of Christ. In this
                short 200 years America has been given extraordinary
                blessings spiritually as well as materially and
                has grown to be the mightiest nation on earth.
                Now America is in the position of the second
                Israel. Christianity and the United States to-
                gether can fulfill God's will and create one
                unified world with all the nations joined into
                one... As with everything, the ideal world must
                have an initial starting point. In the divine
                will, Korea, the final bastion of the free world
                in Asia, is now serving as a link to bring har-
                mony between the civilizations of the East and
                West. Korea will be the ignition point of God's
                final dispensation. Therefore, according to the
                will of God, the United States must safeguard
                Korea--not for Korea's sake nor the United States
                [sic] sake, but for the sake of creating the
                world of unity, harmony and peace... The supreme

> test of America in the will of God is at hand...
> Anerica must return to the founding spirit of the
> nation and rise up as God's instrument to save the
> world. Through a close cooperation between reli-
> gion and state, America must accept the challenge
> to become the co-worker of God in His Kingdom-
> building here on earth. America must be willing
> to sacrifice for God's purpose. She must rush
> forward as God's flag bearer. When America does
> this, her prosperity will be eternal. When
> America fulfills God's will, His blessings upon
> her will increase forever.

Considered strictly from the political angle, Rev. Moon's
ideology of history seems to read the Bible and American
history in order to divise some way--any way--to ration-
alize Korean chauvinism and insure political independence
for the South at the expense of American intervention.
When one knows something about church history, however,
one hesitates to fault a Constantine, a Luther, a Niebuhr,
or a Moon simply because they do their theology in a political context. That particular sin seems to be original
with us all.

Sun Myung Moon, "God's Plan for America, (House Caucus Room
of the United States Congress. December 18, 1975) in
America in God's Providence, (New York, 1976) pp. 21, 25, 26.

9
  Robert N. Bellah, *The Broken Covenant: American Civil
Religion in Time of Trial,* (New York, 1975) esp., 139-163.

GOD IN UNIFICATION PHILOSOPHY
AND IN THE CHRISTIAN TRADITION

SEBASTIAN A. MATCZAK

According to Unification philosophy, we can distinguish two main aspects of our knowledge of God: the
first is God as known in His own infinite reality; the
second is God as known according to our spatially and
temporally conditioned concepts of Him.

GOD AS KNOWN ACCORDING TO HIS OWN INFINITE REALITY

Two basic sources of Unification philosophy, the
Divine Principle and *Unification Thought*,[1] point out emphatically and correctly that God is beyond our concepts
of Him. Unification philosophy clearly states that God,
who is beyond space and time, cannot be exactly expressed
in our categories, which are marked in their essence by
space and time.[2]

Coupled with this extremely important statement is a
series of other, equally important statements which are
reiterated in clear language on many pages of both books:
God is the First Cause, God is the Ultimate Reality, God
is supremely perfect, God is unique, God is the Creator,[3]
God is Trinity.[4] To these ideas Unification philosophy
adds the further, related ideas that God is Logos, that
Jesus is the incarnate Logos, and that Jesus is both God
and man.[5] The existence of the Holy Spirit is emphasized
and the Spirit's specific role and relation to Jesus are

elaborated.[6] The Cross,[7] Resurrection,[8] and Redemption
are also taught.[9]

All these above mentioned ideas are very clearly
stated and emphasized in both main sources of Unification
philosophy. This fact is of considerable importance, for
it demonstrates that there is an essential unity between
the basic teachings of the two main theological sources
of the Unification Movement and the faith of the major
denominations within the Christian tradition.

SOME SOURCES WHICH CONTRIBUTE TO UNIFICATION PHILOSOPHY

The first source of Unification philosophy is the
Bible. The Bible is quoted as simply the last and decisive word: The Bible says so, and that is that! The
Bible is interpreted in particular ways in some instances,
but the authority of the Bible is clearly recognized.

A second source of Unification philosophy is science.
Since the natural sciences are acknowledged as a source
of truth, the explanation advanced on the pages of both
Unificationist texts are intended to be in agreement with
the achievements of the sciences, their recent discoveries,
and their conclusions.[10]

A third source of Unificationist philosophy is common sense. Many issues are discussed and interpreted according to ordinary, every-day sensibleness. According
to both books, we are led to understand God in accordance
with our knowledge of His creatures. We see God reflected
somehow in creation and therefore form our image of God
according to our knowledge of His creatures. This reflection of God in the creation is seen, however, in a way
which does not undermine but rather preserves the mystery

of God. Since it is so clearly stated that God is beyond
our concepts of Him, our understanding of God thus takes
place through the *images* of God which reflect Him in the
created things. These images and concepts, which are in
space and time, are therefore not a perfect reflection of
God, who is beyond space and time.

A final source important for the two basic sources
of Unification philosophy is Oriental philosophy; or,
more precisely, Confusianism, and even better, Neo-Confucianism. A clear indication of this is found in the
Divine Principle where the *Book of Changes* is quoted.
The *Book of Changes*, written ca. 300 B.C., displays a similarity in teaching to some of the characteristic ideas
of Confucianism in its historical development.[11]

The most striking parallel is to be found between
the rational philosophy of the Sung period, of which the
Book of Changes is the basic source, and the Unificationist view. During the Sung period, emphasis focussed on
two concepts: the Great Ultimate and Reason. These two
concepts may be considered to represent God, though not
conceived of as personal. The Great Ultimate moves and
generates *yang*, the active principle. When *yang* develops,
it engenders *yin* the passive, tranquil principle. The
whole of reality thus oscillates eternally between the two
yang and *yin*. Through this oscillation, the visible reality which we witness is produced. This reality then pro-
gressively develops into a coordinated system, the orderly
character of the universe, on the basis of Reason and the
Vital Force. The function of Reason is to combine the
many into one, whereas the function of the Vital Force is
to differentiate the one into many. Reason is embodied

in the Vital Force. The similarity--though not identity
--between these concepts as taught in the *Book of Changes*,
and the Unification point of view is quite clear to one
who has studied both perspectives.

Further similarities lie in the idea of moral order
and the ontological development of the world as developed
in the Mind School of Confucianism during the Ming period.
The moral order consists in the cooperation of the functions of Reason and the Vital Force. This cooperation
makes the universe a cosmos, that is, a beautiful and
harmonious whole. If the whole universe is to be harmonious, then the human moral order must be harmonious too;
it has to function in agreement with the universe. This
agreement is due mainly to that Reason which permeates the
universe and which is expressed in our human minds. The
idea behind the moral order is that if we understand its
reality as deeply as possible, we grasp the essence of
Reason. Reason, then, is the source of our morality: we
ought to work in agreement with Reason. And Reason dictates that we love. Love is the main factor--and this is
a central conclusion taught with great force in the *Divine
Principle* and *Unification Thought*.[12] For both systems of
thought, love is connected with the idea of the brotherhood of all people. All people are brothers and sisters.
Why? Because all people have the same Reason. This idea
resonates to the Christian concept of mankind: all human
beings have the same basic nature and the same kind of
soul and, consequently, the same ontological purpose.

This kind of Neo-Confucianism seems not, however, to
provide people with much training in social responsibility.
It is not interested in government, religious affairs or

priesthood, or in any particular creed.[13] At this point
we observe a clear difference between the Confucian position and the Unification position, since the latter is per
vasively concerned with human social ethics.

All of the above mentioned sources of Unification
philosophy are used with specific modification, interpretation and personal insight of Rev. Sun Myung Moon.
They thus result in a unique position which I am calling
Unification philosophy. Reverend Moon's personal insight
adds to the sources and thus gives to Unification philosophy its own logical unity and basic consistency. There
are gaps within the detailed elaboration of certain specific aspects of the system of thought; but these gaps
are understandably unavoidable within the scope of a tre-
mendous enterprise as vast as Rev. Moon's attempt to unify
the multitude of highly diversified viewpoints within
Christianity and the understandings of the Bible.

GOD AS KNOWN ACCORDING TO OUR CONCEPTS OF HIM IN TIME AND SPACE

To speak about God according to our spatially, temporally conditioned concepts, we must most emphatically
state, is to speak about God according to our limited
understanding and our imagination of God. In the *Divine
Principle* and *Unification Thought,* as I understand those
two books, imagination is strongly emphasized. God is
presented there as an Original Image, a Divine Image, the
Source and Foundation of individual images, and so on.
We must therefore ask the question: On what basis do we
form our image of God?

The answer of Unification theology is that our image
of our understanding of God is based on our observation
of creatures. We observe creatures and from these observations we draw conclusions concerning God. More specifically, our imagination and understanding of God are based
primarily on the observation of a specific kind of creature, namely man and woman in their human family. Thus,
our central concept of God is a family: for, since the
family is the essential constituating factor of mankind,
the human family must reflect the nature of God more accurately than does any other creature or institution.

The other point, which must be equally emphatically
stated, is that Unification philosophy teaches that our
conceptual and imaginary explanations of God are metaphorical only. We must not take them literally and so apply
them to God; they are only figurative representations.
Many religions and especially philosophies are mentioned
and criticized in the *Divine Principle* and *Unification
Thought* with the implication that the Unificationist image
of God as a family is a better explanation than the others.

POSITIVE CONCEPTS OF GOD

I want now to discuss the concrete, positive images
of God as taught in Unification philosophy, first in a
summary way, and then in detail.

In *Unification Thought*, the Divine Image in general
is called Original Image.[14] The specific content of Original Image is called Divine Character, and includes the
notions of Heart, Logos, and creativity. A third category of individual images relates to God's concepts of
particular creatures.

The Divine or Original Image includes three factors: sung-sang (internal character), and hyung-sang (external form), and the individual images of creatures.[15] Sung-sang and hyung-sang together are called the dual character or dual nature of God, and relate to one another as positivity and negativity. The individual images within God, which are neither God's own sung-sang nor hyung-sang, are God's own concepts or ideas of individual creatures external to God.

The basis of these three general features of God is constituted by three specific features of God. God's sung-sang corresponds to God's Heart (Love), His hyung-sang corresponds to His Logos (Word), and the individual images correspond to His creativity. All these features taken together, both the general and the specific, constitute the content or internal character of God.[*]

But, according to Unification theology, in addition to God's internal content, God also possesses His external structure. God's external structure refers to the activity by which God relates from within the depths of His bosom to and with the creatures external to Him. This activity is said to be structured on a four-fold foundation or Quadruple Base. This structure of the Original Image is called the "Order of the Divine Activity;" it can be described from two aspects: from the point of view of Heart, it is called the Quadruple Base centered on Heart;

---

* For further discussion of these themes see the essay by Professor Lewis, *Is the Reverend Sun Myung Moon a Heretic?* which also appears in this volume.

from the point of view of purpose, it is called the Quadruple Base centered on Purpose.   This structure occurs in
terms of four stages of action: (1) Origin   (2,3) Division
(4) Union.

        With this basic scheme before us, we can proceed with
a more detailed explanation of our particular concepts of
God.   The internal content of the General Divine Image consists of dual characteristics.   God is understood to exist
in terms of sung-sang and hyung-sang because we see that
the creatures, who were created in God's image, also exist
in terms of internal and external factors.

        God's sung-sang is the Divine Mind.   The Divine Mind
includes God's intellect, will and affection.   God's intellect comprises principles, names, ideas and laws.   The
Divine Mind, or subjective aspect of God, also has its objective aspect, or hyung-sang.   God's hyung-sang is necessary in order to explain God's external relation to His
creatures and is thus God's outer reality.   Within God's
sung-sang in particular we can distinguish the inner sung-
sang and inner hyung-sang.   The inner sung-sang contains
intellect, will and emotion; the inner hyung-sang contains
ideas, which are the images of created things, and laws,
which are the laws of creation.   The whole sung-sang, composed of inner sung-sang and inner hyung-sang, produces
God's objective aspect or hyung-sang.   This hyung-sang
also comprises its own inner sung-sang, which is undetermined matter, and its inner hyung-sang, which is universal prime energy.   The universal prime energy causes the
actual creation of all things.

        The dual characteristics (sung-sang and hyung-sang)
in God correspond to positivity and negativity, a set of

dual characteristics which can be justified, again, by
reference to the creatures created in the image of God.
The two natural forces, negativity and positivity, are
elemental within all creatures. Atoms exist as protons
and electrons. Minerals display the two aspects of cation
and anion. In plants we see stamen and pistils. Animals
come in twos: male and female. These positive and negative aspects recur among humans, as well. The human body
occurs as a man's body and a woman's body; the human mind
occurs as masculine and feminine components. Natural negativity and positivity recurring universally throughout all
creation must somehow be reflective of God. Consequently,
a divine negativity and positivity are directly posited of
God, i.e., sung-sang and hyung-sang. These features of
God do not occur separate from one another, nor does natural positivity and negativity occur separate from the being
of God; for, all reality is interrelated. When God produces sung-sang and hyung-sang, they are immediately accompanied by positivity and negativity; after this follows
creaturely positivity and negativity, man and woman, and
so on.

God's individual images of created things, which were
mentioned earlier, also belong to sung-sang and hyung-sang
though they may be singled out in a special way to make
clear that God creates through conceiving images. The
ideas and laws of the individual images, as has already
been stated, belong to the inner hyung-sang of the sung-
sang of God. The individual ideas thus do not constitute
a different duality in God, but belong strictly to the
duality of sung-sang and hyung-sang. In this way, a divine

unity is maintained within created diversity.

THE SPECIFIC CONTENT OF THE DIVINE CHARACTER

The specific content of God's internal character is Heart, Logos, and creativity.

Heart is directly related to and even identified with God the Father. The essence of Heart is love, and love is the very core of God's mind, God's entity; thus Heart is most appropriately predicted of the Father. The Heart and love of the Father is the principle of everything. Just as in the human family, the father is the principle which constitutes the family entity, so within God it is the same: the Father is the principle, the source, the love or Heart of the divine entity.

The *Divine Principle* proves its understanding of God's Heart by the Bible. God is first of all the Father; thus, He is Heart. Because He is Heart, God is a person--the person of the Father. This is, according to the Bible and the *Divine Principle*, the most essential characteristic of God: He is the Father, a loving person.

Heart is located in the core of God's being; but, the innermost core of God's essence is the inner sung-sang, which comprises intellect, will and emotion (or, affection). Thus the bosom and origin of all these three factors is love, is Heart. Thanks to Heart, God creates the universe. God's Heart compels Him to create, for God's Heart is looking for joy. His Heart finds its joy in the object of God's own creation. God's creatures are thus the objects of His joy, created with some--though not a perfect--resemblance to Himself. The other two characteristics of God--

Logos and creativity--are means to fulfill the purpose of
Heart.

Logos is the object of God within God. Or, in other
terms, Logos is reason and law. Through the Logos, the
whole universe is created. Since God is both subject and
object, Heart is the Divine Subject and Logos is the Divine
Object. Logos is formed through an interaction between
the inner sung-sang and inner hyung-sang. This explanation
of the Logos reminds us of the concept of Logos in Christianity, according to which the Logos is the eternally be-
gotten, only Son of God. This Logos is the Object of God;
or, to say it more in accord with Christian terminology,
the Logos is the Divine Object of God the Father.

The third internal characteristic of God is creativity.
Creativity issues as a result of the impulses of God's
Heart. Heart establishes purpose; its purpose is creation.
Creatures are created through the Logos, who was produced
before the creatures were made. The Logos, as reason and
law, contains pictures or images or ideas of the creatures.
The Father's Heart thus forces Him through the Logos into
creative activity. I am strongly tempted to call this
creative activity "Holy Spirit," since both books, the
Divine Principle and *Unification Thought,* speak about the
Holy Spirit in this way in describing "Her" relationship
to the Logos. The Holy Spirit is said to be the Object of
the Logos. Since the Logos is conceived here as the masculine element, then the Holy Spirit is the feminine element. In other words, She is His Divine Object just as He
is Her Divine Subject.

The creativity of the Holy Spirit comes about through
the activity of Heart and Logos. This understanding resul

in certain conceptual difficulties. How is the Holy Spirit formed? How does She come into existence? The sources of Unification philosophy are not clear on this matter. At first reading, one gets the impression that the Holy Spirit proceeds from the Father and then from the Logos, in a linear way: first there is Father, from whom the Logos proceeds; then, the Holy Spirit proceeds from the Logos.

This explanation of God's internal character reminds us of the explanation of the concept of the Trinity according to the Fathers of the Eastern Church. Whereas the Oriental Fathers explained procession within the Trinity in this linear way, the Fathers of the Western Church explained procession within the Trinity in a triangular way. The Latin Fathers thus reasoned that the Son proceeds from the Father and then the Spirit proceeds from both the Father and the Son. There is some basis in the sources of Unification philosophy for explaining inner trinitarian procession both ways, though in either event the idea is clearly accepted by the *Divine Principle*,[16] however one chooses to explain it. The creativity of the Spirit is thus a specific push which has its ultimate and original source in the Father but also through and in the Logos. The conceptualization of the Logos as the active principle and therefore the masculine element, and the Holy Spirit as the passive principle and therefore the feminine element more closely resembles, it seems to me, the linear mode of procession as taught by the Oriental Fathers: God the Father, as source and Heart, communicates that energy to the Holy Spirit.

It must be agreed that the Unificationist books are not entirely clear on the matter of the procession of the

triune God *ad intra*. Nevertheless, some positions are
quite clear, namely, that a Trinity of Father-Heart, Logos
and creative energy is the theological foundation of Unifi
cation philosophy.[17] I willingly see the description of
the Divine Image as taught by the sources of Unification
philosophy as a restatement of the Divine Persons of the
Trinity according to the teaching of the Christian Church.
All the necessary elements for a presentation of the Triun
God are contained in the Unification sources. We can thus
conclude that a point-for-point parallel between Unification philosophy and Christian theology exists in the under
standing of the internal character of God: the Divine Per
sons of the Trinity are the basis for the specific Image
of God. The Father is Heart and Love, the eternally begot
ten Son is the Logos, and the Holy Spirit, who proceeds
from the Father through the Son, is the creative energy
and activity of God. This conceptualization of the Trinit
--that doctrine so central to Christianity--is closer to
my understanding of the truth than are many of the other
diverse explanations of the Trinity taught in the various
churches.

THE STRUCTURE OF THE ORIGINAL IMAGE,
OR THE ORDER OF GOD'S ACTIVITY

God carries on two kinds of activities: those activities within Himself, between Heart, Logos, and creativit
and those activities outside Himself through which He relates to creatures in the external world, that is, the
world which is not Himself but which was produced by Himself outside Himself. To understand the nature of God's

activity outside Himself, we must make constant reference
to God's activity inside Himself. And, as we previously
considered God statically, we now propose to consider Him
dynamically. This externality of God's structured activity flows from His internal content and is called the
"Structure of the Original Image" in both Unification
books. I prefer to speak of the "order of the divine activity," for the sake of greater clarity.

The order of the divine activity is an interaction
within God, namely, the interaction of God's sung-sang and
God's hyung-sang. This interaction between God's mind and
object which finally produces the creatures is called, in
Unification philosophy, the action of "give-and-take."
Subject gives something to object and takes something from
it; object takes what subject has given and gives what subject takes. This is the horizontal internal activity of
God; it is the basic principle of any other activity of
God; it is the basic principle of any other activity within God as well as among the creatures. Because give-and-
take action is observed among all creatures, it is introduced into our explanation of God's activity. Give-and-
take action is a specific dialectic, different from the
Hegelian-Marxist dialectic, yet reminding us of it, and
even more so of the dialectic of the *Book of Changes*.

Besides this horizontal activity, there is also vertical activity. Vertical activity occurs between Heart
and its effects, the diversity of creatures. The action
of Heart results in two conditions: it both produces the
multiplicity and diversity of creatures and it also effects
the unity of all the diverse creatures due to Heart's love.
This is the "activity of the quadruple base": Heart

(origin) divides into sung-sang (subject) and hyung-sang (object), which then unite through give-and-take action to produce Heart's desired effect (union).

Heart's activity can be explained another way: since the Heart is the core of everything, Heart is at the center. But Heart is Love. What does Love do? Love does two things: it unites the whole divine essence into a single unity. This is called the "identity-maintaining quadruple base," or the inner quadruple base of God's activity. The Heart also gives identity to intellect, to will, to images, and establishes the union of all these. Thus God is one and God is unity.

The activity outside God related to the external world of creation is called the "outer quadruple base." The outer quadruple base creates (causes) the multitude of creaturely bodies as a result of Heart acting by way of intellect. Flowers and people, stones and the sky are the multiplicity of Heart's effects.

In summary, we thus have a single, basic form of give-and-take action which functions in four ways: horizontally and vertically, both inside and outside God. Heart divide vertically into sung-sang and hyung-sang, which then horizontally maintain give-and-take action and union with each other as a result of Heart's continuing give-and-take action with each of them. Heart thus effects both divisio and union through both vertical and horizontal give-and-take action inside God. Similarly, Heart's give-and-take action with sung-sang and hyung-sang passes on to the crea tures, who also maintain give-and-take action among themselves. The creatures which have come from God must also return to God; thus, the vertical give-and-take action between Heart and creation is made complete. Unity of

Heart and creation is thereby maintained outside God;
unity among the creatures is maintained by horizontal give-
and-take action, the effect of Heart's creativity through
intellect. In all these processes, the quadruple action-
base of Origin-Division-Union has been recapitulated.
     There are two ways of describing the unity of the
quadruple base: the unity of the quadruple base centered
on Heart and the unity of the quadruple base centered on
purpose. Centering on Heart, the quadruple base maintains
unity inside and unity outside because Heart is the origin;
both sung-sang/hyung-sang and the multitude of creatures
are Heart's beloved objects, and Heart is both the unity-
maintaining Love among Heart's objects as well as the ultimate goal to which Heart's effects return. Centering on
purpose, or the goal-object of Heart, the effect of the
quadruple base is to bring all things together in the love
of Heart. There is, once again, the give-and-take activity
between sung-sang and hyung-sang in the production of all
beings, and Heart attains its external purpose through
loving give-and-take with its effects and through maintaining a loving relationship among them as well. Heart,
which has its own inner sung-sang and hyung-sang eternally
unified in the loving action of give-and-take centered on
Heart, thus maintains its own vertical relationship with
its creation as well as maintaining a horizontal relationship
among the many creatures. This accounts at once for both
the diversity of creatures and their unity in God.

UNIFICATION PHILOSOPHY RELATES THE CHRISTIAN
CONCEPT OF GOD TO ORIENTAL PHILOSOPHY

The foregoing explanation of God according to Unification philosophy is a metaphorical explanation of God as we understand Him, or, rather, as we try to understand Him This understanding of God is in essential agreement with the biblical understanding of God: God is a single unity, is Spirit,[18] and is, therefore, simple. Besides this, God is Creator; God is Logos; God is Trinity. Unification philosophy is an attempt to explain all these mysteries of faith contained in the Bible in a way accessible to the human mind. The Unification sources claim that their expl nation is more acceptable to human reason than other expla nations. Perhaps the most important factor in this whole endeavor is that Unification philosophy arrives at this explanation by applying Oriental philosophical concepts to the Christian Bible.

This point is of special importance in our time of ecumenical movements. The two most populous countries of the world, China and India, are Oriental lands in which Christianity found almost no footing, despite its attempts to penetrate them for many centuries. In my opinion, base on my experiences in India, the reason for Christianity's missionary failure in these countries is that Christianity approached these people with the idea of converting them in such a way that they would have to abandon their own philosophies and embrace Aristotelian or Platonic philosop as they embraced the Christian faith. The question I rais then, is whether other philosophies—perhaps Chinese Confucianism or the Indian Vedanta—might not explain the Bib better than Aristotle or Plato. If any philosophy distorts the teaching of the Bible, then it is not acceptable to a Christian. But if these philosophies do not distort the Bible, even if they are Oriental philosophies, they may be acceptable.

The Unification sources, the *Divine Principle* and *Unification Thought*, contain valuable, basic explanations of the Bible's teaching about God, as I have indicated above. The conception of how God is reflected in His creatures, particularly in human family life, deserves special attention and applause, since man and woman and the human family are some of God's most perfect creations. These concepts require, however, further elaboration, refinement, and proof; but, this activity must be undertaken with a clear purpose not to distort the teachings of the Bible. And, in my opinion, if Oriental philosophy--or any other-- seems to explain the biblical concepts of God, man, woman, and the family better than they have been explained until now, such an interpretation is highly welcome. Aristotelian philosophy as applied to the Bible by Thomas Aquinas helped us enormously to understand the Bible and the teaching of Jesus. The same must be said of the efforts of the Fathers of the Church, particularly of the Greek Fathers, who applied Platonic philosophy rather than Aristotelian philosophy. But our ecumenical attitudes may now be extended beyond the boundaries of previous times to include as well unfamiliar and better philosophic perspectives, inclusive of Oriental philosophy. No matter how good the efforts to explain God philosophically of former times may have been, our notions of God always require fur-

ther refinement. I agree that the task is always difficult, since God is infinite and our minds are finite; but
good ideas can always be replaced by better ones. Therefore, other philosophies, in this case Oriental philosophies, are welcome, if they advance a better explanation.

Another reason Oriental philosophies more especially
are welcome is that they are philosophies of long standing;
they have educated millions of people through thousands of
years, producing hundreds of generations of high and diversified cultures. Consequently, it would be quite unreason-
able to compel these peoples to abandon their philosophies
and to insist that they embrace a Platonic or Aristotelian
philosophic interpretation of the teaching of Jesus, who
did not himself use Aristotle or Plato in his teaching but
rather a common-sense philosophy.

THE BIBLE, THE PHILOSOPHIES, AND UNIFICATION PHILOSOPHY

The task before us, then, is to test the consistency
of Unification philosophy as it applies Oriental philosophies to the teaching of the Bible. This is a kind of new
missionary work among Indians, Chinese, and in the Orient
in general. And, as we compare philosophies, perhaps we
can improve them in the light of the Bible and reconcile
Oriental philosophies with the Bible. Perhaps we can use
Unification philosophy as we have learned to use Aristotelian philosophy--in the service of providing a better
explanation of the Bible. There have been other thinkers
before us, especially in India, who accepted Indian philosophies and attempted to modify them in order not to distort the Bible but to explain it clearly. I therefore co

clude that the application of Oriental philosophy to the
Bible, which permeates both the *Divine Principle* and
Unification Thought, is a method which both is highly wel-
come and defines our present task.

At the same time, it seems to me that we shall also
need to modify certain aspects of Unification philosophy,
just as we adjust Oriental philosophy, so as not to run
into contradiction. Particularly the areas concerning
creation, Trinity and the person of Jesus require careful
comparison among the philosophies and close scrutiny from
the biblical perspective.

CREATION

The first contradiction to be resolved relates to the
Unification philosophy of matter. Unification philosophy
seems to teach that because creatures are matter, matter
must therefore exist in God's eternal hyung-sang. This
does not, I hold, necessarily follow. I could agree that
matter might potentially pre-exist in some way in God in
order for God then to be able to create matter outside
Himself. Unification philosophy does not then conclude,
however, that God must be a stone in order to create a
stone. Rather, it reasons that God contains the stone in
an eminent and much superior way to the way in which the
stone actually exists. Because God is the infinitely perfect, completely powerful being, God has the power to
touch the very essence of being as such. God has the power
to create matter itself and the things composed of matter.
This God does simply by His will, by His decision that such
and such "be so!" No one else and no other thing can

create; only infinite being has the power of creating.
Creatures can change existing matter into different forms
of matter, but they cannot produce something out of nothing.

Moreover, God's creation is not God's emanation. This
point is not very clear in the Unification sources. In
the Unification books, it seems that creatures are a kind
of emanation from God and that the universal prime energy
is material and enters into creatures.[19] If, however, we
interpret the Unification sources in this way, we would
be forced to a conclusion of pantheism or panentheism,
which is not the philosophic intention either of the books
or of their ultimate author, Rev. Sun Myung Moon. We must,
therefore, alleviate their unclearness by interpreting them
in another way. If we accept the idea that matter is in
God, we then must conclude that matter enters into the
being of God. In this way, all things--both God and crea-
tures--become the same, i.e., somehow material. This conclusion is, however, specifically rejected by both Unification books in that they teach the essential identity of
God's mind or sung-sang and God's outer hyung-sang or universal prime energy and undetermined matter.[20] If they
were not essentially identical, that is, of the same nature
the inner sung-sang could not sustain give-and-take action
with the external hyung-sang. All these features of God's
nature are of the same divine essence in their inmost
foundation. Creatures, however, are of a different nature
and essence. The difference, then between God and creatures is God's decisive act of creation. Whereas God by
His will decided to create creation, God Himself was not
willed into being. This distinction solves the problem.

TRINITY

The problem of the Trinity within Christianity is perennial.[21] In the last analysis, the Trinity is a mystery;[22] consequently, we do not hope to penetrate to the core of the divine life with our limited intellect. Instead, we accept what Christ told us; but, to understand and explain in rational terms what He said is not easy.[23]

The traditional explanation of the Blessed Trinity within Christianity has been more uniformly and consistently explained by Catholic theologians than by Protestants, since Protestants differ among themselves considerably in this matter. The Catholic Church intends, with the Thomistic-Aristotelian scholastic interpretation of the Trinity, to give a deeper understanding and justification of the concept through philosophy than the ordinary, average person is capable of expressing through a simple statement of faith. The Church therefore teaches that this philosophy does help us in understanding Jesus' common-sense teaching about God.

Though there have been differences in Christian teaching about the Trinity, the one thread that runs unbroken throughout all the centuries is faithfulness to the teachings of Jesus. In a few words, Jesus taught this about God: that God is triune or a trinity. This means that God, who is a single, divine, perfect, and infinite nature can, nevertheless, be distinguished to be three persons. By "person," we understand what Boethius (sixth century A.D.) taught: "an individual substance of rational being (nature)." A person is a being that can reason, and is completely individual and separate from other such ra-

tional beings, so that two such beings do not become confused with one another or mix and mingle together. This
definition is most important for our understanding of
Jesus' teaching about the Trinity.

How, then, do we understand God to be three persons?
First, let me say what God is not. God is not a being wit
three heads. God is a spirit, not a body; and although
matter may be eminent within God, God has not matter. Because God has no matter, God is not extended in space, nor
does God exist by a juxtaposition of parts. God not only
does not have three heads, He does not have even one head.
God is spirit and therefore simple; God is not a quantita-
tive but rather a qualitative being.

God, who is spirit, does, however, exist in three way
as Father, Son, and Holy Spirit. But why do we speak of
"Father" and "Son"? God forms a concept or an image of Hi
self; this concept is thus God's word about Himself. Because the Word is the image from God which God had of Himself, we say that God the Father has a Son (Word, Image,
Concept) of God, since sons come from fathers and sons are
like their fathers. This is the explanation given by
St. John in his Gospel. Furthermore, since the Concept of
God is of Himself, the Image of God has to be perfectly
like God so as to be God Himself. Because God is infinite
when God conceives Himself, understands who He Himself is,
this understanding or concept of Himself has to be equal
to Himself, and therefore equal to His infinite entity.
If the Logos were not equal to the mind that conceived it,
then God would not be understanding Himself, since by a
concept which is not Himself He could not penetrate His
own infinity. He can grasp His own infinity only by under

standing Himself completely; consequently, His concept of
Image or Logos of Himself has to be as infinite as He is
Himself. The Logos of God is therefore as infinite as God;
for, the Son is like the Father.

But what is the difference between the Father and the
Son? Since they have the same divine nature, there can be
no essential difference between them. The difference between them must therefore be a personal difference, the
difference of personal opposition. In the language of Unification philosophy, the Father is the subject and the Son
or Logos is the object; as was said above, God the subject
begets His Son the object by His intellect. But why are
they two persons? Because the Father and the Son are both
rational beings who can be distinguished from each other,
as we have just done. Furthermore, in the language of Unification philosophy, God is persons because humanity is
persons.[24] God has to possess the perfections of humanity
in an eminent way, and this eminent way is God's way of
being persons. God, who is infinite intellect, thus conceives of Himself in an infinite way. This infinite picture of Himself is His Logos or Son, equal to His Father
in infinite perfection. God is, therefore, three infinite
persons.

But why do we say "three"? If we have a loving and
infinite Father and a loving and infinite Son, they must
love one another infinitely. It is impossible for God not
to love Himself. Since God is infinitely perfect and good,
it would be a contradiction in terms for God not to love
infinitely the goodness which He Himself is. Therefore,
the Father loves the Son infinitely; and the infinite object or product of their mutual love is Holy Spirit. Uni-

fication philosophy thus rightly speaks of Holy Spirit as the result of the give-and-take action between the Father, who is Infinite Subject, and the Son, who is Infinite Object.

The Trinity is conceived of in the *Divine Principle* according to the structure of family life. In other words, we can say that humanity is an image of God. The human person is an individual possessing intellect, will, and love (emotion, affection). God also possesses intellect, will, and love. The human person is formed for procreation, for creativity, for multiplication. God also exists to create, to diversify His creatures and to unify them. Human individuals naturally form families in which there is, according to the created nature of humanity, a father, a mother, and a child. God also, within the bosom of the Trinity, exists as the Father who knows Himself and who loves Himself through this knowledge of Himself. God the Father thus produces God the Son through knowledge, and together they both produce God the Holy Spirit through love. Just as we can speak of the inner-relatedness of persons within the family life, so we can also speak of the inner trinitarian relationship within the divine life.

JESUS

The Trinity is one of the mysteries of our faith; yet we try to believe it without falling into contradictions, since we are rational beings. Nevertheless, no matter how hard we try to bring the essence and entity of God closer to us, to understand it somehow, still God surpasses our capability. Therefore, in faith, we look for the causes

of and reasons for our faith. The reasons for belief are
given us in Jesus' teaching, his miracles, his righteous
life, and in his cross and resurrection.

In two particulars--Jesus as the God-man and the resurrection of Jesus--something more needs to be said with
reference to Unification philosophy.

Traditional Christian teaching about the person of
Jesus has been that Jesus as the incarnate Logos of the
Father is the second person of the Trinity. Jesus therefore has a double nature: both divine Logos and created
humanness. As a human, Jesus was like we are, except that
he did not sin and was more perfectly what we are. He
prayed, he became hungry, he died on the cross. As a man,
he rose from the dead. He was fully human in every way,
possessing a body, a soul, the full complement of human
nature. At the same time, this human nature was in a
special way connected to the Logos, the Son of God. The
Logos united himself with the human nature of Jesus and
therefore participated in Jesus' human life. This is a
mystery; we accept it as a fact on the basis of the biblical teachings.

Christians confess that Jesus the man was God. But
what do we mean by this confession? Jesus was and is a
man. If we say that he is also God, we say this only because his human nature was assumed by God the Son of God,
so that the single human person was also unified with the
Logos of God. When we say that Jesus is a divine person,
we say this because divinity is higher than humanity; the
Logos was one with Jesus, and therefore Jesus was divine.
But we do not say this in the sense that Jesus' human nature became divine. Humanity did not become divinity.

Humanity is always human and remains human; Jesus was and
and remained a man; he still remains a man, though united
with the Logos of God. Man will never be changing into
God. This mystery of Jesus' connection with God can be
explained by saying there is more of God in Jesus than in
us. Jesus' connection with God was necessary, if the cros
was to be valuable for the human race.

Unification philosophy explains that Jesus was a man
who was united to God's Logos. The *Divine Principle*
teaches both that "Jesus was not God," and that "Jesus was
God in flesh." By the first statement, the *Divine Principle* intends to teach that Jesus is not God the Father;
by the second statement, it intends to teach that God's
Logos--God's purpose, plan, intention, and perfect image--
came to be unified with the soul and body of the man Jesus
It further teaches that Adam, the first human being, could
also have realized this perfect union with God, if he had
not sinned. But since Adam and Eve did sin, human perfection was reserved for a Second Adam. The *Divine Principle* teaches that Jesus is this perfect, Second Adam who,
attaining the perfection of humanity which God intended fo
Adam, fulfilled God's eternal intention and plan; thus
Jesus was the perfected Logos of God on earth in human
flesh.

Unification philosophy thus teaches an understanding
of Jesus as God's Logos incarnate quite similar to traditional Christian doctrine. The question of Jesus' person
has presented probably more questions than any other problem in Christian thought, due to the traditional understanding of Him as both divinity and humanity. It seems
that the sources of Unification philosophy solve these pro

blems quite satisfactorily. The sources state both truths
--that Jesus is God and that Jesus is human--but do not
enter into philosophical speculations in an attempt to reconcile those seemingly contradictory possibilities. By
maintaining both sides of this Christian teaching, Unification philosophy upholds the traditional value ascribed
to the merits of Jesus' cross, a divine sacrifice with
value for humanity and a human sacrifice with merit before God.

Concerning the other particular, the resurrection of
Jesus, Unification philosophy teaches that the man Jesus,
born naturally mortal like all other humans, would naturally have died a physical death. Just as naturally, Jesus'
spirit-man would naturally migrate to the world of spirits
after his physical death. That Jesus was "raised" and
"ascended" to the spirit world, therefore, comes as no
surprise, since this is the natural course for all human
spirits. Jesus' resurrection, according to the Unification sources, is, then, not the resuscitation of his physical body. Indeed, the sources are not clear on the fate
of Jesus' physical frame. His resurrection is, rather, a
cosmic and historical process of restoring the whole of
mankind to God through a spiritual process of indemnifying
fallen men and women and helping them to indemnify themselves from their disorientation due to sin. In this process of spiritual resurrection,[25] Jesus is greatly aided
by the cooperation of the *communio sanctorum*--the heavens
of angels and the spirits of perfected men and women--who,
with Jesus in his "second coming," return to earth at the
time of the Lord of the Second Advent, a vast heavenly host,
to "raise" the "Body" of Christ from spiritual death and

establish the Kingdom of Heaven on earth. We can state
the Unification philosophy of human salvation in this way:
Jesus accomplished the spiritual salvation of our souls in
his sacrificial ransom on the cross; physical salvation--
political, economic, and social salvation-- is to be accomplished through the historical process of resurrection.[26]
Thus we see that, although a traditional Christian believer
might want to raise some question about the "bodily resurrection" of Jesus, still the net effect of Unification
teaching on the resurrection is essentially compatible
with traditional Christian eschatology. For Roman Catholic
and Orthodox believers, this reappropriation of the *communio sanctorum* in the thinking and experience of a more
Protestant-type philosophy seems most welcome.

CONCLUSION: ACCEPTABILITY OF UNIFICATION PHILOSOPHY

     We have seen that Unification philosophy safeguards
the basic concepts of God common to the Christian traditions and strongly emphasizes some of them. The terminology used to elucidate these concepts by the Unification
sources is, however, new, striking, and sometimes dubious
to the Western reader. The reason for this lies in the
education in Western philosophy, in Platonic and Aristotelian concepts, of the Western reader, to whom Oriental
concepts and other ways of philosophizing are foreign.
Yet, when we clarify the terms, we see that the meaning of
the terms in Unification philosophy does not contradict in
any serious way the Western philosophical tradition. Further, it seems that Unification philosophy can be reconciled with biblical teachings.

For example, we have observed that Unification philosophy teaches about the same God in which the Christian
faith believes, and speaks of that God in basic concepts
maintained by the major branches of Christianity. God's
uniqueness, infinity, personality, simplicity, eternity,
omnipotence, omnipresence, omniscience are some of those
important concepts upheld by Unification philosophy in
common with the Christian philosophic tradition.[27] Concerning God Himself, Unification philosophy insists that
God is above time and space and, consequently, beyond our
concepts of Him. Unification philosophy thus stresses the
value of our "negative knowledge" of God as superior to
our "positive knowledge." This position, known to the
Christian tradition as "negative theology," maintains that
God *melius scitur nesciendo*: our confession that we do
not know God is closer to the truth than our affirmative
statements about God. This is because God is infinite and
we are finite; infinity remains infinitely distant from
any finitude; thus God remains infinitely distant from our
finite concepts of God. This position was defended by
Fathers of the Church[28] both ancient and modern, from
St. Basil and Gregory of Nyssa to Karl Barth. This position is essentially basic to the thought of those who de-
fend positive theology as well, when they affirm that we
form proper concepts of God but must nevertheless conceive
of God analogically.[29] Even defenders of positive theology agree to the strictly mysterious character of God's
intimate life in the Blessed Trinity[30] and the Incarnation.[31]

Further, traditional Christianity also accepts the
position that our concepts of God, even if they are positively applicable to Him, are still derived from observing

creatures, i.e., from the visible world around us. When
these concepts are applied to God, they must be stripped
of the imperfections they contain as finite creatures so
that they may be applied to God in terms of their infinitely increased perfections. Our concepts of God, therefore, may be applicable (proper to Him), but they are
formed not by deriving them from God Himself (*propter ex
propriis*), but rather from visible, common objects which
He has created (*propter ex communibus*).

   This position is very close to the Unification view
since it asserts that our concepts about God must be formed
from things which we experience. Yet the concepts formed
in this way cannot be applied to God literally, but rather
in a broad, more general sense; for He is infinite, but
the concepts are finite. The correctness of this method
is supported by the biblical usage in both Testaments,
where all kinds of perfections observable in the visible
world of creatures are ascribed to God. The Bible uses
ordinary language to describe God's infinity, with the understanding that He is not comprehended by any of the observable perfections ascribable to Him. The Unificationist
way of speaking about God is therefore highly acceptable
to Christianity. Any Unificationist novelty in speaking
of God should therefore be judged by us as an attempt, not
to distort the image of God as presented in the Bible, but
to proceed along the traditional line of approach to God
in order to make a contribution to our knowledge of Him.

   By contrast, however, the concept of God as pure act
and immutable formed on the Aristotelian basis is not itself lacking in serious problems. How does one reconcile
the strong Biblical emphasis on God's compassion, love,
and foreknowledge with an immutable Unmoved Mover?[32]

We Western philosophers must admit to certain logical
inconsistencies in our concepts of God, whom we philosophically describe as pure act and immutable, yet whom we as
Christians confess to be our saviour, the lover of mankind,
and one who suffers with us. The Unificationist view of
God does not present us with more problems than does the
Aristotelian view of God; and the value of Unification
philosophy lies in the effort to make God more intelligible and believable to contemporary men and women of the
East as well as of the West. Similarly, we have seen that
the specific descriptions of God according to Unification
philosophy concur with numerous counterparts in traditional
Christian thought. We reached the same conclusion concerning Unification and traditional Christian teaching
about Jesus. But just as the interpretations of the several theological and philosophical notions about God and
Jesus vary from one branch of Christendom to another, so
the Unification interpretation represents a new interpretation of the basic concepts. We saw above that Unification philosophy accepts the traditonal idea of the Trinity
without expanding upon it in detail.[33] We also could see
the possibility of reconciliation of the Unification philosophy of God with the Roman Catholic or another orthodox
position. Similarly, the basic truths of the Christian
faith are repeated and reinterpreted in Unification philosophy; in addition to this, however, it must be conceded
that a number of controversial points may be raised concerning the Unificationist interpretation of Jesus' second
coming, the fulfillment of His mission, the institution of
His Church and the sacraments. These difficult issues
have, however, been discussed throughout the centuries
among the Christians without reaching a final solution

acceptable to all, or, perhaps, even most.[34]

    Finally, we have also observed a special use of philo-
sophy in the Unification sources--a methodological point
which is possibly more important than any other single
factor. There are some influences of Christian and Aristotelian scholasticism in Unification philosophy (God is
called the "first cause" in both systems, and God's attributes are described alike in both). But the basic philosophical perspective of Unificationist thinking is not
only the Western philosophy, to which we have all become
accustomed, but also a blend of Oriental and common-sense
philosophy.

    The Oriental influence directly touches our metaphy-
sical explanation of God's being. The concepts of sung-
sang and hyung-sang are basic to this explanation. They
are not Aristotelian terms; rather, they are concepts
close to the yin and yang of Confucianism. Unification
philosophy is thus pervaded by notions of the inwardness
and outwardness of things and of God. In Unification
philosophy we have an understanding of the inner content
of things which is of an intellectual and spiritual natu
and the external form of things which is the universal
prime energy and matter. The notions may not, however, b
applied too strictly, since the differences among individual beings require different applications. It seems t
me that what is said, quite simply, is that everything ha
both its inner content and its external form. Whatever
the essence of a thing may be, that thing exists in terms
of inner content and outer form.

    Thus sung-sang and hyung-sang can, quite logically,
be applied to all beings of whatever essence, whether

material, spiritual, humans or angels, and even to God.
Even though these all-important terms of Unification philosophy are not Aristotelian, they seem to be close to the
Aristotelian concepts of substance and accidence. Aristotelian or not, the language is intelligible and illumi-
nating; properly understood, the terms enlighten our understanding of the biblical concepts of God; rightly interpreted, these notions are acceptable to a thinker in the
Christian tradition.

The common-sense philosophical approach of Unification
philosophy also directly touches our understanding of God:
we are told to trust our ordinary, every-day sense of
reality and think about God as we conceive the visible
things of creation. Unification philosophy thus proposes
not an esoteric or abstract philosophical explanation of
God, but rather one much closer to the content of the Bible
and Jesus' teaching--a common-sense understanding of God
for the average man. Jesus taught the masses of people,
used their language and adapted their ideas, accommodated
himself to their understanding, and frequently told simple
little stories to communicate inspired truths. I observe
a similarity of approach between Jesus and Unification
teaching about God. If Unification philosophy uses terms
which seem less familiar to Western thinkers, this is not
because the terms in themselves are esoteric; they are
quite common in the Orient and can be easily understood by
anyone who simply thinks them through.

I therefore conclude on the basis of a comparison of
Unification philosophy and the Christian tradition that
they do not basically differ in their concept of God.
There are differences between the two systems, but they

are secondary and not essential. I agree that certain
tenets, cherished by Christianity, are either inadequately
explained by Unification philosophy (the Trinity) or given
a new interpretation (the role of Jesus). The reason for
these differences is quite obvious when one considers the
degree of disagreement which exists among the variety of
acknowledged Christians on these same issues. This ener-
getic new Unification Movement proposes, however, to unify
divided Christians and to invigorate the Christian tradition. Perhaps it will be as successful at this as it has
been at energizing and invigorating Western philosophy by
its importation of Oriental philosophical concepts.

[1] *Divine Principle,* 2nd ed. (Washington, D.C., 1973).
Hereafter abbreviated *D.P. Unification Thought,* (New York,
1975). Hereafter abbreviated *U.T.*

[2] *D.P.,* pp. 27, 74; *U.T.,* pp. 16, 26-27.

[3] *D.P.,* pp. 20, 40-42, 52, 205-217; *U.T.,* pp. 16-17, 19.

[4] *D.P.,* pp. 205, 213, 215, 217; *U.T.,* p. 15.

[5] *D.P.,* pp. 208-210, see also 211-215; *U.T.,* pp. 42,
162, see also 15, 25.

[6] *D.P.,* pp. 214-216.

[7] *Ibid.,* pp. 140-152.

[8] *Ibid.,* pp. 165-191, 233, 358, 360, 362.

[9] *Ibid.,* pp. 221-270.

[10] *D.P.,* p. 29; *U.T.,* pp. 92-112. See also *International
Conference on the Unity of the Sciences,* 4 vols. (New York,
1974-1977).

[11] Vergilius Ferm, ed., *Living Schools of Religion,*
(Ames, Iowa, 1958) pp. 97ff. See also *D.P.,* pp. 26-27.

[12] *U.T.,* pp. 17-30.

[13] Ferm, *op. cit.,* p. 99.

[14] *U.T.,* pp. 11-12.

[15] *Ibid.*

[16] *D.P.,* pp. 213-218; see above note 4.

[17] *D.P.*, pp. 210-216.

[18] *Ibid.*, pp. 62-63, 87-88, see also 58-61.

[19] See above, 3, a, aa; see below, note 20.

[20] *U.T.*, pp. 23-24; *D.P.*, pp. 31-32.

[21] *D.P.*, pp. 205, 213.

[22] *D.T.C.*, "Trinité," *Dictionnaire de théologie catho-lique*, 15 vols. (Paris, 1909-1967) xv, col. 1797f.; here-after abbreviated *D.T.C.*

[23] *Ibid.*

[24] *D.P.*, p. 27; *U.T.*, p. 11.

[25] *D.P.*, p. 172.

[26] *D.P.*, pp. 48, 100-102.

[27] See above, note 4.

[28] M.J. Rouet de Journel, *Enchiridion Patristicum*, (Friburg i.B., 1937), Minucius Felix, 270; Origen, 450; Cyprian, 603; Hilary, 860-861; Gregory of Elvira, 900; Basil the Great, 923, 931; Gregory Naziamzen, 984, 1041-1042; Didymus of Alexandria, 1075; John Chrysostem, 1125, 1161, 1209; Ambrose, 1266; Augustine, 1505; Theodoret, 216 John Damascus, 2338.

[29] See my *Karl Barth on God,*(New York, 1952) p. 210.

[30] See note 21.

[31] *D.T.C.*, VII, col. 1458f.: see also IV, col. 1606ff.

[32] Jurgen Moltmann, *The Crucified God,* (New York, 1974).

33 See above, note 4.

34 Leo Rosten, ed., *Religion in America,* (New York,
1963) pp. 30, 72, 101, 114, 133, 162, 173, 189, 203, 227,
247, 265 ; see above, note 4, 7, 11.

HEURISTIC INQUIRIES

UNIFICATION ESCHATOLOGY AND AMERICAN MILLENNIAL TRADITIONS: CONTINUITIES AND DISCONTINUITIES

M. DARROL BRYANT

> "'Tis not unlikely that this work of
> God's Spirit, that is so extraordinary
> and wonderful, is the dawning, or at
> least a prelude, of that glorious work
> of God, so often foretold in Scripture,
> which in the progress and issue of it,
> *shall renew the world of mankind.* If
> we consider how long since the things
> foretold, as what should precede this
> great event, have been accomplished;
> and how long this event has been expected
> by the church of God, and thought to be
> nigh by the most eminent men of God in
> the Church; and withal consider what the
> state of things now is, and has for con-
> siderable time been, in the church of God
> and world of mankind, we can't reason-
> ably think otherwise, than that the be-
> ginning of this great work of God must
> be near. And there are many things that
> make it probable that this work will
> begin in America."[1]

These, of course, are the words of America's most distinguished theologian, Jonathan Edwards. They were
penned during the time of the Great Awakening. For
many, this is a part of the Edwards' corpus that we

An earlier version of this paper was presented at a
Conference on the Unification Church in Boston in May,
1977.

would do well to ignore, or at least to pass over
in discreet silence. However, the line of scholarship that runs from H. Richard Niebuhr and Perry Miller
to Alan Heimert has insisted upon the centrality of
Edwards' millennialism to the understanding of Edwards.[2]
Indeed, the argument is not simply that millennialism
is central to Edwards, but that millennialism is the
cradle out of which the American tradition is born.
Although I have reservations about certain aspects
of that scholarly tradition, I do find the larger
outlines of the position convincing.

There are two morals which I draw from this line
of scholarship in relation to the present hullabaloo
concerning the Unification movement and the eschatology
of the *Divine Principle*.[3] First, it strikes me as
virtually axiomatic that a religious movement which
speaks in an eschatological idiom would find great
resonance within the American context--that it would
strike resonant chords in the hearts of America's
offspring. Second, it strikes me as at least ironic,
if not downright deceitful, to suggest, as some have,
that there is something fundamentally "UnAmerican"
about the Moon movement. What could be more fundamentally consistent with the American tradition than a
millennialist movement?

Perhaps, however, these comments come too early
and are too provocative. At the moment, they will
have to stand as an indication of the context out of
which I approach the eschatology of the Unification
movement. In order to further specify that context,
two further comments are in order: one is autobiographical, the other is intellectual.

First, the autobiographical comment. I approach
Unification eschatology as one who was nourished by
and suffered the secular (perhaps better, the civil
religious) millennialism of the 1960's. Living in
and through that period of millennialism, I am deeply
aware that one need only sound the millennial trumpet
in America and many will respond to its clarion call.
An awareness of the appeal of millennialism, whether
in secular or religious dress, resides in this breast.
Moreover, such an awareness is, in the broader contours of American history, not idiosyncratic, but
characteristic of the American tradition from Winthrop's
"City Set Upon A Hill," through the "Dawning of the
New Jerusalem" down to King's "I've Got a Dream" and
even Cox's "Secular City."

This leads, then, to my second prefatory comment,
namely, that my approach to Unification eschatology
is shaped by my study of the Great Awakening in particular and the millenial tradition in America in general. Out of such study, instructed by such diverse
figures as George Bancroft, the 19th century historian,
H. Richard Niebuhr, Perry Miller and, most recently,
Alan Heimert, I have come to see that a constituting
element of the American tradition is its millennialism. Although that is an element which appears now
in one form, now in another, it is always near at hand,
always pulsating in the American psyche. From such
study, I find it hard, even impossible, to comprehend
the American tradition apart from the millennialist
impulse. Millennialism, as this line of scholarship
makes clear, is the matrix out of which America

learned to walk and to make its way in the world.

As I say this I am aware of the curious identification, (some might say confusion) that I am making
between America and the Kingdom of God. That identification needs clarification. The impact of millennialism in the American tradition is not to be
found primarily in ecclesiastical changes, but in the
socio-political order. I am reminded here of the comment by a student of early Christianity that the
early Christian community longed for the Kingdom of
God and got, instead, the Church. The same is true
in the American tradition: instead of the Kingdom
of God on Earth, we got America. This, it seems to
me, is the conslusion one must draw from the line of
scholarship I have indicated above. It is the conclusion present in the subtitle of Alan Heimert's
work on *Religion and the American Mind,* namely, *From
the Great Awakening to the Revolution.*

Against this background, then, I want to make
some comments about Unification eschatology and its
continuities and discontinuities with the millennial
tradition in America.

First, I want to state briefly the main outlines
of Unification eschatology as I understand it. In
these comments I am restricting myself to the text
of the *Divine Principle.* The text runs to 535 pages.
After an introduction, a chapter on the Principle of
Creation and one on the Fall of Man, the rest of the
text focuses on *The Consumation of Human History.* The
problem has been set by the Fall of Man, and the whole
of human history is a history in which God is involved
attempting to restore humanity to its original purpose.

According to the *Divine Principle*, the "purpose of
Creation is to establish the Kingdom of Heaven on
earth."[4] This purpose was frustrated by the fall of
man, in the period of growth. Since to leave man in
this fallen situation would be to "nullify the principle of creation,"[5] the whole of "human history is
the period of the providence through which God intends to save fallen men and have them restore the original world of goodness."[6] Four-fifths of the *Divine
Principle,* then, is devoted to an account of how God is
achieving the restoration of humankind.

In the account of human history as a process of
restoration, the whole of biblical history is reviewed
as well as the history of the Christian church and the
Western world. Unlike Augustine's *City of God,* where
the history of salvation is confined to biblical
history and human history must await the Last Judgment for the unraveling of the City of God from the
City of Man, and unlike Edwards' *History of the Work
of Redemption* which includes both biblical history and
ecclesiastical history in the history of salvation,
but leaves out human history, the *Divine Principle*
includes all three--biblical history, ecclesiastical
history, and secular history in its history of restoration. Thus, in the *Divine Principle* the whole
human drama in all its aspects, is made transparent
to the divine intention. This tracing of the "red
thread" of divine intention through the whole human
drama is not arbitrary and whimsical. Rather, it is
grounded in a complex set of theological principles.

When the *Divine Principle* turns to history it

does so by focusing on four elements: the history
of religion, the history of religion and science,
the history of struggle in human societies, and the
Bible.[7] It is the latter, the Bible, interpreted in
the light of the *Divine Principle,* that provides the
spectacles through which the history of humankind
can be rightly viewed. The Bible, as understood by
the *Divine Principle,* makes clear that the fundamental
human quest is the quest for restoration, for "the
Garden of Eden with the Tree of Life in the Center."[8]
It is the Bible, then, which provides the "archetypes"
and "typologies" through which the inner thread of
history can be grasped. (This, I might say, seems
characteristic of such kinds of literature.) As
with Augustine, it is the Cain/Abel typology which
is central although for Augustine it points to a state
of affairs that persists throughout human history
whereas for Unification thought it is this conflict,
that it is now possible to overcome. This typology
points to the fundamental conflict, namely, God-
centered versus Satan-centered tendencies in the
human breast, in human groups and communities, and
in the world. The *Divine Principle* deftly moves through
the whole of human history in a way that comes to focus
on the present as the "Last Days." Interestingly,
the Last Days are not understood in an apocalytic,
or chiliastic, way. Rather, the Last Days are understood in a cultural sense as a period of decisive transition in the history of restoration. There have been
"Last Days" prior to the present: Noah's days and
Jesus' days. Now, the present world finds itself in
an archetypically identical position such that "the

sinful world under Satanic dominion will be transformed into the world of good sovereignty."[9]

The present situation is described in the *Divine
Principle* as the "Day of the Lord's Second Advent."
Rather than understanding the Second Coming in terms
of the Last Judgment, or in terms of some miraculous
transformation of the earth, the *Divine Principle*
understands the Second Advent in relation to the fulfillment of the "Third Blessing," namely, that humankind may exercise dominion over the world. Now is
the time when the Kingdom of God may be established
on earth. The Lord of the Second Advent completes
the spiritual restoration affected by Jesus with a
physical restoration which will manifest itself through
God-centered individuals, families and nations.

Curiously enough, the whole eschatological drama
has a very definite geography, in addition to the
definite time-table indicated above. The non-Communist
world, the representative of Able-type democracy,
is of course of central importance since it is only
on the basis of "God-centered" nations that the Kingdom
of God on earth can be built. In this eschatological
drama, both America and Korea play a central role.
Korea is the nation in which the Lord of the Second
Advent will come, and America is the nation which will
facilitate the spread of the Message of the Lord of
the Second Advent. Typologically, Korea is the Third
Israel, while America is in a situation comparable
to the Roman Empire at the time of Jesus.

The outcome of the eschatological drama unfolding
in our midst, and through our agency, will be a unified

world. The long-standing, but from the point of view
of Unification thought, mistaken, conflict of religion
and science will come to an end. The longstanding
conflict of Cain and Abel type nations will be resolved through the creation of God-centered nations.
The conflict between capitalism and communism will
be overcome through a "socialistic society centering
on God."[10] The division of Christianity into the
multitude of denominations will be overcome, and the
world's religions will be reconciled. The litany
continues.

       Such, it seems to me, is the eschatology of the
Divine Principle. Much of what appears in the *Divine
Principle* is familiar to those aquainted with the millennial traditions of America. Several of those
continuities can be stated in point form,

       First: Unification eschatology, like the es-
chatology of the Great Awakening, is not apocalyptic.
Rather than heralding the "end of the world" in a
literal sense, Unification eschatology, like the eschatology of the Great Awakening, heralds the transformation of humankind--the dawning of a new era in the
history of the race. Jonathan Edwards' belief that
the dawning of the millennium "shall renew the world
of mankind" is equivalent to the *Divine Principle's*
belief that humankind will now come into it's own and
exercise dominion over the creation.

       Second: Unification eschatology, like the es-
chatology of the Great Awakening, is centered on the
transformation of the socio-political order. Alan
Heimert, for example, has written that "the revival

and evangelical impulse pressed to the goal of a more
beautiful social order."[11] Heimert consequently
argued that the Awakening impulse is not discontinuous
with the American Revolution, but really achieves
its fulfillment in the Republic. Similarly, Unification eschatology is very much centered on the transformation of the socio-political order as the sphere
proper to the kingdom of God.

Third: Unification eschatology, like the eschatology of the Great Awakening, sees the achievement of Christian unity as integral to the achievement
of the millennium. The proper title for the Unification
Movement is "The Holy Spirit Association for the Unification of World Christianity." The underlying idea
in basic continuity with the proposal for Union of
Prayer which grew out of the Great Awakening of the
1740's. Only on the basis of such religious unity
could the millennial order be sustained.

Four: Unification eschatology, like the eschatology of the Great Awakening, does not see any basic
conflict between learning/science and religion. In
Edwards' catalogue of the new age, the blessing of
science ranked high. Similarly, Unification eschatology is not anti-science, nor, curiously, anti-intel-
lectual.

Five: Unification eschatology, like the eschatology of the Great Awakening, is activist. Heimert
wrote that "likeness to God became for evangelical
America a state not of being, but of doing."[12] Likewise, Unification eschatology is adamant about the
role of the true believers in fulfilling their res-
ponsibilities in the achievement of the Kingdom of

God.

The list could go on. But I trust that this will suffice to make my point about fundamental continuities between the Great Awakening and the eschatology of the *Divine Principle*. For me, reading the *Divine Principle* was an encounter with a familiar set of theological ideas, typologies and tempers. However, I was struck at the same time by some fundamental discontinuities. Again, I am simply going to indicate those in point form.

First: Unification eschatology, unlike the eschatology of the Great Awakening, gives a central place to the family in their eschatological vision. Although the consequences of the millennialism of the Great Awakening were profoundly social, the central image for entry into the blessed community was the individual encounter with God. In Unification eschatology, the emphasis is on the family as the context for the creation of a new humanity. One of the problems of the Great Awakening was the unevenness of "New Birth." The ingenious solution in Unification eschatology is the notion of "sinless children." In other words, Unification eschatology believes in a fundamental restoration of human nature that will be effected biologically and nourished in the institution of the family. Through a relationship with the Lord of the Second Advent, the True Parents of Humankind, human nature will be restored to its original state. Hence, Unification eschatology holds a doctrine of physical restoration that overcomes the "waiting upon the Holy Spirit" that plagued the millennialism of the Great Awakening. (Parenthetically,

one could note similarities here with an indigenous
American religion: Mormonism).

Second: Unification eschatology, unlike the
Great Awakening which is post-millennialist, introduces a new category in the "Lord of the Second Advent." This figure, necessary to the accomplishment
of the New Order, is identified "archetypically"
with Jesus, but not personally. In other words, the
Lord of the Second Advent is necessary to the establishment of the Kingdom of God on Earth, but his relationship to "Jesus" is ambiguous. For the Great Awakening,
the millennium would be established prior to Jesus'
return, but the Messianic role of "Jesus" is unquali-
fied.

Third: Unification eschatology, unlike that
of the Great Awakening, offers a geography in which
Korea is the critical nation. For the Great Awakening,
this role tended to fall on the New World. However,
Unification thought comes close to Great Awakening
eschatology in that it sees America as the forerunner
of the unified world. Thus, there is a strange continuity between Unification eschatology and Alan Heimert's interpretation of the Great Awakening as
achieving its fulfillment in the creation of America.

When viewed in relation to the millennial traditions of America, the eschatology of the *Divine
Principle* appears as the latest in a series of eschatological visions of the future we should both
work and hope for. The eschatology of the *Divine
Principle* is centered on the vision of *unification,*
a vision which is at all times powerful, but perhaps

even more so in our present situation. Rather than
regarding the eschatology of the Unification movement
with suspicion and hostility we would do well to
examine it in relation to the visions of the future
that have inspired other groups within America in the
past. Viewed in that light, the eschatology is certainly no worse than others and may even be in some
respects more desirable. Surely, for example, the
internationalism, the unification of the peoples and
cultures of the world, that is so deeply imbedded in
the eschatology of the *Divine Principle* and embodied in
the community that has emerged around Rev. Moon has
much to recommend it. Indeed, such elements could
serve to correct the implicit provincialism of the
dominant eschatologies of America.

Moreover, the Christian traditions would do well
to accept the challenge posed by the eschatology of
the *Divine Principle*. What is the future that we
hope for? Do we still believe that a significant
future awaits us either in this world or the next?
What is the vision which can inspire our vocations
in the world? These questions bear our serious consideration. Consequently, Christian communities
should be wary of dismissing the challenges posed
by the eschatology of the Unification movement. The
doctrine of eschatology within the Christian traditions has yet to achieve either a creedal or dogmatic
definition that would justify outright dismissal of
the eschatology put forth by the Unification movement.
The eschatological vision of the *Divine Principle*
with its universality, its affirmation of a significant
future, its inclusiveness in relation to science and

other religions, its affirmation of the family and its
determination to create a restored world should not
be dismissed or lightly set aside. Rather, it should
at least challenge Christian communities to rethink
their eschatological commitments.

Although the eschatology of the *Divine Principle*
is open to formal critique, that critique must be balanced by an awareness that this eschatological vision
has called into being a commendable community of men
and women around the world and here in America.
Every eschatology must be evaluated in at least two
ways: formally and functionally. An eschatology is
not simply the formal compliment of the doctrine of
creation; it is also the horizon which focuses and
orients the life of the believing community in time.
The Unification community is, in my experience, a
vital, highly energized, theologically open and
focused community. Consequently, it is my conviction
that we are witnessing the emergence of a significant
religious movement which may enrich the whole range
of Christian traditions and, if successful, could
chasten the provincialism of American millennialism
with a needed internationalism.

[1]   Jonathan Edwards, *Some Thoughts...in the Great Awakening,* ed. C.C. Goen, (New Haven, 1972) p. 353.

[2]   See the classic statement by H. Richard Niebuhr, *The Kingdom of God in America,* (New York, 1959), Perry Miller, *Errand Into the Wilderness,* (New York, 1964) and Alan Heimert, *Religion and the American Mind, From the Great Awakening to the Revolution,* (Cambridge, Mass., 1966). See also M.D. Bryant, "America as God's Kingdom," in *Religion and Political Society,* J. Moltmann, et. al., (New York, 1975).

[3]   The *Divine Principle* is the principle text of the Unification movement. All references to the *Divine Principle* 2nd edition, (New York, 1973).

[4]   *Ibid.,* p. 102.

[5]   *Ibid.,* p. 104.

[6]   *Ibid.,* p. 105.

[7]   *Ibid.,* pp. 105-111.

[8]   *Ibid.,* p. 110.

[9]   *Ibid.,* p. 111.

[10]   *Ibid.,* p. 444.

[11]   Heimert, p. 96.

[12]   *Ibid.,* p. 313.

THE HUMANITY OF GOD AND THE DIVINITY OF MAN:
REFLECTIONS ON UNIFICATION'S THEOLOGY OF CREATION

HENRY VANDER GOOT

Before I begin to deal with the subject matter proper of this paper, I would like to offer a few general observations above Unification's Theology of Creation as a
whole. The first is that Unification theology understands
that an adequately theistic system "begins" its theological reflection with the story of Adam and Eve, not with
the story of Jesus. Unification thought tries to be a
genuinely *theological* system, and it realizes that such
an intention can only be fulfilled where the various theological "*loci*" are developed from the prospective glance
of the doctrine of creation. Any other perspective is
necessarily "retrospective," and by that token invariably
anthropocentric.

Furthermore, Unification theology also discerns that
to lend concreteness to the doctrine of sin and subsequently to the doctrine of salvation, creation must be defined in terms of specific structures. This is where all
theological reflection either gets started on an adequate
footing or goes amiss. Not only does Unification theology
affirm the priority of creation, but it also displays con-

This lecture and subsequent discussion are reproduced with permission
from *Exploring Unification Theology*. The discussion took place at a
theological conference convened at the Unification Theological Seminary in Spring, 1977. The participants are identified in the listing
of contributors in this volume, see page 321.

siderable sensitivity to the fact that even the founda-
tional assumption of creation is subject to ideological
distortion.   If vaguely formulated, the theological assumption of creation is as susceptible of being swallowed
up by an alien structure as Christology and eschatology
have been in the contemporary theological discussion.   To
prevent this, Unification theology sees that the theology
of creation must be lent a certain concreteness.   An analysis of cosmic structures is required, and Unification's
notion of the three four-position bases (of the individual,
the family and society) performs this indispensible function.   It is at this level that a specific sense is prepared for Unification's subsequent conception of sin and
restoration.

Finally, to a considerable extent Unification theology, though it recognizes the indispensability of an
analysis of concrete structures, nonetheless has succeeded
in preventing its theology from being swallowed up in an
alien philosophy.   This is indeed unique in the contemporary theological context.   The worthiness of contemporary
theologies is increasingly judged by the measure to which
they can make their concepts concrete without being assimilated to alien philosophical analyses.   These philosophical
analyses prove to be covers for a narrative portrayal of
life which comes into conflict with the theologies to which
those philosophical analyses have been attached.   In the
Protestant and Catholic worlds the search is on for dis-
tinctively "Christian" ontologies.   Unification theology
participates in that search.

Recognizing the crucial relevance of the theology
of creation, I should now like to turn to the topic proper of this paper.   This topic is the relationship of Unification doctrines of creation and restoration.   A rather
cursory perusal of the *Divine Principle* makes manifestly

obvious the fundamentality of the so-called "Restoration
motif" in Unification thought. According to the *Divine
Principle,* redemption is the restoration of the original
creation; it is emphatically not a radically or absolutely new start.

However much this restoration motif might be attractive——especially to Reformed Calvinists——our enthusiasm
must be tempered by a more thorough-going analysis of
what specifically is meant by "restoration." Theologically,   many options are possible within even a restoration-
ist framework. In other words, we might say that the
logical fundamentality of creation in relation to redemption can itself be variously understood.

For example, such widely historically separated and
signally different theologians as Irenaeus and Luther formally concur in asserting the theological priority of creation over redemption. Both Irenaeus and Luther share (at
least formally speaking) the conviction that salvation can
be understood only against the background of God's more
primitive work in creation. Yet the specific meaning of
this principle of the logical originality of God's work in
creation has a different actual meaning in each case. In
fact this is already indicated by the use of two distinct
terms of their common stress on the essentiality of God's
original work: namely "creation" in the case of Irenaeus
and "law" in the case of Luther.

Though Irenaeus and Luther stand together over
against theologians who "begin" their theological reflection with the story of Jesus, Irenaeus and Luther stand
together only in an abstract and formal sense. The specific difference between Irenaeus' conception, on the other hand, and Luther's on the other, must not be neglected.

For Irenaeus the essence of Christianity is best

described in terms of the "duality of creation and recapitulation." However, for Luther this same essence is
understood in terms of the "dialectic of law and gospel."

In the theology of Irenaeus, recapitulation releases
and sets free the uncorrupted life of the original creation. The new is the old, for the goal of salvation is
the restoration and re-establishment of the lost goal of
creation. For Irenaeus, then the form of the relationship
that exists between creation and redemption is one of harmony, unity and continuity. Recapitulation frees humankind *for creation*.

By contrast, in the case of Luther the essential
form of the relation that exists between creation and redemption is conflict. The law-gospel formula stresses
the contrast between its two constituent terms. Thus,
Luther's formula emphasizes the radical uniqueness of the
gospel.

This is not to deny that for Luther law and gospel
are in some sense harmonious. They are, indeed, both activities of the same God. They are two ways in which the
one God rules. Yet, this dimension of the law-gospel relationship is not the point that qualifies it and lends
it its specific sense. The uniqueness of the law-gospel
relationship is that the two terms form an antithesis.
The law-gospel relationship highlights the principle of
dissimilarity. The Word bestows forgiveness, and the law-
gospel formula thus stresses man's freedom from the burden
of guilt more than his actual possession of new life. The
new is opposed to the old, for the old is what is overcome. The gospel frees humankind *from that law*.

My point thus far has been to demonstrate the importance of asking what Unification thought means by "creation" in asserting that salvation is its "restoration."

Though it is theologically difficult to quarrel with res-
torationism as such, the discussion cannot be allowed to
end at this point. For the concrete concept of creation
involved in Unification thought may itself pose new problems.

     For example, my assessment is that Unification the-
ology's concrete concept of creation comes finally to vi-
tiate the restoration motif itself. Unification theology
maintains a notion of creation as the differentiation of
the inner life of God, a notion that finds no easy reconciliation with the motif of restoration in its most precise sense. Restoration thus becomes "Return to God" in
a literal sense, and this is divinization, not the repetition or re-establishment of "creaturehood." In Unification theology restoration cannot be the republication of
creaturehood because "creaturehood" is not adequately
ontically distinguished from the being of God and cannot
be assigned, therefore, an intermediate character or nature of its own. Therefore, the question of how "it" can
be "restored" is immediately suggested. The following
pages will be devoted to a clarification of this argument.

     The *Divine Principle* opens its theological discus-
sion of Unification thought with the idea of the "Dual
Characteristics of God." [20] This duality of God is the
polarity of positivity and negativity. Furthermore, it
is a reciprocal relationship corresponding to the dualities of interiority and exteriority, subject and object,
character and form, and masculinity and femininity. [24]

     In addition, the *Divine Principle* asserts that the
world was created in God's image. Like God, the world
displays the polarity of positivity and negativity at the
fundamental ontic level. "The Universe," says the *Divine
Principle*, "...has its own internal character and external

form."

But, according to Unification thought, the world is
more than a metaphor. It is more than a reflection of
the divine life. Indeed, the strong claim is made that
the universe has God as its center. The created order is
the external form of God; or God is the inner character
or deepest energy of the world. Says the *Divine Principle*: "In relation to the whole creation, God is the masculine subject representing its internal character." [25]

Though God is transcendent, according to the *Divine
Principle* He is also the *dynamis* of the created order.
In fact the *Divine Principle* calls Him the "Universal
Prime Energy."

Energy is, of course, motion, not just extension in
space and duration in time. In Unification theology the
notion of energy (which is God) explains how the creation,
though fundamentally and at the highest level of general-
ity intelligible in terms of positivity and negativity,
specifically becomes a multiplicity of concrete, dual
structures. God's being is the base of the cosmic process
through whose "give-and-take" secondary, tertiary and
quaternary purposes emerge. Says the *Divine Principle*:
"When, through Universal Prime Energy, the dual essential-
ities of God enter into give-and-take action by forming a
reciprocal relationship, the force of give-and-take action
causes multiplication." [31]

Finally, this process of differentiation is desig-
nated the "origin-division-union (O-D-U) action." Little
has to be said about how basic this three-tiered "ontology" is to Unification thought. It is the overall structural framework within which Unification thought concretely
articulates (1) its doctrine of sin as the vitiation of
personal integrity, familial order, and social community;

(2) its notion of the mission and failure of Israel; (3) its doctrine of the work and failure of Christ; and finally (4) its very this-worldly conception of the personal, familial, and world-political calling of the community of the regenerate. Upon the children of God rests the awesome responsibility of bringing about fulfillment at every level in the wake of the failures that have characterized the past.

Crucial to my purposes is the initial assumption that the three four-position (O-D-U) bases constitute the horizontal structure of creation, and that they are in effect actually (ontologically) the unfolded objectification of the inner life of God Himself. Creation is actually the life of God; or, the inner, dynamic, organizational structure of the universe is the Divine Being Himself.

This theological position is nowhere more vividly indicated than in Unification's conception of God's Joy and Love, and Unification's corresponding notion of the centrality of the base position of family and marriage. The group constituted by God, male and female, and children is the concrete foundation from which the base of human society flows and in terms of which the base of the human constitution (God, mind and body, perfect man) acquires its real significance.

According to Unification thought God is Heart (Love) and His desire is the experience of Joy. God can only fulfill Himself by objectifying Himself in His creation, whose center base is marriage and the family. Only through man, through his experience of love and joy, can God's own desire for fulfillment and Joy be realized. Man is the vehicle through which God (the Lover) relates Himself to the world (the Beloved.)[1]

If man fails, God does not experience Joy. But as

man achieves perfection, says Prof. Kim, "the *incarnation* of God is at last fulfilled."[2] As we follow man's efforts to attain to the purpose of creation at every level or base position, we are in effect observing the development of God's own life. The evolution of creation is God's own history.

But this growth of creation is also man's history, man's autobiography. However, since the life of the world is preceded by God and since it comes again to be drawn into Him, man's perfection really comes to life beyond the *restoration* of creaturehood. Says the *Divine Principle:* "The man whose mind and body have formed a four-position foundation of the original God-centered nature becomes God's temple...and forms one body with Him....This means that man attains *deity*." [43, emphasis added.]

Another way of indicating the same thing might be to say that since the life of God is also the life of man, man "precedes" himself and in principle should be destined to become more than he was actually created to be. What he was created to be has no specifiable boundaries. For example, in Unification theology marital love is sacred, so that, as Prof. Kim herself observes, "When a man and woman unite in perfection, they are in a sense a *new higher being* even closer to God."[3]

It should be apparent that Unification theology regards as a single continuous reality the life of God and the being of the creation. If deification is not the final goal of creation, then surely creation is in principle at best only an intermediate and subordinate metaphysical part of the Divine Being.

But what has become here of the notion of Creation? What has become of the idea that God is Creator, not creation? What has become of the idea that there is an abso-

lute void between God and what He calls into being? What
become of the idea that there is nothing God Himself that
can or must ensue in creation? And, if we allow these
ideas to disappear, can we still speak in a theologically
respectable way of "Creation?"

Furthermore, when the infinite difference between
God and creation is ignored, is not the precise sense of
"restoration" also jeopardized? Is it not the case that
if God and creation are somehow only interrelated and
structured through one another, then the creation can
have no finally definable nature, just as God can finally
have no incomprehensibility, or dignity and majesty?

It is my impression that if the indelible line of
demarcation that separates God from His creation is
eclipsed, then restoration cannot be the recapitulation
of creaturehood either; for there is then no such reality
as "creaturehood," at least as distinct from the being of
God Himself. Restoration must become the transformation
and translation of humanity into the divinity of God. The
concrete sense of restoration becomes qualified by the
notion of divinization, and restoration becomes specifically "Return to God" in a substantive or metaphysical
sense. The notion of "Union with God" is inevitably
turned into a cosmological process.

My criticism of Unification theology is that while
it tries to honor the language of restoration, it viti-
ates this effort by failing adequately to honor the ontic
difference between God and His creation. This difference
is the key assumption of the doctrine of creation. Creation stands or falls with this idea.

Furthermore, the restoration motif goes hand in
hand with creation. Where creation becomes confused with
the actually incomprehensible majesty of God, creation

loses its nature as a "self-identical" reality, and the
sense of restoration becomes deification or actual metaphysical "Return to God." Unification theology must
choose between creation and restoration on the one hand
and the principle of the bi-polarity of the Divine Being
in terms of positivity and negativity on the other. The
two are incompatible concepts.

DISCUSSION

Lloyd Eby: I want to ask a question. At the end
of your paper you say that "the difference between God
and His creation is the key assumption of the doctrine of
creation." What is that key?

Dr. Vander Goot: I'm talking about classical Christian theology. It seems to me that within Christian
thought that assumption has to be made and is the point
of the doctrine of creation. God is one thing and that
which He calls into being is quite another thing. From
the point of view of being, God and Creation do not over-
lap. God *is* absolutely. There is nothing within Him, or
before Him, or alongside Him out of which creation flows.
God *is* absolutely. That means in effect, that God is one
thing and creation is another.

Dr. Clark: Your criticism of Unification thought
is that the distinction between the Creator and the creation is confused. Yet when you were speaking I found myself thinking that much of what you said Unification theology is sounds like Greek Orthodox thought. Would you
make this same criticism of Greek Orthodox theology?

Linda Mitchell: It is my understanding, the *Divine
Principle* and Greek Orthodox thought seem very close. I
understand Greek Orthodoxy to say that there are two

aspects of God: His essence and His energies. Man can
never become one with God in essence, but he can become
one with God's energies. The *Divine Principle* never asserts that man will become one in being with God, but
simply that he will be united in heart with God.

Dr. Vander Goot: Okay, but how does that stand
theologically with the fact that there is the persistent
argument in the *Divine Principle* that God is the "Center"
of the universe? This is not, it seems to me, a metaphor,
but an ontology.

Dr. Richardson: How do you differentiate that from
the Orthodox way of saying that the world is dependent on
God, that man is made in the image of God, that God's
purposes are worked out in creation, and so on? Why are
you criticizing Unification theology for a way of talking
about these considerations that is very much a part of
traditional Christian language?

Dr. Vander Goot: To say that the creation is totally dependent on God is not to say that there is no
distinction between the Creator and the creation. It is
simply to say that the creation has no absolute identity
or being in or of itself, and that creation must constantly be referred to that which lies beyond it.

Dr. Richardson: But is it as clear as you assume
that the *Divine Principle* confuses creation with Creator?
For example, creation falls. There is at least one case
in which there obviously is some distinction between God
the Creator and His creation.

Dr. Vander Goot: Yes, that's true. There is another fact, too, that constitutes a break from the divinization motif, namely, the stress on the doctrine of the
Christian life and the physical coming of the Kingdom. I
find that these two things contravene the more ontologi-

cal presupposition with which the *Divine Principle* begins.

   Dr. Richardson: Perhaps we have two doctrines of creation in Unification theology. Is there one articulated and stated doctrine of creation which is not a doctrine of creation at all, but a doctrine of emanation? And then do we have an implicit doctrine of creation in Unification's stress on the doctrine of sin? Is it only there implicitly? Could you draw it out and put it over against the expressed and articulated doctrine of creation one finds in Section One of the *Divine Principle?*

   Farley Jones: But I'm not convinced that the *Divine Principle* does not distinguish between the Creator and creation. Early in your paper you write, "In fact, the *Divine Principle* calls Him, God the Universal Prime Energy." But now, in the *Divine Principle,* we read that "God is the Creator of all things. He's the absolute reality, eternally self-existent, transcendent of time and space; therefore, the fundamental energy of His Being must also be absolute and externally self-existent. At the same time, He is the source of the energy which enables all things to maintain their existence. We call this energy (that is, the energy which enables all things to maintain their existence, which God is the source of) Universal Prime Energy." So there is, in the *Divine Principle,* a distinction between God and Universal Prime Energy.

   Dr. Vander Goot: But the problem is right there. God is called energy, right? Even if God is distinguished from Universal Prime Energy, He is called energy. Now that is the problem. Philosophically, God is described in terms of a condition that belongs to the creation itself.

   Dr. Richardson: But wouldn't we have to know, then,

how they understand that: whether ontologically, or meta-
phorically, or mythically?

Dr. Vander Goot: You've got to take the whole context and come to a judgment on what the sense of the
statement actually is. The *Divine Principle* claims that
God is energy, absolute transcendent energy, although He
may be distinct from Universal Prime Energy.

Klaus Lindner: May I add something? There is energy which enables God to create, but the energy which is
created out of "give and take action" is a different energy from the energy which enables God to create. Energy is
part of God's existence, but the energy out of which the
universe is created is a different energy.

Dr. Vander Goot: But that's exactly the point.
You're saying that there's something in God which finally
explains the creation. There is a principle within Him,
namely, energy, that finally enables Him to create Universal Prime Energy, right? That is a highly dubious conception.

Dr. Richardson: You mean to say that Christian
teaching is that there is nothing in God that would explain how it is possible for God to create?

Dr. Vander Goot: There's nothing like a philosophical or metaphysical principle that would explain it, no.

Dr. Richardson: But the question is whether this
is a philosophical or metaphysical principle or a theological mode of speaking which every Christian would use.
Suppose you say, "God can create because He possesses the
power to be creative."

Dr. Vander Goot: You're being unprincipled if you
think you're explaining creation by using naive language
like that. (laughter)

Dr. Richardson: Surely the point is that the cause
has to be sufficient to produce the effect.

Dr. Vander Goot: God's not related to the world as cause to effect.

Dr. Richardson: I might say then that you're not talking any longer about Christian dogma, but that you're proposing one philosophical or theological interpretation of the Christian dogma of creation. It's perfectly clear, for example, that one type of Christian theology uses the cosmological argument, and other kinds of Christian theology argue from degrees of perfection. It may well be the case that theologians can argue whether its right to use these arguments or not, but clearly, in the Christian tradition, these arguments are used in order to explain what it means to say that God is the creator.

Dr. Vander Goot: But there's nothing uniquely Christian about that argument. That's my point. That argument was, in effect, used by the Greeks. There's nothing that differentiates the Greek conception of the relationship with God from the Christian conception.

Dr. Richardson: Yes, but don't you see that some Christian theologians have always thought that we had some arguments that were also used by the Greeks, and that we didn't need to make them up for ourselves. (laughter) It's an advantage. (laughter)

David Jarvis: The *Divine Principle* is operating in an Eastern philosophical mode in which it's more common to speak of God in terms of energy. I was going to say that I agree with your perception that the *Divine Principle* is saying that God in some way creates the tangible world out of Himself, out of His own energy. But I lose you at the point where you say that means that we cannot say that God is different from creation. I'd like you to clarify that distinction. Why must we choose between our ontical idea of God's creating out of His energy and our idea of God?

Dr. Vander Goot: Because the idea of God's creating out of His energy is not a doctrine of creation, but is really a doctrine of emanation. It seems to me that when you stress restoration as much as you do, you imply a classical doctrine of creation which cannot go hand in hand with the notion that the creation is really the external form of God who is its inner character. There's an inconsistency here.

David Jarvis: I don't see that. I don't even see the inconsistency of that last point. I think we're saying that God is energy, but we stress that God's energy is only one aspect of His Being. I think some of the people have brought this out. Energy is only a small aspect of God's Being. There's also intelligence, will, love, other kinds of being in God. To say that God is the creation or that we're equating God and the creation wholly is probably incorrect.

---

[1] See Young Oon Kim, *Unification Theology and Christian Thought,* rev. ed. New York: Golden Gate, 1976, pp. 23-25.

[2] *Ibid.*, p. 38, emphasis added.

[3] *Ibid.*, p. 49.

A LECTURE TO STUDENTS AT THE
UNIFICATION THEOLOGICAL SEMINARY IN BARRYTOWN, NEW YORK

HERBERT RICHARDSON

Today I am interested, not so much in offering
an interpretation of the *Divine Principle* as in showing
you how a systematic theologian, like myself, goes
about reading, analyzing and interpreting a work with
which he may or may not agree. As a Protestant who
also teaches in a Catholic seminary, I have constantly
to deal with books which present Catholic arguments or
viewpoints. While I may or may not agree with these
views, I must still try to understand them. In a sense,
my own agreement or disagreement with these views
is irrelevant to the task of understanding them.
My goal today is to attempt to understand the *Divine
Principle* as a systematic theologian.

In any analysis of a text, we have to bring to that
text certain categories and questions which are not
found in it. This is also necessary in order to understand the *Divine Principle*. To analyze this work, we
have to employ certain principles of classification
that are not employed in the book itself. Some such
principles of classification are the following: "What,

This lecture on the *Divine Principle* as systematic theology was given by Professor Richardson in the fall of
1976.

in most general terms, is the structure of Rev. Moon's
theological thinking?" or, "What is the chief doctrine?"
or, "What principle of interpretation does Rev. Moon
use in dealing with the Bible?" These are the kinds
of questions I shall discuss today.

I'm sure you will agree with me that Rev. Moon
is important not only as a prophet, but also as a theologian. These are two different things. Because they
are different, one might agree with Rev. Moon's theology
without believing in his spiritual Fatherhood, or one
might believe in his spiritual Fatherhood without agree-
ing with all of his theology. This fact is a real source
of strength within the Unification movement. It means
there is a room for theological openness; you and I
can debate, and even reject Moon's theology, without
rejecting the man. This is the case because, as I
understand it, the function of Rev. Moon within the
Unification Movement is not primarily as a theologian,
but as a True Father through whom the new humanity,
the new family of man, is to be formed.

Rev. Moon's Fatherhood is obviously his more important function. He is spiritual Father first, and
theologian second. I might say that this was also true
of Jesus. Whether or not we possess any actual words of
Jesus is a debatable matter, but whether or not Jesus
is Messiah is not a debatable matter within orthodox
Christianity. All Christians agree that Jesus is Messiah even though they may disagree about his theology.
So you need not feel anxious if I criticize the *Divine
Principle* as theology because that does not directly
affect your relation to Rev. Moon in his role as Father.
For my part, I, as a Presbyterian, can learn a great

deal from the *Divine Principle* as theology without
having to resolve the question as to whether the Rev.
Moon is my spiritual Father also.

    In approaching Rev. Moon as if he were a theologian,
I should begin by saying that I regard the *Divine Principle* to be the most interesting theological treatise
I have read in twenty years. It may even be the most
important theological treatise of the twentieth century.
Time will tell. The work of Karl Barth is comparable
to it in systematic power. But Barth never managed
to give us a short comprehensive statement of his whole
theological system as Moon has done. In its compact-
ness, inclusiveness, and systematic power the *Divine
Principle* resembles Calvin's *Institutes*. It also resembles Calvin's *Institutes* because of its Biblical orientation.

RELATIONAL THINKING

    As a mode of thought, the Rev. Moon's theology is
of primary importance to us in America because it is
relational. That is to say, his thinking is structured through relational categories. There are three
different ways in which thinking may be structured:
relationally, individualistically, or holistically.
One thinks relationally by defining things in relation
to other things that also are reciprocally related
to them. One thinks individualistically by isolating
things and looking at what they are by themselves
("essences"). One thinks holistically by the character
of this whole. In the Western tradition, and especially
in America, theology has tended to be extremely

individualistic.

As an example of how Rev. Moon's thought proceeds differently from individualistic Western thought, let us take his notion of love. The Western tradition of thought searches for the essence of love. In trying to *define* love, it moves into psychology. Isolating love as an individual thing, it defines it as a psychological feeling. By contrast, Rev. Moon thinks about love relationally. That is, he correlates love with an external, or objective, term. That term is beauty. He then offers a relational definition of love in terms of beauty and beauty in terms of love. In Moon's theology, love determines a disposition or orientation towards beauty, an external form.

One great strength of Rev. Moon's relational, or correlative theology is that it directs all thought toward action. That is because his way of thinking orients everything that is in the subject to something that is objective and external to it. Moreover, such a theology does not end merely in action towards this external object; rather, because there is a give-and-take (a reciprocal back and forth) between the subject and the object), the object becomes itself a stimulus for deepening the understanding and action of the subject. A give-and-take relation is a reciprocal temporal process of action and reflection which produces new things on both sides. Such give-and-take is the source of a healthier personality generally and the source of human growth. Because he holds to this give-and-take theory, Rev. Moon attributes to the external world, or the world which science studies, a value which is equal to the internal or spiritual world. He sees

these two worlds, the spiritual and the physical, as
needing each other and as building each other.   In
this way, Moon's ontology is radically different from
western ontology which, in its Greek roots, gives
higher value to the spiritual than to the physical
world. Greek thought emphasizes reason's dominion over
nature rather than the influence of nature on man.
The western tradition has not generally interpreted
the action of man on nature as leading to an *interaction* of nature on man that would deepen the human spirit.
This is why, in western theology, being religious has
traditionally meant leaving the world behind.

      Rev. Moon's understanding of the essential function
of the objective world in strengthening and deepening
character in its inner spiritual life involves a fundamental challenge to western philosophy and psychology.
Moon is not a totally radical innovator in this respect.
Moon's insight is also acknowledged within Calvinism.
In fact, in the healthier version of the Calvinistic
work ethic, there is a conviction that a person's
spirit or character grows and is strengthened through
his external activity or work.   (Calvinists believe that
work shapes character.)   But Moon's thought is distinguished by a philosophical or a structural foundation
to these affirmations that is not found in most Calvinist theological texts.   Relational thinking, then,
is a key characteristic of Rev. Moon's mind.

                        GOD AS FATHER

      Let me now explain how this relational way of think-
ing is manifested at a most general level in the *Divine*

Principle. Here we face a theological problem. The
problem is, "How many units are there to a book which
deals with the whole of Christian theology?" In traditional Christian theology, the answer has tended to
be either three units or four. In a theology of three
units the major topics are the Father, the Son, and
the Holy Spirit. In a theology of four units the
topics are the Father, the Son, the Holy Spirit and
the Church. Some theologies have as many as ten units
in their system: the Father, the Son, the Holy Spirit,
the Church, forgiveness, resurrection, life everlasting,
the Christian life and so forth. Once one starts analyzing in this way, it is easy to jump from ten to
forty-seven. For example, the great Catholic theologian,
Bernard Lonergan, is a man whose mind tends toward such
analytical precision that, in reading him, one occasionally finds him saying "And in the 37th place..." Here
is a commitment to thoroughness that has run to weeds!

How many units does Moon's theological system have?
Three? Four? His theology has only <u>two</u> major parts.
Of course, the *Divine Principle* is divided into many
sub-units, but it has only two major parts. The two
parts are the Doctrine of Creation and the Doctrine of
Restoration.

The greatest theologian of modern times, Frei-
drich Schleiermacher, also divided his theological system
into two parts: a doctrine of creation and a doctrine
of redemption. So a twofold division is not novel.
In fact, it has great systematic power, for the two
facts of the system can always be held in tension with
each other. Let us, therefore, see how this works.

First, let me say that it is a difficult thing

for a theologian to think consistently and to develop
all the implications of his fundamental commitments.
It is doubly difficult to be consistent when trying
to treat all the doctrines of the Christian faith.
To see a theologian discuss all the Christian doctrines
in a thoroughly consistent way is a very exciting thing.
It is like hearing a great symphonic work. It is
exactly this excitement I experience in reading the
Divine Principle--and for this reason, here are some
of the things I see.

For a surprise, think about this. Rev. Moon's
theology does not have an independent doctrine of God.
Remember I told you how traditional western Christianity
had a three or four topic theology, and the first one
was always "God the Father." Rev. Moon does not talk
about God in this way. The first part of Moon's theology is not "God," but creation. Of course, as part of
his discussion of creation, Moon does talk about God.
But this means that he never talks about God abstractly,
but always as *related to us*. We know God always *within*
our relation to Him as our Father, our Creator, and
never apart from this relation, from outside. It
is as if you were in a group of people who were talking
about a man--and suddenly you realized they were talking
about *your father*. You *know* you never could feel or
talk about your father from "outside" in that way.
Even though other people address Jimmy Carter as "Mr.
President," Amy says "Daddy." For her that is *exactly
right*. In the same way, because Moon thinks we only
know God in this Father-child relationship, he contends
that it is *exactly right* for us to call God "Father."
In traditional Christianity, because it tried to

define God first as one separate from His creation,
it was denied that we could call God "Father" in an
exactly right (or "univocal") way. Traditional Christianity said that when we say "Father," we mean it in
a less than exact way. We mean it "analogically." That
is, God is not really our Father. But traditional
Christianity adds that there is a kind of Fatherhood
in God (variously explained), so we can use the word
anyway as long as we do not presume on it too much!

Rev. Moon's decision to begin with the concept of
God as Creator-Father is brilliant because it orients
us immediately to the purpose of our lives: namely,
perfect creaturehood, or becoming perfect images of
God. Perfect creaturehood is my word, but it expresses
Moon's direction. If we ask, "What is perfect creaturehood?" that is, "What is it for us to be created to be
images of God?" the answer is that we are to become
divine spirits. This means that we are ourselves to
become creators.

How can we be creators if God is creator? Rev.
Moon's answer is that God as creator has created a world
for us to be creators in. God has created both a spiritual and a temporal world and has created us with both
a spirit and a body so that we can mediate between
the two worlds. Because we have bodies, we can be
creators in the world of time and history just as God
is creator and Father in the spiritual world. Thus,
we are creatures in relation to God, but we are also
purposed by God to be creators as He is Creator.
I might here add that God, our Father, has also created
us to become *Fathers*, too. This follows logically.

It means that Unification stresses not the Father/child relation, but the Father/child becoming-father-too relation. Fathers should help children grow up. Few theologians dare affirm that man is created to become a creator as God is a creator. Usually "Creator" is a name reserved for God alone and therefore used to contrast God with man, who is a "creature". But the *Divine Principle* sees man's becoming a creator as a perfecting of the image of God in man. What is theologically interesting, however, is how Rev. Moon explains that man can be a creator like God. The explanation lies in his doctrine of the spiritual world.

MAN AS CREATOR

Let me here caution you against misinterpreting the meaning of the word "spiritual." It would be an error to think that the *Divine Principle's* teaching about the spiritual world is a spiritualism. It is, rather, the way that Rev. Moon explains how man can be a creator. According to Moon, God has created both a spiritual world and a material world. God rules over the spiritual world directly, and over the material world indirectly, i.e., *through* the persons who live in the spiritual world (such as angels and perfected humans). According to Moon, God has created this twofold order so that man may have the possibility of being the *immediate* lord over the physical world, just as God is the *immediate* lord over the spiritual world.

God has created man to be a creator and therefore has given him the condition of creativity: a physical life in space and time. The direct dominion over

space and time can only be exercised by beings who
are free physical beings. We are free because we are
spiritual. But we can act *directly* in the material world
because we have physical bodies. Because we are souls
and bodies, i.e. both spiritual and physical, we can
become *creators* in the material order. To do this is
to fulfill God's third blessing.

I think Rev. Moon has made an original and remark-
able use of the idea of the spiritual and material creation. Moreover, his view is entirely orthodox, for
spirit means to him the reality of man's freedom, and
God's "indirect direction" over the material world is
what classical theologians used to call the "world
logos". Given this approach, it is easy to understand
why Moon can have such a high valuation of science.
The function of science is to assist man in creating the
world through the process of bringing happiness and peace
to the family of mankind.

Let us summarize. The *Divine Principle* is a theology primarily oriented in terms of the question:
Why did God create the world? In this, it differs from
many theologies which cannot even ask this question
because they assume that God is totally self-sufficient
and needs nothing else at all. Rev. Moon's general
principle of the correlation of subject and object
enables him to see the world as created by God so that
(and this is not Moon's language) God might see His
own character reflected back to Himself. Moon's principle of correlation (give-and-take) justifies his
doctrine that God created the world in order to have
an image of Himself.

In Rev. Moon's view, the purpose of creation is

to give joy to God. This is not so removed from the
language of traditional western theology in which the
purpose of creation is to give glory to God. In traditional theological language, the purpose of all life
is to return to God what God is and what God seeks.
It is significant that Moon's theology is a radically
theocentric one, that is, a theology ordered in terms
of the divine purpose. It is significant, too, that
what keeps this radically theocentric theology from
becoming oppressive of human life is its principle
of double creation, its notion that God seeks to have
an image of His own purpose by creating creators.
God does not need us as creatures; He desires us to
become free creators, too.

Traditional western theology has never solved this
problem of radical theocentricity without diminishing
humanity because, usually, when creation is understood
as an object, it is understood to be less than God.
In Rev. Moon's theology, however, creation, understood
as an object, is understood to be equal to God because
of the give-and-take relation. That is, Moon sees
that creation should return to God what He has given it,
and that God finds joy in this response. I find such
a view theologically imaginative and psychologically
healthy.

Considered structurally, Rev. Moon's theology
contains not only the relationality of the creator/
creature relationship, but also relationality within
God himself. This relationship posits within God a
dyad of principles: positivity and negativity. These
principles are not understood to be absolutely ultimate
because there is also a primal principle of origin.

Why does Rev. Moon assert in addition to the
positivity/negativity dyad, a primal principle of origin?
His primal principle does not function, it seems to me,
as something that transcends and is more than the dyad
of powers. Rather, it functions in a formal way as
the sheer unity of the two dyadic powers. This primal
principle of origin is the insurance that, in the last
analysis, the two poles interact creatively and har-
moniously rather than in such a way as to produce an
ultimate conflict. In this way, Moon avoids the problem of dualist Manichaeism, which posits two principles
but no ultimate principle of unity holding them together.
In Rev. Moon's theology, the primal unity is not in-
voked as a principle of transcendence, but as a principle
of creative harmony between the two powers of God. It
is the principle of the relationality of the two.

This may seem abstruse or unimportant to you.
But, in fact, Moon's solution is a brilliant one to an
enduring and terribly destructive dilemma within western
thought. Let me show you how.

What are the two powers in God that one holds in
creative harmony by this primal principle of origin?
The answer is positivity/negativity, masculinity/feminin-
ity, subject/object. None of these sets is familiar
to the western tradition. But how about this one:
Reason and Will (or word/wisdom). Here is a set of
ultimates that has created havoc within western philosophy and theology.

Plato set up the problem. Is justice good because
it is willed by God or is it willed by God because it
is good? Which comes first: reason or will? Which
is the origin of the other? Thomas Aquinas said "reason"
and developed "natural law;" Calvin said "will" and

affirmed "predestination." Rationalists and volun-
tarists have fought with each other through 2,000 years
of western theology. The fight made sense because it
could always be shown that reason or will is ultimate.
To say they were different, but ultimate, seemed like
dualism. No one saw what Rev. Moon has seen, namely
that Reason and Will are two different ultimate powers
which exist *only in relation to each other*. That
relation is the primal principle of origin. Who else
in Christian theology has seen and solved this problem?
What Moon has done is show the deepest meaning of the
Christian assertion that God is trinity.

THREE METAPHYSICAL PRINCIPLES

Rev. Moon develops his theory of a primal dyadic power
within God, which in the principle of God's creativity
into a doctrine concerning three metaphysical ultimates:
the principle of Give-and-Take relation, the principle
or Origin-Division-Unification, and the Four-Position-
Foundation. These are Moon's three metaphysical principles. Something should be said about why they are
metaphysical principles. They are metaphysical principles because they are absolutely general and universal,
applying to everything that exists whatsoever.

In fact, these principles are so general and universal that there can never be anything at all except in
dependence upon them. There cannot even be disorder
and sin except as a form of the principle of origin,
division, union. This means that even sin depends upon
the structure of goodness. Therefore Rev. Moon repeatedly insists on something that all Christian theologians

hold: namely, that conscience is never eradicated
from man, and that evil can never exist except in dependence upon good. The realm of Satan exists only
through its exploitation of the structure of creation itself. This is the source of its peculiar
power as well as the source of the certainty that
Satan's realm must eventually be overcome. Thus, Moon
asserts the traditional Christian view that all disorder
depends upon order.

It is necessary to clarify why Moon's three metaphysical principles are so important for a theological
understanding of life and reality. They are important
because they mean that we do not encounter power, or
reality, as one. Rather, we encounter power and reality
as plural and differentiated. Theologically, this
means that the thing which makes the creation creation
and not God is its plurality. True unity exists only
in God. In the creation there is only plurality, even
though it is ordered plurality.

When Rev. Moon talks about Subject-Object, Give-and-
Take - Action, the Four-Position-Foundation, and Origin-
Division-Union, he is introducing multiplicity into
the creation. These terms help us see that reality
is differentiated and, therefore, a sphere that is appropriate to human action. This is the great strength in
Rev. Moon's philosophy (specifically his philosophy
as opposed to his theology). He does not begin by presenting us with a totally undifferentiated conception
of God and reality, such that we have to come to terms
with everything all at once, or retreat from the differentiated, complex world. Rather, he presents us with
a conceptual apparatus which sets out many things to

which we can relate in a gradual and ordered way.

Rev. Moon is concerned with the order of life, and with ordering life. This kind of concern does not overwhelm people, but is something in which they can actively participate. This idea is an evidence of Moon's Calvinism--his fundamentally pluralistic experience of life. In Moon's differentiated conception of life and reality, God becomes directly related to life in each and all of its many parts.

Let me mention two other philosophical points here. A consistently relational thinker like Rev. Moon faces two metaphysical problems. One is how to conceive substance as relation. For a consistently relational thinker, a substantial reality is not an individual entity, but a relation. You will recall that the Greek philosophers saw reality in terms of individuality; that is they identified reality with individual things, and thought of individual things as discreet "chunks" of matter. The Greeks, therefore, saw relations as derivative rather than as primal. For instance, they would understand the relationship of marriage as re- sulting from the joining of two individual bodies. On this view, the marriage relation, since it *derives* from two individuals, is less real than the individuals it relates.

Rev. Moon, on the other hand, argues that individu- ality derives from rationality since relations are more real than individuals. He therefore regards a body as a relation or network of relations. In the same way, he regards a marriage, or a family, as substantially more real than the individuals who belong to it. Rev. Moon does not hold that individuals are unreal; he

holds only that their individuality derives from the
set of relations to which they belong. On this point,
Rev. Moon is in agreement with the best of modern
sociology--and with the best theologian that America
has produced: Jonathan Edwards*

   (*In the question period, a question regarding Rev.
   Moon's relations to Jonathan Edwards was raised.
   The reply was as follows:

   There are many similarities between the *Divine
   Principle* and Edwards' theology, especially their
   theories about why and how God created the world.
   Like Moon, Edwards was a consistently relational
   thinker. For the moment, let me urge those of you
   who want to explore a way of dealing with Moon's
   notion of substantial reality or body in this relational language to read Jonathan Edwards's early
   writings on the mind. Edwards developed his notion
   of substantial reality as relational in direct dependence upon the work of Isaac Newton, and Newton
   understood that the reality of every living thing
   is determined by gravity, and that gravity is nothing other than a force determining a network of
   relations. So, following Newton, Edwards says that
   an individual body is inevitably a relational entity.
   This notion should be developed and extended, not
   only metaphysically, but also sociologically, in
   terms of the reorganization of all institutions in
   American society. America is sick to death of individualism. The development of Moon's relational
   theology is one of the great possibilities for your
   group and could be an important contribution to theology and social theory today.)

The second problem a consistently relational thinker
must face is how to conceive individuality. In fact,
Rev. Moon does have a concept of individuality, which
he relates to the first of God's three blessings to Adam:
"Be fruitful, multiply and have dominion over the earth."
How is it that "being fruitful," the first of the

three blessings, is related to the development of in-
dividuality? Well, first of all, we should see that
Moon is here interpreting the scriptures symbolically.
Second, we have to see that he is not intending "be
fruitful and multiply" as one statement, but as two.
What he is saying is that you cannot have relationality
("multiplying") without first having individuality.
That is the relational principle.

There is a sense, then, in which Rev. Moon understands individuality as prior to relationality. It
is in this sense: the individuality to which he is here
referring is the development of the individual through
his relation to God. This developed individuality is
the foundation of his capacity to multiply, that is,
to have good social relations. (So what for him is
first in the order of time is not first in the order
of nature.) One implication of this priority of individuality for your practice should be that preparation
of any person for marriage would include a lengthy
period of spiritual training to perfect that person's
individuality. Marriage should be regarded in your
group not as a way to help individuals grow up, but as
something that mature individuals are ready to undertake. Marriage, therefore, is a second task derived
from the second blessing. I think from what I have
heard, that these are your views.

WHY SATAN SINNED

To develop a theological system one must focus
ideas in terms of a single scope and, in Rev. Moon's
case, this is the doctrine of creation. Creation is

Rev. Moon's central concern. A theology which, by
contrast, focusses on Jesus alone, inevitably neglects
everything except what leads us to Jesus: e.g. faith,
speaking in tongues, the sacraments. But Rev. Moon's
theology wants us to center our lives not in one person,
but in the whole world. God's purpose is for man to
have dominion over the earth. This happens through
God's transmission of His creatorship. We have already
discussed how this takes place. Now, we will begin to
discuss Moon's notion of sin and show how it, too, is
dependent on this theory of creation.

Moon's conception of the fall and the structure
of sin follows from his three metaphysical ultimates:
the principle of Give-and-Take relation, the principle
of Origin-Division-Unification, and the Four-Position-
Foundation. Thus, the fall of many occurs through
Lucifer's seduction of Eve by using the principle of
Give-and-Take. The fall effects a division, or separation, even though not a good one. The realm of Satan,
like the realm of God, also depends upon the Four-
Position-Foundation, but in a defective and antagonistic
form.

One thing that Rev. Moon does not explicitly deal
with is the reason for Lucifer's jealousy of Adam and
Eve, the reason behind his seduction of Eve. While
Moon suggests that Lucifer perceived that God loved
Adam more than himself, I do not think this fully ex-
plains Lucifer's jealousy and anger. At this point,
I am going to proceed with an internal criticism of
Moon's theology.

Suppose now, that I granted Lucifer was angry
because he perceived God had a greater love for Adam;

then I would still have to ask "How did God show his
greater love for Adam?" The answer that Rev. Moon,
as a systematic theologian, should give to this
question is the following: "No creature can possess
love without possessing beauty. If God loved Adam
more than he loved Lucifer, it was because God saw more
beauty in Adam than he did in Lucifer." But what more
beauty did God see in Adam than he saw in Lucifer? What
more did God give to Adam that he did not give to Lucifer? The answer is this. God gave to Adam the power
to become a creator and to have direct dominion over
the physical world. Lucifer, therefore, was jealous
not only of God's love for Adam, but of Adam's creativity. More particularly, Lucifer was jealous of Adam's
body because Adam's creativity derived from the fact
that he had a body and existed in the physical as well
as the spiritual world. This made it possible for him
to become a creator within the physical world.

Now, Lucifer does not have a body. At least he
does not have a body in the way that Adam does. So
we can say that Lucifer is jealous of Adam's body.
The question now arises: How can Lucifer get a body?
Lucifer can get a body only by seducing, or uniting
with someone who has a body. So Lucifer seduces Eve.
He seduces Eve because he needs a body in order to be
creative. Hence, just as Eve gained a certain wisdom
from her relationship to Lucifer, so Lucifer gained
a physical body and progeny from his relationship to
Eve. Through this relationship, Lucifer usurped
Adam's place, and in doing so made himself into a creator. So, the motive for sin is more than merely Lucifer's jealousy. I think that Rev. Moon would agree

with me on that.

But let me mention one implication of Lucifer's
jealousy of Adam's creativity and of his desire to be
a creator. Since the realm of creation for Adam, that
is, for humanity, is especially the realm of science
and technology, this is also the realm that Satan especially covets. Therefore, man must be very alert to the
demonic tendencies within the area of human creativity
embraced by science and technology. (You can see how
I am generating an ethic out of my theological analysis.)
But is the Unification Church sufficiently alert to the
demonic tendencies in modern science and technology?
Does it invest them too uncritically with Messianic
significance? I think so, for I have not seen a single
critique of technology from your group. One of you
should write it. I have given you already the theological rationale.

WHAT IS SIN?

From the above, we can see that Satan sinned because he coveted the power to be a creator like Adam
and Eve. His sin was not primarily a rebellion against
God but an attack on man! This means that the Unification doctrine of salvation will stress the "liberation"
of man from evil powers that hold him in bondage,
rather than man's needing forgiveness for sins against
God. Sinful man is in a *sorry* condition, not a *bad*
condition. God fights against Satan to redeem us all.

To understand how God redeems and restores us to
our original position in the universe, we must know
what Satan did to us when he led us into sin. Since

restoration requires undoing what was done, we have
to know what was done. A systematic theology always
has a clearly specified understanding of sin. This is
because, in a systematic theology, the concept of sin
has to be systematically related to the concept of the
act of salvation. So what is Rev. Moon's doctrine of
sin?

Rev. Moon emphasizes that his understanding of sin
is novel. He regards his understanding of sin as a
radically new theological discovery. What is Moon's
radically new discovery about sin? It is that Lucifer
established the Give-and-Take relation with Eve.
Through this, Lucifer and Eve became one. That is,
Eve receives Lucifer's nature and (this is my theological discovery!) Lucifer receives hers. As I have said,
this is how Lucifer gets a body.

Moon's discovery is that there is a spiritual
intercourse between man and angels or, more specifically,
between Eve and an evil angel, Lucifer.*

(*Question: Do you think these ideas about angels
can be used in theology today?

Answer: Only the great theologians dare to talk
about the role of the angels in the fall of man.
Why is this the case? Because only those theologians
can talk about the angels who themselves know the
angels. And only those know the angels who have
attained to spiritual maturity or divinity. I know
that Moon knows the angels, that he talks with them,
and that this discourse has formed his theology.
I should add, too, that Moon is not alone in knowing
the angels. St. Anselm knew all about the angels,
as is evident from his book called *Fall of Satan*,
and Jonathan Edwards, too, knew the angels a little
more circumspectly, as did Swedenborg, who conversed
with them.

According to Moon, this evil intercourse between Lucifer
and Eve resulted in the establishment of a satanic
family on earth, a family quite literally under the
headship of Satan. The logic here is that just as
Lucifer's characteristics are transmitted to Eve through
their conjunction so Eve transmits Satan's characteristics to Adam through their conjunction. And so on
and so forth. In this way, the human race is turned
into "Satan's family." Within this system of relations
which has Satan at the head, sin may be structurally
defined as "unprincipled love." This definition of sin
is imaginative and useful. Let me explain the usefulness
of the idea by contrasting it with the Protestant theory
of Adam's sin as *disobedience*.

WHAT IS THE SAVING ACT?

In Protestant theology Adam's sin is usually defined as an act of disobedience against God which
offends Him. This definition has systematic consequences
because the task of the Messiah must be defined as
undoing the original sinful act. In Protestant theology (and, for example in the theology of Anselm of
Canterbury), it is then argued that there must be
some amends or penalty for Adam's disobedience. Adam
cannot be forgiven until this indemnity has been paid.
Hence, the Protestant (and Anselmian) doctrine of atonement requires that an indemnity be paid by the Messiah
in order that forgiveness be given. Thus we have the
following correlation: sin is Adam's disobedience for
which he is guilty, requiring forgiveness; his salvation
comes through payment of a penalty for that sin. On

On this theory Christ's death is that payment, the bene-
fits of which are imputed to us through God's forgiveness.
Here, then, you have a traditional notion of sin correlated with a notion of redemption. It is also a
theory that requires God to send the Messiah for the
explicit purpose of being crucified.

   Now, Rev. Moon rejects the notion that original
sin is Adam's disobedience, and so, quite consistently,
he also rejects the notion that the crucifixion was
intended by God as a means of Adam's redemption. Rev.
Moon then draws the conclusion (once again consistent
with his position) that Jesus did not perform the full
messianic work. The world still awaits the Messiah.
But what Messiah, then, does the world await? The world
awaits the Messiah who will rescue man from original
sin in its full meaning. Here is the key to Moon's
whole theology, and the reason for his excitement
at discovering Adam's sin. By his discovering the
true nature and definition of sin, Moon has also discovered the true nature of redemption.

   We have seen how the sin-redemption correlation
works in some traditional Christian theology. In traditional theology, (1) Adam's disobedience makes him
guilty, (2) his guilt requires Christ's death, (3)
Christ's death leads to God's forgiveness; hence (4)
Jesus is the Messiah in an ultimate sense. By contrast,
in Moon's view, the first act of sin is Satan's seduction of Eve rather than Adam's disobedience. So another
kind of redemptive act (rather than crucifixion) is
required.

   Let us now reflect on the act through which Adam
and Eve originally sinned. Before discussing what

they did let us first ask how they had the power to do
it. In traditional Christian theology, Adam and Eve
had a perfected power of freedom from the first moment
of creation. That is, they knew right and wrong and
were able to choose the right. Only on such a presupposition could Adam's sin be called disobedience. But
Rev. Moon does not agree that Adam and Eve possessed this
perfect and mature freedom when they were created.
Rather, they were like children in whom there are strong
desires but not yet the knowledge of *reasons* (principles)
to govern their actions.   Children act "unreasonably."
They do not think; they *desire*. According to Moon,
such "unreasoning" or "unprincipled love" was in Adam
and Eve. They were immature children--growing towards
perfect freedom--but still susceptible to being *misled*.
That is how Satan "seduced" Eve.

Now if Adam and Eve did not fall through "disobedience" (because they lacked perfect freedom) then "forgiveness" will not accomplish their redemption. What
humanity--like lost children--needs, according to Rev.
Moon, is restoration--restoration and *not* forgiveness.
Just as when a child misbehaves through his immaturity
he is helped by being restored to his family, so humanity, fallen through its immaturity, requires restoration
to its original relationship to God in the true human
family. Restoration, then, is how Moon defines redemption. Humanity has fallen out of the family for which
God intended it, and fallen into another family--the
family of Satan.

How can this restoration take place? We have said
that the act of redemption must be correlative with
the act of sin. So, Christ's death is of no use in

solving the fundamental human problem. What is needed
is the creation of a new family. But how is a new family
to be created? The answer is: through a principled
love. Just as unprincipled love created the fallen
human family, so principled love creates the new human
family. What is needed is a give-and-take relationship
now deriving from one who becomes the new father of the
human race and, in this way, displaces Lucifer as the
father of us all. Around this new father, there will
be created a new family.

The question arises: What form will this saving,
principled love take? The saving act must be exactly
correlated with the act of original sin. Therefore,
it will be a give-and-take relationship which exactly
reverses the sinful intercourse between Eve and Satan.
It will be an intercourse, both spiritual and physical,
of a man and a woman, such that the man will be the
father of the new humanity and the woman the mother.
The salvific act, then, is a healthy marital relationship in its fullest sense. It is spiritualized sex
and not crucifixion which is the act of redemption.
Only this principled marital love, this restorative
marital give-and-take relationship, can restore humanity.

WHO IS THE MESSIAH?

Traditional Christian theology discusses the topic
of the correspondence between "the person" and "the
work" of Christ. This means that whatever Christ does,
he must be a person capable of doing this thing. Applying this formula to Unification theology, it means
that whoever undertakes to establish the specific

give-and-take relationship between a man and a woman
which leads to the new family of mankind must himself
be personally capable of this undertaking.

Who, then, would such a person be? He would
have to be a person equal to the angels, equal to Lucifer. He cannot merely be an immature human being.
Rather, he must be a perfected person who, in order to
establish his equality with Lucifer, will have to undergo
a long period of personal trial, tribulation, and suffering equivalent to the period of temptation and suffering of Jesus in the wilderness. (It is in the wilderness that Jesus meets Satan and demonstrates his equality
with and even his power over him.) Since Rev. Moon strives
to become this Messiah, it would be most interesting to
know more about his own spiritual autobiography, for
a person is perfected only through trial and suffering.
Only the love of such a perfected person will be *perfectly* centered in the purpose of God for the created
universe.

That brings us to the interesting question of whether or not the woman to whom this person is married
would also have to be a perfected person. Could it be
that this woman would receive her wisdom from her
husband in the same way that Eve received Satan's wisdom? Or does this woman have to become a perfected
human in her own right before the relationship of principled love can take place? Clearly, this woman would
have to be a perfect spirit; there is no question about
this. But whether she would have to be this *in her own
right,* before her relationship with the perfected man
could begin or whether she could become such through
his leadership, is a matter that is not totally clear

within Moon's theology. I think that the tendency
of Moon's theology is to argue that only the Messianic
man must achieve this perfection by himself but his partner could achieve it through him subsequently. Then,
when she also had attained this   perfection, the two
of them would become the mother and father of the new
human race. In their love, or through their love, the
establishment of the new family of mankind would take
place. But here I am just speculating.

CONCLUSIONS

Let me remind you that, while the *Divine Principle*
defines what redemption is and how it is to be achieved,
it does not tell us who the Messiah is. I think it is
reasonable that the theology ot the *Divine Principle* and
the person of Rev. Moon should be kept separate. This
separation allows us to think the matter through ob-
jectively. We can think about the theory Rev. Moon
is proposing without having to believe he is, or is
not the Messiah. I think his theory has integrity and
it is not clear to me how orthodox Christianity should
reply to it. Moreover, it does deal with the two issues which I, personally, believe are most urgent for
the Christian church today.

The first issue is that the Messiah must be both
a man and a woman. We cannot have a single male Messiah
anymore for two reasons: (1) it is too individualistic;
and (2) the masculine principle is not fecund without
the feminine principle. It is perfectly clear that
the Christian Messianic doctrine must be transformed
to acknowledge the co-equality of man and woman. This,

of course, is the theological issue at stake in the or-
dination of women.

The second issue that I would argue with equal
passion is that Christianity has been a western religion
for too long. While there is strength in the west,
there is also a great lack. Christianity has been,
for too long, a western religion. It must be strengthened and renewed by prophets from the east. Why, then,
not by prophets from Korea?

CONTRIBUTORS

M. DARROL BRYANT, a Lutheran, is a Professor of Religion and Culture at Renison College, University of Waterloo, Waterloo, Ontario, Canada. He contributed to *Religion and Political Society* and is the author of the forthcoming *History and Eschatology in Jonathan Edwards*.

ELIZABETH CLARK, Professor of Religion at Mary Washington College, is the author of *Clement's Use of Aristotle: The Aristotelian Contribution to Clement of Alexandria's Refutation of Gnosticism; Jerome, Chrysostom, and Friends: Essays and Translations;* and, with Herbert Richardson, *Women and Religion: A Feminist Sourcebook of Christian Thought*.

RICHARD DeMARIA, a Christian Brother, is a Professor of Religious Studies at Iona College, New Rochelle, New York. He is the author of *Communal Love at Oneida: A Perfectionist Vision of Authority, and Property, and Sexual Order*.

LLOYD EBY, a member of the Unification Church for more than five years, is enrolled in the graduate program in philosophy at Fordham University. He has been a member of the faculty of philosophy at the State University of New York at Albany.

JOSEPH H. FICHTER, S.J., is a sociologist at Loyola University, New Orleans. His works include *Social Relations in the Urban Parish;* and *One-Man Research: Reminiscences of a Catholic Sociologist*.

FRANK FLINN, a Roman Catholic, is Chairman of the Department of Religious Education, St. Louis University. He has contributed to *Women and Religion* and is the author of a forthcoming book on the thought of George Grant, a Canadian social thinker.

DAVID JARVIS, a 1977 graduate of the Unification Theological Seminary, holds two B.A. degrees and is now doing graduate work at the Divinity School of the University of Chicago. He has been a member of the Unification Church for more than five years.

FARLEY JONES received his B.A. in English from Princeton University. A member of the Unification Church for more than ten years, he graduated from the Unification Theological Seminary in 1978.

WARREN LEWIS comes out of the Church of Christ. He is a Professor of Church History at the Unification Theological Seminary, Barrytown, New York. He is the author of the forthcoming *The Unification Church* and his textual study on Peter John Olivi is forthcoming.

KLAUS LINDNER, from Regensburg, Germany, is a graduate of the Unification Theological Seminary and is presently a graduate student in church history at Harvard University.

SEBASTIAN MATCZAK, a Roman Catholic priest, is Professor of Philosophy at St. John's University, New York. He is the author of many books, most recently, *God in Contemporary Thought: A Philosophical Perspective*.

LINDA MITCHELL, a former Unification Church member, studied at California State University and graduated from the Unification Theological Seminary in 1978.

HERBERT W. RICHARDSON, a Presbyterian, is a Professor of Religious Studies at the University of Toronto, Toronto, Ontario, Canada. He is the editor, together with J. Hopkins, of the theological works of Anselm of Canterbury and the author of *Towards an American Theology*.

RODNEY SAWATSKY, a Mennonite, is Professor of Religious Studies at Conrad Grebel College, University of Waterloo, Waterloo, Ontario, Canada. He writes extensively on the Mennonite tradition and is the author of a forthcoming study of the place of the writing of history in Mennonite self-identity.

WILLIAM C. SHEPHERD is a member of the Department of Religious Studies at the University of Montana. His most recent book is *Symbolical Consciousness: A Commentary on Love's Body*, and his recent articles appear in the *Journal of the American Academy of Religion* and the *Journal for the Scientific Study of Religion*. A companion piece to the present essay will be published by *Sociological Inquiry*.

BART TESTA, a Roman Catholic, is presently a lecturer on the new religions at the University of California, San Diego. He is also a professional journalist specializing in popular myths and cultures. His writing appears in *Crawdaddy, Rolling Stone* and elsewhere.

HENRY VANDER GOOT, is an Assistant Professor of Religion at Calvin College. He has edited and translated Gustaf Wingren's *Creation and Gospel*, to which he also contributed an introduction.